MW01034947

ART, ARTISTS AND PEDAGOGY

This volume has been brought together to generate ideas and provoke discussion about what constitutes arts education in the twenty-first century, both within the institution and beyond. *Art, Artists and Pedagogy* is intended for educators who teach the arts from early childhood to tertiary level, artists working in the community, or those studying arts in education from undergraduate to Masters or PhD level.

From the outset, this publication is not only about arts in practice but also what distinguishes the 'arts' in education. Exploring two different philosophies of education, the book asks what is the purpose of arts in the twenty-first century. With specific reference to the work of Gert Biesta, questions are raised as to the relation of the arts to the world and what kind of society we may wish to envisage. The second philosophical position comes from Deleuze and Guattari, looking in more depth at how we configure art, the artist and the role played by the state and global capital in deciding on what art education has become.

This book provides educators with ways to engage with arts, focusing specifically on art, music, dance, drama and film studies. At a time when many teachers are looking for a means to re-assert the role of the arts, this text provides new ideas with reference to case studies and in-depth arguments from some of the world's leading academics in the arts, philosophy and education.

Christopher Naughton has lectured in education and the arts at the University of Exeter, UK, and the University of Auckland, New Zealand. Currently Chris is researching artists working in education following a two-year, funded project *Move, Act, Play, Sing (MAPS)*.

Gert Biesta (www.gertbiesta.com) is Professor of Education and Director of Research at the Department of Education of Brunel University London, UK.

David R. Cole works as an educational researcher at Western Sydney University, Australia.

'Reframing fundamental, enduring issues in arts education, this collection of papers on the arts, artists and pedagogy is fresh, timely, insightful, at times provocative, always compelling.'

–**Liora Bresler**, PhD, University of Illinois, Urbana-Champaign, Professor in the College of Education, Curriculum and Instruction, and the School of Art and Design

ART, ARTISTS AND PEDAGOGY

Philosophy and the Arts in Education

Edited by Christopher Naughton, Gert Biesta and David R. Cole

Routledge
Taylor & Francis Group

LONDON AND NEW YORK

First published 2018
by Routledge
2 Park Square, Milton Park, Abingdon, Oxon OX14 4RN

and by Routledge
711 Third Avenue, New York, NY 10017

Routledge is an imprint of the Taylor & Francis Group, an informa business

© 2018 selection and editorial matter, Christopher Naughton, Gert Biesta and David R. Cole; individual chapters, the contributors

British Library Cataloguing in Publication Data
A catalogue record for this book is available from the British Library

Library of Congress Cataloging in Publication Data
A catalog record for this book has been requested

ISBN: 978-1-138-50051-8 (hbk)
ISBN: 978-1-138-50060-0 (pbk)
ISBN: 978-1-315-14388-0 (ebk)

Typeset in Bembo
by Out of House Publishing
Printed and bound by CPI Group (UK) Ltd, Croydon, CR0 4YY

This book is dedicated to all those who teach the arts, and who wish to embrace nature, art and the politics of change.

CONTENTS

Preface   *ix*
Acknowledgements   *xi*
List of contributors   *xii*

1 Philosophy and pedagogy in arts education   1
   Christopher Naughton and David R. Cole

2 What if? Art education beyond expression and creativity   11
   Gert Biesta

3 Dicing the meat: bacon in the middle of an arts-based sandwich   21
   David R. Cole

4 Artists, presence and the gift of being unteacherly   31
   Mary Ann Hunter

5 The implications of 'percepts, affects and concepts'
   for arts educators   43
   Christopher Naughton

6 Jazz departures: sustaining a pedagogy of improvisation   52
   David Lines

7 Bodily connectedness in motion: a philosophy on
   intercorporeity and the art of dance in education   61
   Nico de Vos

8 Thinking school curriculum through Country with
Deleuze and Whitehead: a process-based synthesis   71
David R. Cole and Margaret Somerville

9 From the artist to the cosmic artisan: the educational
task for art in anthropogenic times   83
jan jagodzinski

10 Towards 'grown-up-ness in the world' through the Arts as
critical, quality pedagogy   96
Robyn Ann Ewing and John Nicholas Saunders

11 Authentic teaching assessment in graduate teacher
education: becomings of pedagogical artistry and leadership   107
Julianne Moss and Anne-Marie Morrissey

12 Beyond belief: visionary cinema, becoming imperceptible
and pedagogical resistance   115
Jessie L. Beier and Jason J. Wallin

13 Flight from flight: composing a pedagogy of affect   127
John Roder and Sean Sturm

14 Weak subjects: on art's art of forgetting—an interview with
John Baldacchino by Gert Biesta   137
John Baldacchino and Gert Biesta

15 Walking the museum: art, artists and pedagogy reconsidered   147
Gert Biesta

Index   *157*

PREFACE

This book began with a chance meeting between Mary Ann Hunter (University of Tasmania), Robyn Ewing (University of Sydney) and myself, at the 2011 Australian Association for Research in Education (AARE) in Hobart, Tasmania. After our initial discussion and subsequent online exchange, the work of Gert Biesta seemed to resonate well with our common interests in arts education. In the following year, 2012, the three of us presented a paper at AARE with Michael Gard (University of Queensland), specifically referencing Biesta in respect to our research with students and artists.

In 2013, Gert made an appearance at the Philosophy of Education Society of Australasia (PESA) conference in Melbourne, so we took the opportunity to share our work and look at possible collaborations. Through continued dialogue by 2015 we were in a position to obtain funding through the Philosophy SIG at AARE, to enable Gert to join us and present at a Featured Symposium at AARE in Perth.

While the development of closer ties between Gert and the Australian research-ers progressed, the *Move, Act, Play, Sing* (MAPS) project had begun in Auckland, New Zealand. This project brought together David Lines and John Roder at the University of Auckland, both already familiar with the work of Gilles Deleuze and Gert Biesta in relation to the arts in education. The symbiosis of my work, Biesta's and Deleuzian philosophy opened up new territories in the MAPS project in many unexpected and productive ways. It appeared more was to follow.

In 2014 on another visit to AARE, I met David R. Cole who was acting as chair for a Symposium on Deleuze. It was only a matter of time before the two currents of Biesta's work and Deleuzian scholarship converged into a publication which started to evolve in 2016 with the award from AARE to attend the American Educational Research Association (AERA) conference. Gradually, others joined the roll call of authors so that there was a sufficient number of contributors to embark on a publication, and *Art, Artists and Pedagogy* is the result.

This excursion into Biesta and Deleuze presents many challenges, working with two overlapping and yet at times quite distinct philosophical positions. The hope is that at a time when the arts are having to reinvent themselves and their worth, this text may offer educators insights into the arts and resolve to fight on, but to do so on new terms of engagement.

Christopher Naughton
4 May 2017

ACKNOWLEDGEMENTS

The editors are particularly grateful to John Quay and the AARE board, for enabling Gert Biesta to attend the 2015 AARE conference and for providing funding for AERA conference participation in 2016. This helped to develop a sense of fellowship and connection within the research group.

From my own perspective, I would like to acknowledge the persistence and patience shown by my colleagues in the evolution of this project. Alongside virtual discussions and on-going informal conversations on Deleuze, the immersive experience of last year's Summer Institute at Western Sydney University with David R. Cole helped in developing a sense of purpose, bringing together the different strands from Biesta and Deleuze.

The final acknowledgement has to be to the two co-editors Gert Biesta and David R. Cole, who have been remarkably consistent throughout the process of fashioning *Art, Artists and Pedagogy*. Their ability to undertake long-haul flights, present at international conferences, complete many other research obligations and discharge their commitments to preview scripts, support writers and completing their own chapters – on time – is a tribute to their scholarship and their commitment to producing this publication.

Christopher Naughton
4 May 2017

CONTRIBUTORS

John Baldacchino

Professor of Arts Education: Director of The Arts Institute

University of Wisconsin-Madison

John Baldacchino is Chair of Arts Education at the University of Wisconsin-Madison. His work focuses on art, philosophy and education. He is the author of *Post-Marxist Marxism* (1996), *Easels of Utopia* (1998), *Avant-Nostalgia* (2002), *Education Beyond Education* (2009), *Makings of the Sea* (2010), *Art's Way Out* (2012), *Mediterranean Art Education* (with Raphael Vella, 2013), *Democracy Without Confession* (with Kenneth Wain, 2013), *John Dewey* (2013), and *My Teaching, My Philosophy: Kenneth Wain* (with Simone Galea and Duncan Mercieca, 2014). He is currently editing volume I of the *Wiley-Blackwell's Encyclopedia of Art & Design Education: Histories & Philosophies*, and writing two new books, on Giambattista Vico and on Ivan Illich. *More information*: www.johnbaldacchino.com

Jessie L. Beier

Faculty of Education at the University of Alberta

University of Alberta

Jessie Beier is a teacher, artist and PhD Candidate at the University of Alberta in Edmonton, Alberta. Beier's interests in visual and sonic ecologies have led to a research–creation practice that works to think of pedagogy, in its many forms, as a power for overturning cliché and dismantling common-sense habits of interpretation and understanding. Beier's most recent projects can be found in the forthcoming edited books *Sound Thinking* (Ed.: B. Herzogenrath, Bloomsbury), *The Precarious Future of Education: Risk and Uncertainty in Ecology, Curriculum, Learning, and Technology* (Ed.: j. jagodzinski, Palgrave Macmillan) and *What is Art Education? Essays After Deleuze and Guattari* (Ed.: j. jagodzinski, Palgrave McMillan).

Gert Biesta

Professor of Education; Director of Research

Department of Education

Brunel University

Gert Biesta (www.gertbiesta.com) is Professor of Education and Director of Research at the Department of Education of Brunel University London. He writes on the theory and philosophy of education and educational research, with an interest in curriculum, teaching, pedagogy, democracy and the arts. Recent books include *The Beautiful Risk of Education* (2014), *The Rediscovery of Teaching* (2017) and *Letting Art Teach: Art Education 'after' Joseph Beuys* (2017).

David R. Cole

Associate Professor in Literacies, English and ESL

University of Western Sydney

Associate Professor David R. Cole works as an educational researcher at Western Sydney University, Australia. He is currently the theme leader of Globalisation research at the Centre for Educational Research (CER). He has dedicated his career to understanding how the work of Gilles Deleuze and Félix Guattari can be used to critique, enliven and change educational practice. This endeavour has led to more than 100 publications and 13 books in this field. Cole thinks in an international context and has completed 12 major research projects that have investigated how the ideas of Deleuze and Guattari work in an empirical sense. Cole's latest monograph is *A Pedagogy of Cinema* (with Joff P.N. Bradley), Sense Publishers, Rotterdam.

Robyn Ann Ewing

Professor of Teacher Education and the Arts

University of Sydney

Initially a primary teacher, Robyn Ewing AM is currently Professor of Teacher Education and the Arts, Sydney School of Education and Social Work, University of Sydney. Passionate about the role that the arts can play in transforming learning, Robyn's teaching, research and extensive publications include a focus on the use of drama strategies with literature to enhance students' English and literacy learning. She has worked in partnership with Sydney Theatre Company on the *School Drama* teacher professional learning programme to develop primary teachers' confidence and expertise in using drama strategies with literature since 2009. Teacher education, especially the experiences of early career teachers and the role of mentoring, sustaining curriculum innovation and evaluation, and the use of arts-informed, particularly narrative, inquiry in educational research are also current research interests.

Mary Ann Hunter

Senior Lecturer

Faculty of Education

University of Tasmania

Mary Ann Hunter works across academic, industry and community-based contexts and is currently Senior Lecturer in Education at the University of Tasmania. Alongside national and international consultancy work in arts and education, she has been national evaluator of the Australian Government's Artist in Residence and APRA-AMCOS Songmakers Programs and publishes in the fields of arts education, arts-based peacebuilding and youth cultural development. Her current research interests are in the role of curiosity and presence in applied and educational arts settings.

jan jagodzinski

Professor of Visual Art and Media Education: Faculty of Education

University of Alberta

jan jagodzinski is a Professor in the Department of Secondary Education, University of Alberta in Edmonton, Alberta, Canada. He is the author of 15 books and Series Editor of *Educational Futures.* Sample books include: *Youth Fantasies: The Perverse Landscape of the Media* (Palgrave, 2004); *Musical Fantasies: A Lacanian Approach* (Palgrave, 2005); *Television and Youth: Televised Paranoia* (Palgrave, 2008); *The Deconstruction of the Oral Eye: Art and Its Education in an Era of Designer Capitalism* (Palgrave, 2010); *Misreading Postmodern Antigone: Marco Bellocchio's Devil in the Flesh (Diavolo in Corpo)* (Intellect Books, 2011); editor of *Psychoanalyzing Cinema: A Productive Encounter of Lacan, Deleuze, and Žižek* (Palgrave, 2012); *Arts Based Research: A Critique and Proposal* (with Jason Wallin) (Sense, 2013); editor of *The Precarious Future of Education* (Palgrave, 2017); editor of *What is Art Education? After Deleuze and Guattari* (Palgrave, 2017); editor of *Athropocene, Ecology, Pedagogy: The Future in Question* (Palgrave, in process, scheduled for 2018).

David Lines

Associate Dean Academic: Creative Arts and Industries

University of Auckland

David Lines, PhD (Education) is Associate Professor of Music Education at the University of Auckland. His research is in the area of educational philosophy and the arts, particularly music, working with philosophers such as Deleuze, Nietzsche and Heidegger. He has written on early childhood arts education, improvisation and education, creativity, music technology and music education as cultural work. David plays in an instrumental jazz ensemble and has contributed to five recorded albums and numerous performances. His music teaching career has spanned primary, secondary and tertiary levels.

Anne-Marie Morrissey

Senior Lecturer in Education (Early Childhood): Faculty of Arts and Education

Deakin University

Anne-Marie Morrissey is currently a Senior Lecturer in Early Childhood Education at Deakin University. She is a qualified and experienced early childhood professional, with extensive experience in teaching across a range of early childhood settings and primary schools in Victoria, NSW and the United Kingdom. She has also taught in both the TAFE and University sectors in early childhood education and gifted education. Anne-Marie has research interests in areas of quality in early education and care, the role of play in learning and development, gifted development and education, and natural outdoor learning environments.

Julianne Moss

Professor in Pedagogy and Curriculum: Faculty of Arts and Education

Deakin University

Julianne Moss is Director of REDI (Research for Educational Impact), Deakin University's Strategic Research Centre in Education. She holds a personal chair in Pedagogy and Curriculum and is immediate President of the Australian Association for Research in Education. Her research interests lie in visual research and the intersection of these methods with student diversity, teacher professional knowledge and social change.

Christopher Naughton

Academic Consultant

Auckland University of Technology

Christopher Naughton has lectured in education and the arts at the University of Exeter and the University of Auckland. Currently Chris is researching artists working in education following a two-year funded project *Move, Act, Play, Sing* (MAPS). Chris has contributed articles to the *Australian Journal of Music Education*, *British Journal of Music Education*, *Action Criticism and Theory*, *Education Philosophy and Theory*, *Studies in Philosophy of Education*, *ACCESS*, *International Review of Research in Open and Distance Learning*, *E-Learning and Digital Media* and the *Journal of Distance Learning*. He is a regular presenter at the Philosophy of Education Society of Australasia (PESA) and the Australian Association for Research in Education (AARE) and many other international conferences.

John Roder

Senior Lecturer: Faculty of Education and Social Work

The University of Auckland

John Roder is a senior lecturer in the Faculty of Education at the University of Auckland. He works with teachers and pre-service students in early childhood education as well as compulsory sector settings, teaching amongst other things teacher inquiry, reflective practice, play pedagogy and educational leadership. Themes around complexity, relationality, emergence and structure as they affect pedagogy, leadership and context run through John's research interests. His current scholarship has moved towards more post-humanist perspectives, particularly the philosophical work of Gilles Deleuze, to address questions arising around these themes as they appear and are produced within digitally fluid worlds. His current project involves the 'playful' university.

John Nicholas Saunders

Education Manager

Sydney Theatre Company

John Nicholas Saunders is the Manager of Education at the Sydney Theatre Company. Previously John worked as a secondary drama teacher and Head of Department for the Arts. He co-wrote the Senior Drama Syllabus with the Queensland Studies Authority and is currently the President of Drama Australia, and a board member of National Advocates for Arts Education and Playlab Press. His research and teaching concentrates on the role of Drama pedagogy in improving student academic and non-academic outcomes. In 2014 John was awarded the CHASS Australia Prize for a Future Leader in the Humanities, Arts and Social Sciences.

Margaret Somerville

Professor of Education

University of Western Sydney

Margaret Somerville is Professor of Education and Director of the Centre for Educational Research, Western Sydney University. Her approach to research is informed by feminist post-poststructural and post-human theories and Aboriginal onto–epistemologies. She has collaborated with Aboriginal knowledge holders, artists and researchers for over 20 years, publishing internationally acclaimed books in the area including *Singing the Coast* (2010) and *Water in a Dry Land* (2013). She is interested in alternative and creative approaches in research and writing and applying new theories of space, place and body in educational research and practice, such as in her most recent book, *Children, Place and Sustainability* (Somerville & Green, Palgrave, 2015).

Sean Sturm

Head, Academic Development Group

The University of Auckland

Sean Sturm is Deputy Director of the Centre for Learning and Research in Higher Education at the University of Auckland. He researches teaching and learning in the university through the lens of critical theory and post-qualitative methodology.

Nico de Vos

Professor of Participation and Society

HU University of Applied Sciences Utrecht, the Netherlands

Nico de Vos, PhD, is a philosopher and professor of Participation and Society. He concentrates on the 'bodily' themes of Art & Creativity and Sport & Physical Activity, in the context of Participation & Community Development in an urban environment, at the HU University of Applied Sciences Utrecht, the Netherlands. He holds a PhD in Philosophy of Art and Culture / Human Movement and Dance. Previously, he studied Physical Education (Bachelor, Master of Science, *cum laude*) and Philosophy (Bachelor, Research Master of Philosophy, *cum laude*). In his philosophical activities, de Vos explores the connections between the fields of art and sport and the wider social and educational domains. Practically, he is interested in the possibilities of social-ecological change. Philosophically, he likes to combine the study of literature with innovative forms of qualitative-empirical research, such as participatory, narrative and arts-based research. In short, he pursues a kind of empirical philosophy.

Jason J. Wallin

Faculty of Education

University of Alberta

Jason J. Wallin is Associate Professor of Media and Youth Culture in Curriculum in the Faculty of Education at the University of Alberta, Canada, where he teaches courses in visual art, media studies and cultural curriculum theory. He is the author of *A Deleuzian Approach to Curriculum: Essays on a Pedagogical Life* (Palgrave Macmillan), co-author of *Arts-Based Research: A Critique and Proposal* (with jan jagodzinski, Sense Publishers), co-editor of *Deleuze, Guattari, Politics and Education* (with Matt Carlin, Bloomsbury), and co-producer of the 2016 extreme music documentary entitled *Blekkmetal* (with David Hall, Vivek Venkatesh and Owen Chapman, Handshake Inc.).

1

PHILOSOPHY AND PEDAGOGY IN ARTS EDUCATION

Christopher Naughton and David R. Cole

Introduction

Art, artists and pedagogy are too often treated as separate and sometimes irreconcilable activities. This book brings these three key creative capacities together by deploying philosophy at its most impactful, as truly creative thinking 'in the now'. The theme of this book is 'arts education as philosophy', and it is to teachers working in whatever capacity, from early childhood to tertiary level, to researchers, artists in the community, or those studying arts in education that this combined text is aimed; it has been brought together to generate ideas and provoke discussion on what constitutes arts education in the twenty-first century, both within the institution and beyond.

There are two primary sources that form philosophical points of reference in this arts education text. Gert Biesta provides the first chapter from his book *The Rediscovery of Teaching* (2017), a phenomenologically informed work, that is questioned and reworked in each chapter through the introduction of the second philosophical stream that works through the text, that of Gilles Deleuze (1925–1995). Deleuze's philosophy of immanence provides a theoretical platform for a shift in thinking around the arts in education in terms of the conceptual. Biesta's work enables educational thought connected to concepts that he introduces such as 'grown-up-ness' and 'the middle ground'. Each chapter, building on these philosophical streams, is designed to be informative and challenging, offering ways to re-think arts education from these two intellectual perspectives.

Deleuze and Guattari: curriculum and affect

Deleuze wrote many texts with Félix Guattari (1930–1992), and their combined work has become the basis for studies in the reconceptualisation of pedagogy as they offer alternative, shifting bases of relationality. This is in part a reconciliation of any perception of 'the child' seen as a potential 'unit of production' (de Alba et al., 2000), or subject in the field of capitalist exploitation of surplus value. Deleuze and Guattari (1987) provide us with a sophisticated analysis of the ways in which capitalism captures the imagination from an early age and potentially commodifies the arts as part of this 'apparatus of capture'. The juxtaposition of Deleuze and Guattari (1987) with Gert Biesta's (2017) chapter in the same volume creates a unique opportunity for a provocative rethinking of the arts along philosophical lines by reconciling art, artists and pedagogy.

For those unfamiliar with Deleuze and Guattari (1987), it is valuable to first consider one of their key concepts, 'territoriality', and think how it relates to the arts. In education, the notion of territoriality has been usefully employed by such writers as Olsson (2009) and Sellers (2013), when observing children creating their own versions of a song or inventing make-believe characters in their dramatic play. Deleuze invented the term 'deterritorialisation', which explains the process of taking a territory and remaking it differently, such as the song or characters, to suit the child's context. Having deterritorialised the song or dramatic play, children then 'reterritorialise' as they settle on a new set of characters or new version of the song, as they invent and reinvent, often with others, before the process begins again. While capitalism decodes, recodes and distributes products for sale through the exploitation of surplus value, including those psychic codes present in education as learning, Deleuze and Guattari (1987) simultaneously present deterritorialisation as a potentially singular and/or collective form of engagement, that can be characterised as inquiry of a multiple nature leading to social, political and personal change. In effect, the term, deterritorialisation, which is central to capitalist functioning, has many levels, and is not solely exploitative, therefore opening up the concept as a potential arts-based fulcrum for understanding key processes in the world from an innocent and playful perspective.

This small example of the concept of territory serves to show how Deleuze and Guattari (1987) ask educators to think with and deploy new concepts, and to constantly exercise their imaginations in coming to terms with a philosophy which is always in flux. What is especially valuable for teachers and researchers is the idea that Deleuzian scholars are determined to remove and deny the constant reiteration of binaries in education. For example, labelling children as successful or failing, correct or incorrect: in art – 'a good likeness' or 'not a good likeness'; in music – 'in time' or 'not in time'; in drama – remembered your 'words' or forgot your 'words'; in dance – the 'correct step' or the 'incorrect step'. Instead, the application of Deleuzian concepts to arts education allows for a connected middle ground to emerge, around the 'and … and … and', instead of the 'either … or'.

Another problem faced by arts educators and the various curricula are the strict definitions and hierarchies produced for the student in assessment. For example at the launch of the 'Task Group on Assessment and Testing' (TGAT) in 1988, a dance teacher asked Professor Paul Black: 'How can you evaluate a dancer moving to the floor in the terms of the National Curriculum?' The answer was simply to reiterate the curriculum orders, to reduce the dancer and her actions to a description of the 'elements' of height, speed and duration. This short exchange typifies the way in which at the outset – since the TGAT report became the basis of the National Curriculum for England, the *affective* in the arts has been removed. One could say that *affect* and to be affected could have interfered too much with the assessment process. Thus the *move* to the floor was not seen as *affect*, but became, as Deleuze would describe it, an ordered, *striated* response, that could only be seen in terms of a curriculum descriptor, and by proxy as maintaining the legitimacy of the State machine.

What Deleuze and Guattari (1987) offer is a means to reinstate *affect* and to be affected in arts education. Not to close doors on what the artwork can be, but to go beyond it. Rather than work always 'within boundaries', a favourite riposte by those seeking closure, Deleuze and Guattari see the arts as going beyond boundaries, where new *striations* or limits form within new territories, in part through the concept of *immanence* (1994) – a state of constant change where there is no beginning, or end, and only a coming from the middle.

The primary set of philosophical ideas in this book comes from Gert Biesta, who provides not only two chapters and an extended interview in this publication, but a set of ideas to which each author responds. Biesta (2017) offers a different but complementary philosophical position from Deleuze and Guattari (1987), which sets up an anomaly and disjunctive synthesis within the same book, as a productive difference or philosophical position. To acknowledge difference fosters debate, something with which arts educators are starting to engage far more readily. Biesta elaborates on philosophical ideas taken from Dewey, Levinas, Foucault, Arendt, Derrida and Heidegger. His work has been widely read and valued by practitioners seeking a philosophical means to stem the tide of global standardisation and the capitalist enfeeblement of education.

What does this book have to offer by way of insight into the role arts can play in education? *Art, Artists and Pedagogy* is not a literal 'how to teach' the arts book; the ideas presented here are to encourage the educator to question practice and to reinvent pedagogy along philosophical lines. The book is not a philosophy text *per se*, in that the concepts do not remain in a space of pure philosophy; it is philosophy applied to arts education. Different theoretical framings by each contributor show what they see as productive and critical in the context of the twenty-first century and arts education. Above all, this book consistently works with difference to (un) recognise how we view the world, and sets up arts-based thinking practice that informs art, artists and pedagogy, without embracing what is tired and/or what has gone before.

Gert Biesta, in Chapter Two, reflects on the absurdity of education locked into an endless cycle of measurement and competition. Biesta produces an argument for the arts that avoids the pitfalls of individual *expression* and *creativity*. Referring to 'creativity', Biesta shows how the arts have been instrumentalised – to 'only' be seen as serving some other attributes, be it mathematical skill or other area of learning. Biesta continues by maintaining that the view of art as a place to 'express yourself' is a deception, when the reality is an insignificant amount of time offered to subjects in diminishing supply. Bound by rigid assessment procedures, this 'express yourself' lobby achieves little for the student. The choice of what the student engages in as art and the quality of that art are taken up by Biesta who asks, how do we ensure quality, and what or who governs such quality? In turning to the *subject*, Biesta suggests the *we* becomes in and with the world. This implies an acceptance of living with others, acknowledging our own as well as others' desire. Likening this *existing* to a dialogue with the world, Biesta touches on the need for resistance in how we engage with others, where to be *grown up*, we must accept a 'middle ground' in coming to terms with desire. As a corollary, to not undertake this task is characterised as 'infantile'. This chapter usefully begins our discussion of *Art, Artists and Pedagogy* in education, confronting two of the most pressing claims that educators face on a daily basis: how to resist the repeated mantras that amount to a fabrication such as 'creativity and expression', and the courage necessary for teachers to take a risk, and encourage students to an encounter *with* the world.

In Chapter Three, 'Dicing the meat', David R. Cole undertakes a detailed analysis of several Deleuzian concepts in the context of art taught in school. Taking as a point of reference *Portrait of Michel Leiris* by Francis Bacon, Cole considers Deleuze's concept of 'rhythm'. Rhythm is the 'dynamic movement' between space and process, providing for 'co-constitution' or the opposite, the potential to disintegrate. Rhythm is not easily quantified or measured; it is something that is felt, in the onlooker and artist. This depiction of rhythm includes the myths and legends that may surround a subject, brought into play in Bacon's portrait. Cole then employs the concept of the 'body without organs' where the sensation of the artwork is felt, a process, Cole suggests, that can form practice in the classroom – looking for the affective in a painting through unconscious feelings. This working with art removes the predictable, to see what may come next. In a reference to Deleuze, Cole suggests that examining a painting such as Bacon's Michel Leiris is a chance to engage with and not to deny sensation. Finally, Cole produces a number of recommendations for what can be done at this point in schools given the curriculum restraints. These include working with teachers to examine Bacon's paintings to see what might work in extraordinary ways, with extraordinary objects, in a cross-disciplinary context.

The theme of visual and tactile art forms the basis of Chapter Four by Mary Ann Hunter. Although there might be conventional attitudes to artists working in schools, Hunter carefully observes how the two artists that she selects, Selena De Carvalho and Laura Hindmarsh, work in a quite a different manner, not aiming to bring something *to do* with the students, but looking to engage with students in the school environment. The presence of the artists and how the artists work with the students holds a fascination for Hunter, who looks at the way that *interruption* – taking her cue from Biesta – absorbs her in what makes education *good*, beyond curriculum frameworks. This area of the work process that the artists engage in has received little attention according to Hunter, who follows the artist moving from a teacher, and multi-purpose individual, to one who is in the school being an artist rather than performing a *teaching-instructor-training role*, allowing for the potentialities of what may arise in the school space, and allowing for *change* and *to be changed* by what occurs. In a discussion of the tensions between the valuing of personal knowledge and the school, Hunter cites the pressures of the high stakes testing regime, and the need for a counterbalance in line with an understanding of 'grown-up-ness'. Countering the terms of achievement, Hunter asks if the curiosity aroused by the artist is the gift that is offered, which makes the interruption matter.

Turning from visual art, Christopher Naughton, in Chapter Five, looks at Deleuze and Guattari's last book, *What Is Philosophy?* (1994). Identifying the three areas that form the subject of the book – 'percepts, affects and concepts' – Naughton examines the non-human impact in the derivation of the artwork. Percepts are seen as the primordial, the before man, Deleuze and Guattari seeing the materiality of the artist's engagement with an as yet unclear work. This first process leads the artist to the experience of 'becoming' as the material envelops the artist, as in Cezanne's landscapes or Thomas Hardy in his depiction of the moor in his novels. Affect is the transformation of the initial percept into a form, and here 'blocs of sensation' become recognisable. At this point the recognition of *affect* occurs so that colours, feelings, mood – create *affect*. An illustration is given that places dance in a context where making is allowed to become, with the material interaction of the dancers. The impact of Deleuze and Guattari's philosophy in relation to Immanuel Kant (1724–1804) is examined, where the conditions for making are linked to profound thinking in relation to fixed and non-hierachical states of being. This argument is then worked back to pedagogy and the impact immanence may have on what it is to teach beyond the imposition of curriculum taxonomies.

A pedagogy of improvisation becomes the theme in Chapter Six on jazz improvisation, by David Lines. Citing his own experience in playing jazz, Lines, with reference to the *refrain* in *A Thousand Plateaus* (1987) by Deleuze and Guattari, discusses the act of improvisation and the sense of not knowing where the improvisation will go. Affirming a form of making that can be seen as an apprenticeship, each player unsettles the taken for granted in responding to each other in the music. Seeing free jazz as a way of life, an embodiment, Lines refers to this as 'cultural work', stimulating movement. Alluding to Biesta, Lines sees an act of responsibility played out in free jazz improvisation, where players lose their sense of direct control, or as Lyotard described it, a 'synchronic' relation connecting to the music requiring an openness and a 'grown-up' approach. As in Biesta, Lines suggests that we be alert to the 'middle ground' where resistance is actioned between others. With reference to the origins of jazz, Lines sees the politics in the rhizomatic, nomadic movement away from capitalist enslavement transforming the educational process. It is through art that Lines suggests we may challenge educational theory, exemplifying this through his illustration of musical elements. Lines calls for a re-appraisal of relations in education, an alertness to the political and cultural educational space and the unforeseen, so that a new image of thought may arise to capture transformation as it occurs.

The subject of dance, in Chapter Seven, forms the discussion of art in Nico de Vos' writing on connectedness and intercorporeity. De Vos writes that it was Maurice Merleau-Ponty (1908–1961) who first saw the body in relation to a pre-reflective level of consciousness – while the subject remained at the centre. De Vos leads from Merleau-Ponty to Jean Luc Nancy (1940–), in whom he finds meaning only in the gathering of more than the one – where the body becomes singular and plural, touch emphasising the materiality of the dance. De Vos then refers to Jean Francois Lyotard (1924–1998), and how the affective is explored as the observation of the artwork, occurring before thought, having a physiological effect on the reader of the work. The final point from de Vos is to affirm the value of the relationship in contrast to the 'I' and 'we' of Cartesian thought, to advance that for students, it is vital to learn the value of the *inter* in relations, the 'between' that physical movement in dance can achieve.

In a paper entitled 'Thinking school curriculum through Country with Deleuze and Whitehead: a process-based synthesis', David R. Cole and Margaret Somerville, in Chapter Eight, consider the parallels between Deleuze and Alfred Whitehead (1861–1937) in the context of an Australian Aboriginal perspective and the restrictive curriculum that diminishes the Aboriginal culture. Employing Deleuze, Cole and Somerville explain a 'flat ontology', where forces and the underlying human and non-human identities are recognised as relational, without creating hierarchy, looking for 'real experience' or the 'world as it is lived'. This ontology has been termed 'immanent materialism'. The story of Chrissiejoy Marshall and how she undertook her PhD offers an interesting account of how a recognition of Country became her methodology. Cole and Somerville describe Aboriginal ancestral rites and the connection to place and spirituality and how this became a series of paintings in Chrissiejoy's thesis. This chapter explains how an Aboriginal Australian might embark on a sophisticated enquiry true to her own cultural process, with linkages to Deleuzian theory being explained in detail, to verify the significance of the encounter between two very different worlds and spiritual views.

Chapter Nine references many texts within Deleuzian scholarship, as jan jagodzinski embarks on a response to the overt humanism that does not recognise the inherent problems facing the world today. With reference to the *Anthropocene*, jagodzinski outlines the impact of the degradation of the world's resources, climate change and the attendant natural catastrophes that have been wrought by capitalism. In a plea to look no longer at fabled humanist solutions, jadogzinski undertakes an instructive text in how to re-fashion arguments in the face of technologies that threaten our survival as a race. Looking to Deleuze and Guattari, their characterisation of the avant garde is seen as working below the level of consciousness, disrupting our sense of orthodoxy and conventions in art. Recognising the Earth as Nature, we find the most profound reality, asserts jadogzinski, referring to passages in *What is Philosophy?* He continues by distinguishing the elemental in how the artwork is formed through percepts and affects in a molecular fashion to become blocs of sensation. In taking the sense of *What is Philosophy?* the artist becomes the scientist, artist and philosopher – a new 'thought brain'. As a result of the inheritance of the artist, jadogzinski sees life creation and its survival, endurance and death as the key concerns of the artist. Citing Paola Antonelli, the senior curator for the Museum of Modern Art in New York, jadogzinski links hidden arguments in her exhibitions mimicking nature through use of nano-technological processes using biodegradable materials, acting as a critique of current global abuses. Works by Catts and Zurr, the TC&A, and Cohen and van Balen are cited as they create a capitalist critique while exploring problematic natural questions. Ending with his own position jadogzinski looks to the educator, to question the use of synthetics from new 'materials and proto cells', to embrace the difficult task of looking to a future with 'little certainty beyond a felt conviction'.

Robyn Ewing and John Saunders, in Chapter Ten, report on a drama project working with primary school age children, developing drama workshops from literature. They see this process as embodying both Biesta's 'grown-up-ness' and Maxine Greene's call for looking at the world through another's eyes. Advocating a whole-school approach to developing an arts-rich curriculum, Ewing and Saunders relate to Dewey in the use of drama to open possibilities by creating an empathetic environment for children. Some of the insights in the dialogue between the children and the interviewers reveal an intensity in the exchange as the children discuss their process of making. For the teachers, the act of co-creating drama work with the children, not knowing in which direction the story will go, creates a new openness, as they join with the children in solving the problem, developing *resilience* through the task.

Juilianne Moss and Anne-Marie Morrisey in Chapter Eleven place Biesta's existence, between 'my' existence and the world, in the context of global performative based teacher education. Focusing on an example of 'authentic' practice, they examine the changing theorisation of *subjectivity* as opposed to *identity*, pointing out that the relation to oneself developing a curiosity about how *subjects* are formed is an essential component of the emerging teacher. After relating the official text regarding authentic learning, Moss and Morrissey provide examples of a 'still life' art class undertaken by a student and her commentary, revealing how her desires as a teacher had to match the desire of the children. Through the account of the teacher we see her coming to terms with herself, her desires, and those of her students as she learns to mitigate her own knowledge and skills with those of her class.

Beier and Wallin repeat Deleuze's observation that what we lack is belief in the world. In Chapter Twelve they delve into the premise of the world as it is already given, denying any variation in contemplating the future. In pedagogical terms they see this as curriculum reform, based on the existing dominant discourse with a pervasive awareness of having 'seen it all before'. The overriding sense is that anthropocentric (*human centred*) and anthropomorphic (*human representation*) thinking presupposes the reality of human thought and cognition, without any doubt being expressed. Looking for new ways to believe in the world, Beier and Wallin, through a reading of Deleuze, turn their focus on film as a way to see beyond our 'ordinariness', and our usual way of being. The cinema, they maintain, acts as a means to reflect on our current pre-occupations, to be critical; a way to re-think the world. How then, Beier and Wallin ask, might we envision cinema as a means to re-think the educational task with reference to Biesta? Taking examples from cinema, an exploration of the potential of film to re-think subjectivity, to 'disrupt', and seek new approaches to believing and existing in the world, is undertaken. Using *Ant-Man* (2015) and previous cinematic techniques, such as Vertov's space and time displacement, reference is made to Biesta in how *suspension* can be considered as a facet of re-learning. Here it is not teachers telling the child which desire is desirable, for this becomes a question the child must answer. Reflecting on the *Anthropocene* we are asked how education might then proceed, when we consider the future of human survival. The question is posed as to how can we, as educators, adjust to an Earth without us?

Beginning with the reaction of early childhood teachers to 'letting go', John Roder and Sean Sturm, in Chapter Thirteen, address *otherness* and the task of teachers to challenge and provoke. This is signified in the recognition of the other and the act of 'grown-up-ness' in making this acknowledgement. The task of the teacher becomes one of opening up spaces, where the student can engage their desire, which in turn requires the teacher to allow for a suspension in time. Roder and Sturm indicate how just as Deleuze demands much of the reader, the student must engage in struggle to comprehend ways of being. Using the reference to suspension, Roder and Sturm cite Deleuze's seminars, where *suspension* was used to allow the thought of the lecture to dwell, and so allow ideas to evolve. This concept is exemplified in an account of a teacher creating an *interruption*, an unsettling event, in children's dance. Roder and Sturm play out a sequence from a video featuring the dancer Adrian Smith, scripted as a story board for the reader to create their own suspension in following their text. In so doing, Roder and Sturm reinforce Biesta's claim for the role of the teacher, in their account of the dancer's interruption of children's work.

In an interview with Gert Biesta, John Baldacchino, in Chapter Fourteen, explains his research focus on 'unlearning'. This term is discussed with reference to John Dewey and many others, while considering how students are allowed to err to 'break into the unknown', allowing them to form a representation of their own reality. Touching on art and *aporia*, or contradiction, an argument is made that art engages between what may be perceived as existing, and different kinds of reality. Continuing this argument Baldacchino states that the *real* is perceived by our aesthetic response to engaging in 'illusion', to transcend from which we can then unlearn by creating a critique of certainty. In a useful comparison of new and old technology, a discussion around *mannerism* is conducted in which it is urged we seek a place in which to remove ourselves from our immediate context, to 'roam' back and forth to seek art through unlearning, removing any 'expectation' in the art event.

Chapter Fifteen is a discussion chapter in which Gert Biesta reflects on *Art, Artists and Pedagogy* through the analogy of visiting an art gallery. Likening the act of reading the book chapters to seeing an exhibition, Biesta observes how some paintings may appeal in different ways, while we are not so sure about others. Biesta sees how this may be the reaction of readers to the chapters in this book, where recognition might invite a certain sense of joy, or raise our curiosity to go back and revisit the text. After putting his case for accuracy in those 'portraits' that depict himself, Biesta comments on the ways in which the different concepts he has contributed were taken up by the authors. This is an absorbing, at times humourous, though scholarly account of the main arguments that Biesta has presented, undertaken in an improvisatory style of writing, touching on art, dance, music, film and drama, bringing the book to a lively and audacious end.

Conclusion

Rethinking philosophically around art, artists and pedagogy does not offer one simple way forward. Rather, this text seeks to avoid the imminent threat to the arts in education, which may be figured in myriad ways, such as those practised by financially motivated, techno-bureaucratic machines that often run schools, colleges and universities. In the end, to avoid the harsh reality of being sidelined in the curriculum because the arts do not return sufficient profit, or because they are too messy and their processes are too difficult to evaluate, educators have to reinvent new means of resistance to a dominant and often unasked for reality. As Deleuze (1994) has said about repetition, 'we die a little every day without the arts' (p.45), talking about the capacity of drama to be more than a representation of life, but to have the capacity to stir up the very forces of life. Education in its many guises has become 'the' exemplary practice reduced to repetitions of the same, and is therefore in dire need of the arts. Hopefully, this book can provide an antidote to the ubiquitous use of textbooks (now often uploaded and stored in e-clouds), to outcomes-based educational scripts with aims and pre-given methods, to standardised testing, to teachers not questioning their lessons, and producing student responses that are robotic and disengaged. When Deleuze (1994) says that we need the arts to stave off death, he is not making a relative statement, for death is apparent in the universal culture produced by current global capitalism. In many ways, thinking with the arts is about saving education from the repetition of the same; it is about changing the fear of experimentation, of the unknown and risky; it is about doing something new which truly engages with the life forces of the locale (Cole, 2011).

References

Biesta, G.J.J. (2017). *The Rediscovery of Teaching*. New York: Routledge.
Cole, D.R. (2011). *Educational Life-forms: Deleuzian teaching and learning practice*. Rotterdam: Sense Publishers.
de Alba, A., Gonzalez, E., Lankshear, C. & Peters, M.A. (2000). *The Curriculum in the Postmodern Condition*. New York: Peter Lang.

Deleuze, G. (1994). *Difference and Repetition* (P. Patton trans.). New York: Columbia University Press.

Deleuze, G., & Guattari, F. (1987). *A Thousand Plateaus: Capitalism and schizophrenia* (B. Massumi trans.). London: University of Minneapolis Press.

Deleuze, G., & Guattari, F. (1994). *What is Philosophy?* (H. Tomlinson & G. Burchell trans.). New York: Columbia University Press.

DES. (1988). *National Curriculum: Task Group on Assessment and Testing*. London: Department of Education and Science.

Olsson, L.M. (2009). *Movement and Experimentation in Young Children's Learning. Deleuze and Guattari in early childhood education*. London: Routledge.

Reed, P. (Director). (2015). *Ant-Man* [Motion picture]. United States: Walt Disney Studios Motion Pictures.

Sellers, M. (2013). *Young Children Becoming Curriculum. Deleuze, Te Whāriki and curricular understandings*. London: Routledge.

2

WHAT IF?

Art education beyond expression and creativity

Gert Biesta

Introduction: what was that all about?

When, perhaps in a hundred years from now, educational historians look back at the turn of the millennium, they may well ask 'What was that all about?' They may well wonder how, in a rather short period of time, almost the entire globe became obsessed with measurable learning outcomes, with league tables, with comparison and competition, and with creating education systems that, in the name of lofty ambitions such as that every child supposedly matters, were actually producing insurmountable hierarchies and inequalities where few could win and many would lose. They may well wonder how the OECD managed to become the McDonald's of twenty-first century education, not just as the organisation that suddenly was everywhere when matters of education were being discussed (as an 'obligatory passage point' – see Callon, 1986), but also as the organisation that successfully promoted a rather narrow educational 'diet' – perhaps effective in terms of what can be measured but not very nourishing. And maybe some educational historians may also wonder how the arts became caught up in all this – how art became redefined as creativity, how creativity became redefined as a skill and, for some, a 'twenty-first century skill', and how such skills were deemed to be important for survival in the uncertain world created by global capitalism. They will also conclude, with a sigh of relief, that in the 30s – the 2030s that is – the educational globe came to its senses, realising that, in its search for effectiveness and excellence, it had been creating an unsustainable monster that was doing the very opposite of what education should be doing – serving humanity in its struggle for meaningful and peaceful coexistence within the boundaries of what the earth can sustain – but instead had become an aim in itself, always asking for more.

If future historians can look back with a sigh of relief, we are, of course, still in the middle of all this, not just wondering how it all happened – and perhaps how we all let it happen – but also trying to find a way 'out', an 'exit pedagogy' (Baldacchino, 2012), or maybe just looking for a way forward and, ideally, a *better* way forward. In this chapter I offer some reflections on the potential of the arts for navigating the complex realities of contemporary education, steering a course in between the Scylla of the high instrumentalisation of the arts in education – that is, the idea that the arts should be useful for what supposedly really matters in education – and the Charybdis of educational expressivism – that is, the idea that the educational mission of the arts in a time of 'exam factories' lies in allowing children and young people to express themselves and find their unique voice and identity. The educational significance of the arts, and perhaps the educational urgency of the arts, lies in art education *beyond* expressivism and creativity. At least, that is what I will seek to argue in what is to follow.

Art in the picture, a mixed blessing?

When we look at the attention for and the place of the arts in the curriculum in many countries, the situation, at least at first sight, does not look too bad. But the 'at first sight' is crucial here, because what matters is not *whether* there is attention for the arts, but *what kind* of attention there is. Here I see two problems. One has to do with what we might refer to as the potential disappearance of *the arts* from art education, while the other has to do with the potential disappearance of *education* from art education.

The argument about the potential disappearance of art from art education is relatively easy to establish, as it is visible in the ongoing presence of *instrumental justifications* for the arts in education. Such justifications usually take the form of a statement in which it is claimed that engagement with the arts is *useful* because of its potential significance for or proven impact on 'something else' (for an all too comprehensive overview of such arguments see Winner, Goldstein & Vincent-Lacrin, 2013). In education there is a wide range of options for this 'something else'. This includes the suggestion that engagement with the arts will drive up testable performance in specific curricular domains (most often those that appear to have a high status, such as language, mathematics and science), and the claim that engagement with the arts will promote the development of a range of apparently desirable qualities and skills, such as empathy, morality, creativity, critical thinking, resilience, and so on. Nowadays, claims about the alleged usefulness of the arts are quite often made 'via' the brain, and sometimes even just plainly in terms of the brain, that is, as the claim that engagement with the arts promotes brain development.

Aside from the fact that arguments like these reveal strong curricular and societal hierarchies – where, after all, is the research that shows that doing mathematics will make you a better musician or doing physics will make you a better dancer? – the issue here is that instrumental justifications for the arts do not really care about art and are therefore quite vulnerable. After all, if researchers or policy makers were to find other – which usually means: cheaper or faster – ways to achieve a similar 'impact,' art would quickly be removed from the curriculum as too expensive, too onerous and too slow. Or art would only remain because it makes schools look 'nice' – which, of course, is a public relations argument, not one about art or education.

It would appear, then, that the only way to counter instrumental justifications is by way of *non*-instrumental justifications, that is, the idea of art for art's sake. This would mean, in other words, that the only viable case for the role of the arts in education would be to claim that art is fundamentally *useless*, that is, without any value *beyond* art. Such a move would only be inevitable, however, if we were to accept that the only way in which we can speak meaningfully about education is in terms of its usefulness, that is, in terms of a discourse that starts from the assumption that education is a techne (τέχνη) in the Aristotelian sense of the word (Aristotle, 1980; Biesta, 2015a), that is, a process aimed at the production of *things*. Yet the educated person is not a thing or a product, but a human being with an altered outlook. Or as Richard Peters (1963) has put it: 'To be educated is not to have arrived at a destination; it is to travel with a different point of view' (p.110). This means that asking questions about the usefulness of education amounts to what philosophers refer to as a *category mistake*, where we apply categories that are inappropriate for the topic at hand or, in more plain language, that simply miss the point of the topic.[1] Rather than asking what education *produces*, we should be asking what education *means*. And rather than asking what education *makes*, we should be asking what education *makes possible* (see also Biesta, 2015b).

The argument about the potential disappearance of education from art education has to do with wider developments in contemporary education, particularly developments that continue to steer education in the direction of the production of a small set of measurable 'learning outcomes' in curricular domains that apparently 'count'. It is in the context of such attempts to turn schools into 'exam factories' (Coffield & Williamson, 2012) that another argument for the role of the arts in education has been emerging. In response to approaches that tend to turn children into objects to be managed in such a way that they produce the most favourable outcomes for the education system,[2] the arts are brought in because of the opportunities they provide for children and young people to express their own voice, to give their own meaning, to discover their own talents, to enact their own creativity, and express their own, unique identity. In educational systems that reduce children to test scores, that stifle creativity or only allow creativity if it generates the 'right' outcomes, that are not interested in the voice of the student, and do not allow for the exploration and expression of the student's own unique identity, the arts definitely have an important role to play.

What if? From expression to education

But it is here that we encounter a crucial and in my view often overlooked issue that has to do with what, above, I have referred to as the potential disappearance of education from art education. While it is definitely important, not least in education systems that just focus on a narrow set of 'outcomes', to provide opportunities for children and young people to express themselves, that is, to appear as individuals in the world, and while the arts have an important contribution to make in this regard, *expression in itself is never enough*. And the reason why this is so becomes clear when we ask a number of 'What if?'-questions, such as: What if the voice that expresses itself is racist? What if the creativity that emerges is destructive? Or what if the identity that poses itself is egocentric or, with the words of Emmanuel Levinas (1991, p.44), ego-logical, that is, just pursuing the logic of the ego? These questions indicate that the educational concern can never be about the expression of voice, creativity and identity *as such*, but has to engage with the far more important and also far more difficult question of the *right* voice, the *right* creativity and the *right* identity.

Conceptions of art education that remain 'expressivist' in their approach, that is, conceptions of art education that see their ultimate aim as that of providing opportunities for expression without engaging in questions about what we might term the *quality* of what is expressed, run the risk of obliterating the educational dimension from art education. The quality that matters here is not the aesthetic quality – or at least not the aesthetic quality *per se* – but what we might term the *existential quality* of what and who is being expressed, a quality that has to do with how children and young people can exist *well*, individually and collectively, *in* the world and *with* the world.

It is one thing to say that education should be concerned with questions about the right voice, the right creativity and the right identity, but an entirely different matter to determine what would count as right. We have been told that in the past people would look at powers outside themselves for an answer to these questions. In some cases religious and spiritual powers were supposed to be able to provide final answers to questions about life, living and human destiny. In other cases secular powers were deemed to be able to do this. And there has also been the hope that scientific inquiry into the nature and condition of the human being would tell us how we ought to live our lives – an ambition perhaps still visible in the 'neurophilia' (Smeyers, 2016) of contemporary neuroscience.

It belongs to the modern experience, perhaps more so than to the postmodern one (see Habermas, 1987), that we have become increasingly aware of our own responsibility – individually and collectively – in engaging with the question as to what might count as right and good in our lives. And most of all, this is perhaps because we have witnessed on a global scale what can go wrong when we deny or surrender this responsibility and let powers outside ourselves decide. In this regard our educational age is indeed the age 'after Auschwitz' (Adorno, 1971, pp.88–104).

It is at this juncture that we encounter the question of what it means to exist as *subject* – as subject of our own actions, our own intentions and our responsibility – and not just as object of what others are inclined to decide or would like to decide about our lives. It is crucial to see, however, that to exist as subject does not mean that we just do what we want to do, without ever considering what our actions mean for, and do to, the opportunity for others to act as well. To exist as subject does not mean to simply escape from any external determination, but to ponder the question of limits and limitations, the question of when, how and to what extent we should limit and transform our own desires in face of the desires of others and in the face of an environment – a planet – that just isn't able to give us everything we want. To exist as subject thus means to exist *in dialogue* with the world; it means being 'in the world without occupying the centre of the world' (Meirieu, 2007, p.96).

This way of looking at education is obviously not child-centred, but it is also not curriculum-centred; it is not aimed at getting a curriculum 'inside' the student. Perhaps the best 'label' for it is to call it a 'world-centred' approach (see Biesta, 2015c), focusing on what it means to exist as subject, in, with and in dialogue with the world, material and social. From this angle, the educational 'task', which is a task for the educator not the one being educated, might be described as that of arousing in another human being the desire for wanting to exist in and with the world as subject, that is, wanting to exist in a 'grown-up' way (see Biesta, 2017b, chapter 1). As all educators know, we can never force another human being to exist as subject, because in doing so we would deny the very 'thing' that we seek to promote, namely that another human being exists as subject rather than object. That is why the educational gesture must remain hesitant and gentle (Biesta, 2012).

Existing as subject: resistance and dialogue

Existing as subject is precisely that: it is about how we, you, me, each of us, *exists*. It is not about what we have – our skills, our competencies, the things we have gathered and learned – nor about who we are. This means that the question of subjectness is very different from the question of identity. To exist as subject is about what we do and about what we refrain from doing. It is, in short, not about *who* we are, but about *how* we are or, more realistically, how we are trying to be. But to exist as subject, in and with the world, does not mean that we simply do what we want to do, that we simply follow our desires. This rather means that we acknowledge and come to terms with the reality of what and who we encounter in the world or, to put it in more precise terms: of what and who we encounter *as* world. Existing as subject thus requires that we try to exist *in dialogue* with what and who is other – in the world without occupying the centre of the world.

Hannah Arendt is helpful here as she has pointed out that to exist as subject does not just mean that one is the originator of one's own initiatives – the subject of action – but that, in order for those initiatives to come into the world, they must necessarily be subjected to what others, as subjects in their own right, do with our initiatives. That is why existing as subject means that we are subject 'in the twofold sense of the word, namely, [as] actor and sufferer' (Arendt, 1958, p.184). To exist as subject thus means that one is 'turned' towards the world or, in educational terms, that one is *being* turned towards the world, that one is being shown the world.

The encounter with the world – material or social – manifests itself in the experience of *resistance*. When we encounter resistance, when something or someone resists our intentions, our actions or our initiatives, we experience that the world is not a construction, and particularly not *our* construction, but that it exists in its own right. We encounter and experience, in other words, that the world is *real*. Experiencing resistance is in many ways a frustrating experience, as it shows us that there is something 'in our way', something that prevents us from realising – literally: making real – what we want to do or bring about. So the key question in relation to what it means to exist in the world is what we do when we encounter resistance, how we respond in the face of the experience of resistance. There are, broadly speaking, three options.

One is that our frustration energises us to push harder and harder in order to make our intentions and ambitions real. Sometimes this is indeed what is needed to get something done, but there is always the danger that if we push too hard, if we have too little consideration for the integrity of what we encounter, our intentions and ambitions will result in the destruction of what we encounter, the destruction of what offers resistance. At one end of the spectrum we thus end up in the destruction of the very world in which we seek to exist.

But the opposite scenario is also conceivable. This is where the frustration of encountering resistance leads us to withdrawal. We abandon our initiatives and ambitions because we feel that it is too difficult, not worth the effort, too frustrating, and so on, to pursue them. If the first response runs the risk of destroying the world, the second response runs the risk of destroying ourselves, destroying our very existence in the world, our existence as subject. We literally disappear from the world.

To exist in the world, to exist as subject, thus means that we try to stay away from these two extremes, although they are always on the horizon if we try to exist in the world. It means that we try to stay in the middle ground between world-destruction and self-destruction. Existing in this middle ground can be described as dialogue – as being in dialogue – as long as we do not think of dialogue as conversation but see it as an existential 'form', a way of existing in the world – not withdrawing from it – without putting ourselves in the centre of the world but leaving space for the world itself to exist as well – hence existing *with* the world. Dialogue is not a dispute or a contest where there is always, in the end, a winner. Dialogue – trying to be in dialogue, trying to exist in dialogue – is precisely where winning is not an option; it rather is an ongoing, lifelong challenge. It is the challenge to exist with what and who is other; it is the challenge to exist as subject in the world.

The middle ground between world-destruction and self-destruction is therefore a thoroughly *worldly* space. It is also, then, a thoroughly *educational* space, not because there may be all kind of things one can learn there, but because it is a space that *teaches* you something that is fundamental about human existence, namely *that you are not alone.*

Art, dialogue and education: towards grown-up existence

There are, of course, many definitions of what art is and many discussions about why such definitions are either essential or futile. Some definitions of art are explicitly expressivist in their orientation in that they see the 'point' of art from the perspective of what artists seek to express: emotions, intentions, ideas, feelings, concepts, an inner self, and so on. Such definitions tend to focus on the conceptual 'quality' of art, that is, on the *meaning* that artists seek to express through works of art. They thus position those who are at the 'receiving' end of the spectrum – as spectators, as perceivers, as listeners, as onlookers – as being in search of understanding, of aiming at getting 'the point' of what is being expressed.

I am interested in looking at art – across the whole spectrum of art disciplines – differently, *not* in terms of the logic of intention-and-reception, but in terms of the *doing* of art or, more precisely, encountering the doing of art. And what I tend to see there is that art is precisely this ongoing, literally never-ending exploration of the encounter with what and who is other, the ongoing and never-ending exploration of what it might mean to exist in and with the world. The ambition there is not to master or domesticate – which would ultimately lead to the destruction of the reality one is encountering – but to come into dialogue, to establish dialogue, to stay in dialogue. Encountering the reality of paint, stone, wood, metal, sound, bodies, including one's own body, encountering resistance, in order to explore possibilities, meet limits and limitations, and out of this create forms, establish forms and find forms that make existing-in-dialogue possible, that is what I see in the 'doing' of art.

Viewed in this way, art itself appears as the ongoing exploration of what it means to be *in* the world, the ongoing attempt at figuring out what it means to be here, now; to be – here – now.

Existing as subject, existing in and with the world, thus requires that we do not simply follow our desires, not simply do what we want to do, but that we always 'measure' our desires, bring our desires into dialogue with the world, with what offers resistance to our desires. Here we encounter an important but often ill-understood educational distinction between what we might term 'infantile' and 'grown-up' ways of being and the point I wish to make here is that to exist as subject in and with the world means that we try to exist in a grown-up way.

There are several caveats here. It is first of all important to see that the distinction between the 'infantile' and the 'grown-up' should not be understood in developmental terms, that is, as a trajectory from the infantile to the grown-up, but should be understood as two different ways of being, two different ways of existing. 'Infantile' refers to a way of being that is totally determined and controlled by our desires as they present themselves to us – and the latter is important because the question of where our desires actually come from, how many of our desires are really our 'own' desires and how many of them are fabricated by forces beyond our control, remains an open question. Nonetheless, the desires are there and it is up to us to do something with them.

If the 'infantile' refers to ways of being that are totally controlled by our desires, the 'grown-up' refers to a way of being where we try to give an answer, through our thinking and our doing, to the question of which of our desires are the desires we ought to have, which of our desires are *desirable*. To exist in a grown-up way is therefore not something that we can claim to have achieved at a certain age or stage in life or after a certain amount of learning. It rather describes a way of being, a 'quality' of existing, where we are not *subjected to* our desires – we might also say: where we are not just an object of our desires – but where we are *a subject in relation to* our desires.

The key educational question, therefore, is whether what I desire is what I should desire, whether it is desirable for my own life, my life with others, on a planet that only has limited capacity for fulfilling our desires.

Pondering the question of whether what we desire is desirable, whether it is what we should and can desire, is not aimed at suppressing or destroying our desires, but about selecting and transforming them so that they can be a force for our attempts at existing as subject, in the world, in a grown-up way. Our desires are after all a – and perhaps even *the* – main driving force, the main source of energy in our lives, so that the very thing that should not happen in our engagement with the question whether what we desire is desirable, is that we give up our desires altogether, most fundamentally our desire to want to exist in the world, our desire for wanting to be here, now. Gayatri Spivak's formulation of education as a process of the 'uncoercive rearrangement of desires' (Spivak 2004, p.526) is helpful here, although the question of coercion is perhaps a bit more complicated than what this formulation suggests.

One interesting implication of the argument I have tried to present is that the experience of resistance is not just an encounter with what is real – to which I have referred as 'the world' – but is at the very same time an encounter with our desires, because when we experience resistance we experience that what we desire in relation to what offers resistance is not 'smoothly' possible. This is why art is not just an exploration of what it means to be in dialogue with the world – it is not just 'outward facing', so to speak – but is at the very same time an exploration of our desires – and in this regard it is also always 'inward facing'. Art makes our desires visible, gives them form, and by trying to come into dialogue with what or who offers resistance, we are at the very same time engaged in the exploration of the desirability of our desires and in their rearrangement and transformation.

To put it more boldly then: just as art *is* the dialogue of human beings with the world, art *is* the exploration and transformation of our desires so that they can become a positive force for the ways in which we seek to exist in the world in grown-up ways. And that is where we may find the educative power of the arts.

In conclusion

There is, of course, much more to say about the topics I have raised in this chapter,[3] but what I hope to have achieved is to outline an approach to art education that neither reduces art to an instrument for the production of outcomes that 'really' count, nor advocates that the educative potential of the arts lies in providing opportunities for the expression of voice, creativity and identity *per se*. The educational task is, as I have indicated, a more difficult one. I have not only suggested that in order for art education to remain educational it needs to take the task of grown-up existence in and with the world seriously; I have also suggested that the arts provide unique possibilities for engaging with this task.

Notes

1 In this context see also Jan Masschelein's penetrating critique of 'productive' thinking about education (Masschelein, 1991).
2 Note that on this logic it is no longer a question of what schools can do for their students, but what students must do for the league table position of their school and their country, a point well made by Michael Apple (see, for example, Apple, 2000).
3 For more detail see Biesta (2017a) and Biesta (2017b).

References

Adorno, Th.W. (1971). *Erziehung zur Mündigkeit: Vorträge und Gespräche mit Hellmut Becker 1959–1969*. Frankfurt am Main: Suhrkamp Verlag.

Apple, M.W. (2000). Can critical pedagogies interrupt rightist policies? *Educational Theory* 50(2), 229–254.

Arendt, H. (1958). *The Human Condition*. Chicago: The University of Chicago Press.

Aristotle (1980). *The Nicomachean Ethics*. Oxford: Oxford University Press.

Baldacchino, J. (2012). *Art's Way Out: Exit pedagogy and the cultural condition*. Rotterdam: Sense publishers.

Biesta, G.J.J. (2012). No education without hesitation: Thinking differently about educational relations. In C. Ruitenberg et al. (Eds), *Philosophy of Education 2012* (pp.1–13). Urbana-Champaign, IL: PES.

Biesta, G.J.J. (2015a). How does a competent teacher become a good teacher? On judgement, wisdom and virtuosity in teaching and teacher education. In R. Heilbronn & L. Foreman-Peck (Eds.), *Philosophical Perspectives on the Future of Teacher Education* (pp.3–22). Oxford: Wiley Blackwell.

Biesta, G.J.J. (2015b). Freeing teaching from learning: Opening up existential possibilities in educational relationships. *Studies in Philosophy and Education* 34(3), 229–243.

Biesta, G.J.J. (2015c). Wereld-gericht onderwijs: Vorming tot volwassenheid. *De Nieuwe Meso* 2(3), 54–61.

Biesta, G.J.J. (2017a). *Letting Art Teach: Art education 'after' Joseph Beuys*. Arnhem: ArtEZ Press.

Biesta, G.J.J. (2017b). *The Rediscovery of Teaching*. New York: Routledge.

Callon, M. (1986). Elements of a sociology of translation: Domestication of the scallops and the fishermen of St Brieuc Bay. In J. Law (Ed.), *Power, Action and Belief: A new sociology of knowledge?* (pp.196–233). London: Routledge.

Coffield, F. & Williamson, B. (2012). *From Exam Factories to Communities of Discovery: The democratic route*. London: UCL-IOE Press.

Habermas, J. (1987). *The Philosophical Discourse of Modernity: Twelve lectures*. Cambridge, MA: MIT Press.

Levinas, E. (1991). *Totality and Infinity: An essay on exteriority*. Translated by Alfonso Lingis. Dordrecht: Kluwer Academic Publishers.

Masschelein, J. (1991). Die ergebnislose und funktionslose Erziehung. Gemeinschaft, Oeffentlichkeit und Immanenz. *Zeitschrift für Pädagogik 37*(1), 65–80.

Meirieu, P. (2007). *Pédagogie: Le devoir de résister*. Issy-les-Moulineaux: ESF éditeur.

Peters, R.S. (1963). Education as initiation. In P. Gordon (Ed.), *The Study of Education: A collection of inaugural lectures*, Vol. 1 (pp.273–299). London: Woburn.

Smeyers, P. (2016). Neurophilia: Guiding educational research and the educational field. *Journal of Philosophy of Education 50*(1), 62–75.

Spivak, G.C. (2004). Righting the wrongs. *South Atlantic Quarterly 103*(2/3), 523–581.

Winner, E., Goldstein, T.R. & Vincent-Lancrin, S. (2013). *Art for Art's Sake? The impacts of arts education*. Paris: OECD: Educational Research and Innovation.

3

DICING THE MEAT

Bacon in the middle of an arts-based sandwich

David R. Cole

Introduction

Even a cursory analysis of Gilles Deleuze's (2003) book on the Irish artist Francis Bacon (1909–1992) reveals the disparity between the resultant philosophy, his paintings, and most contemporary arts-based educational practice. Bacon was a tortured individual with an alcohol problem, and inner demons that propelled his art into the depiction of ever more contorted, self-distorting strangeness. However, even though his work was often lampooned and ridiculed whilst he was alive, his reputation as being perhaps one of the major British painters of the twentieth century has continued to grow since his death in 1992. In contrast, arts-based practice in schools tends to 'play it safe', conforming to normatively pre-defined ideas of 'what art can be'. This chapter will argue that an analysis of Deleuze (2003) in the context of Bacon could help to change the ways in which the arts are currently represented and practised in schools, especially in terms of 'subjectivity' and learning. 'Subjectivity' and 'meat' are powerfully inter-linked in Bacon's paintings and for Deleuze, and point to the visceral and transversal representations of identity, practice and thought that the artist's work affords. For the purposes of this chapter, the example of Bacon's work which will be referred to is the *Portrait of Michel Leiris* (1976).[1]

What is the meat?

The body in Western art is usually addressed in terms of 'the nude', or representational thinking about the human body as a mode of analysing anatomy, desire, sexuality, eroticism or bodily aesthetics, and therefore furthering an appreciation of the intricacies of the human form (Sorabella, 2008). Such thinking about the body pervades arts-practice in education, even though the extension from a mode of human representation to a relational analysis of erotics or sexuality is often censured or stymied in education. This is primarily due to moral considerations and learning-limitations on feeling anything bodily in/through education. By contrast, Lorde advocates: 'In touch with the erotic, I become less willing to accept powerlessness, or those other supplied states of being which are not native to me, such as resignation, despair, self-effacement, depression, self-denial' (as cited in Anton & Schmit, 2007, p.259). The liberational aspects of 'body-feelings' are most often suppressed in education, due in part to the moral censorship of such feelings, but also due to the psychological, developmental model of childhood that is frequently placed on the subjectivity of children at school, wherein and through which they are designated as (sexless/unsexual) learners (e.g., Deci & Ryan, 2000). In contrast, the analysis of the meat, taken from Deleuze's (2003) reading of Bacon's paintings, looks to unlock any liberational sensations that may become internalised in the young body and as the body ages, and as the cloak of invisibility spreads due to contorted feelings that are mixed up, often in a complicated way, with body-sensation.

Psychoanalysis has gone some way to address the issue of the bar to understanding the sexuality of children, though as Deleuze and Guattari (1983) state, even though psychoanalysis opens up questions about the development of the sexuality of the child, it simultaneously locks these questions in timeless mechanisms, such as the Oedipal complex. The expression 'the meat' that Deleuze (2003) uses in his book about the Irish painter, Francis Bacon, is employed in a non-psychoanalytic rendering of the body, that attempts to express the complex vitality of the lived body over time (including, but not pointedly referring to its sexuality). At the same time, all other possible poetic and convulsive aspects of the body are kept in the meat, which are often excluded from overly rational philosophical/educational thought (including non-human relations) and would therefore misunderstand portraits such as that of Michel Leiris: 'Meat is not dead flesh; it retains all the sufferings and assumes all the colours of living flesh. It manifests such convulsive pain and vulnerability, but also such delightful invention, colour, and acrobatics' (Deleuze, 2003, p.23).

Beyond, through, as part of, and co-existent with the 'meat' in Deleuzian terms, and essential to understanding how learning with the arts works in this chapter, is *rhythm*. 'Rather than being a specific space or process, rhythm is the dynamic movements that are always already between any space and process, and that allow for their co-constitution and the possibility of their dissolution' (Russell, 2015, p.345). Thus rhythm is part of the 'in-between' focus in Deleuze, and not defined through magnitude, polarity, range or the extent to which the rhythm happens (as it is already there, and our concern therefore is not to measure, control or to simplify it). Deleuze mentions the importance of rhythm in *A Thousand Plateaus*, in the context of understanding and responding to the complex inter-relatedness of life as 'planes of immanence', and later returns to rhythm, when describing how Bacon is able to produce movement from painting beyond/in/through 'the meat'. The rhythm of the meat in the portrait of Michel Leiris is a dark, foreboding movement, that distorts half of the face, whilst playing with the image of the other. Even though one could argue that Bacon is primarily a painter of contorted human portraits and figures, and the pain and inner demons that these figures emit, he could also be credited with inventing a singular mode of using and portraying the body as meat, which has running through it distinct and powerful rhythms, which are indicative of complicated and far-reaching life and thought processes:

> The lived body is still a paltry thing in comparison with a more profound and almost unliveable Power [puissance]. We can seek the unity of rhythm only at the point where rhythm itself plunges into chaos, into the night, *at the point where the differences of level are perpetually and violently mixed.*
>
> *(Deleuze, 2003*, p.44, emphasis added*)*

Deleuze at this point is emphatically showing how rhythm can lead to non-equilibrium understandings of phenomena. Even though Deleuze could be understood as a materialist philosopher (Cole, 2012), and therefore offers a material analysis of rhythm, his frequent application of theological concepts such as the transcendental, immanence, the univocal and haecceity, indicates his concern to sketch a materialist philosophy that has a substantial connection to metaphysics. The 'rhythm of the meat' is part of this metaphysics, in that Deleuze assigns a mode of becoming to meat which includes the non-equal actions of ghosts, past memories, dreams, random, often fleeting traditions, frequent half-truths and superstitions; all of which could be said to 'haunt' the portrait of Michel Leiris. Deleuze (2003) does everything possible to extend his philosophy to include the darker and more complex side of life, as can be understood through his analysis of Bacon.

This Deleuzian move to reanimate and extend the actions of 'the meat' with transcendental features that play with the shadows of the mind, is parallel to Joseph Conrad's (1857–1924) writing in *Heart of Darkness* (1899), which portrays a haunted, supernatural quality to and of the meat: 'that commingling of absurdity, surprise and bewilderment in a tremor of struggling revolt, that notion of being captured by the incredible which is the very essence of dreams' (Conrad, 1995, p.50). Conrad invented a mode of writing that effectively described the loss of certainty and what it was like for a white, male colonialist to plunge into black Africa in the nineteenth century, through the invention of a vertiginous meta-language. Deleuze's philosophy is similarly interested in vertigo; however, the vertigo involved with the 'rhythm of the meat', in Deleuzian terms, is a reciprocating play and mode of experimentation, which works by sensing how to tap into natural and unconscious processes, that are intimately and simultaneously enwrapped in and as part of the meat. Transposed to contemporary arts practice, the meat can be teased out through non-clichéd or disjunctive repetitive explorations of body/flesh/life interactions. In terms of the portrait of Michel Leiris, the subject stares at us, but this stare is not even rational or 'foreclosed', indeed, it is nearly impossible to stare back, given the intensity of the expression that comes out of the painting. These entwined processes lead to an understanding of a central Deleuzian concept, which he took from the writing of Antonin Artaud (1896–1948), and is repeated in his analyses of capitalism and schizophrenia, and the painting of Francis Bacon: that is, the 'body without organs':

> A wave with a variable amplitude flows through *the body without organs*; it traces zones and levels on this body according to the variations of its amplitude. When the wave encounters external forces at a particular level, *a sensation appears*. An organ will be determined by this encounter, but it is a provisional organ that endures only as long as the passage of the wave and the action of the force, and which will be displaced in order to be posited elsewhere. 'No organ is constant as regards either function or position'.
>
> *(Deleuze, 2003, p.47,* emphasis added*)*

The body without organs sits behind and across from the meat. It is a deeper conception of the body, which sets up encounters with invisible force fields that are passing through the body/flesh/meat at any given moment (Voss, 2013). Once the body without organs interacts with external forces, one feels something, which is exactly what is required in contemporary arts-practice along Deleuzian lines. This type of 'feeling-enhancement' can be produced through the use of paintings such as the portrait of Michel Leiris as a classroom prompt, or as a focus for getting beneath the skin of contemporary arts practice. The meat is important as a means to understand how the body contorts and transforms the visual field, and explains what one sees when, for example, confronted with a Bacon painting such as the portrait. Whilst the meat extends to the visual field, and can be sensed on the optic plane as suffering, pity, fear, confusion in life, a more thorough analysis takes us to the unconscious and historical forces that are provoking and distributing this play of the senses, in combination with the deep sense of rhythm through and as part of the invisible body in time:

> These primordial movements are conceived in terms of an ovoid form—'the egg of the world' *(aduno tal)*—within which lie, already differentiated, the germs of things; in consequence of the spiral movement of extension the germs develop first in segments of increasing length, representing the fundamental seeds of cultivation, which are to be found again in the human body.
>
> *(Griaule & Dieterlen, 1999, p.84)*

The body without organs give one a sense of the coordinates of rhythm, emergence and extension without determining in advance what exactly they might be. Rhythm stands alongside the body without organs, as learning stands beside the organism, not as its determination, but in a reciprocal relationship that shows us how we might start to understand 'subjectivity' according to this schema, and that we can apply to arts-practice. In terms of using the portrait of Michel Leiris, this means trying to comprehend his history, and what the precise distortion of his features does to us as viewers, and whether or not we ourselves are thus distorted in the viewing.

At this point, one is inclined to link the philosophy of Deleuze to that of Whitehead, who also sketched out a philosophy of how subjectivity works as the dynamics of the organism. He didn't go as far in his analysis of the body, though provides a useful theoretical companion to the direction of Deleuze that furthers the metaphysical linkage between the body, rhythm and learning, and that is applicable to arts-based education as 'process thought'. Deleuze has been named as a process philosopher (Barker, 2009) along with Whitehead (1929), which shows how for both philosophers, the organism is not a fixed or static object, but critically responds to elements of motion, rhythm, and the many elements of entwinement which could be dismissed as background noise. As Whitehead tells us, his 'philosophy of the organism is the inversion of Kant's philosophy … For Kant, the world emerges from the subject; for "the philosophy of the organism", *the subject emerges from the world*' (as cited in Sherburne, 1995, p.852, *emphasis added*). The rhythm inside and as part of the body, through and by which learning happens, is explained by Whitehead as a spiralling and repeating aspect of the three inter-related processes of romance, precision and generalisation. Romance was for Whitehead (1967) the basic motivational force, after and due to which all knowledge-work can proceed. Whitehead summarizes: 'romance, precision, generalization, are all present throughout. But there is an alternation of dominance, and it is this alternation which constitutes the cycles' (Whitehead, 1967, p.28). Or, stated differently:

> During the state of precision, romance is the background. The stage is dominated by the inescapable fact that there are right ways and wrong ways, and definite truths to be known. But romance is not dead, and it is the art of teaching to foster it amidst definite application to an appointed task.
>
> *(Whitehead, 1967, p.34)*

This art of teaching is a coordination of and modulation with sensation that Deleuze speaks of with reference to the meat of Bacon, as wave patterns hit the body/flesh/meat, and potentially turn it inwards towards the body without organs and the plane of intensity. By connecting Deleuze's analysis of Bacon through rhythm and the metaphysical, process philosophy of Whitehead, one encounters a profound and multi-levelled educational philosophy, that is, however, seldom practised. In terms of the portrait of Michel Leiris, this educational philosophy involves alternating between contemplation of the full effects of the painting, and how these effects can be translated into enhanced and ongoing arts-practice.

> *Sensation is vibration.* We know that the egg reveals just this state of the body 'before' organic representation: axes and vectors, gradients, zones, cinematic movements, and dynamic tendencies, in relation to which forms are contingent or accessory. 'No mouth. No tongue. No teeth. No larynx. No oesophagus. No belly. No anus.' It is a whole nonorganic life, for the organism is not life, it is what imprisons life.
>
> *(Deleuze, 2003, p.45, emphasis added)*

The problem with modern, contemporary educational practice in these terms is that learning rarely gets the chance to delve deeply or consistently enough to reveal the type of 'feeling experiential knowledge' or 'primordial insight' as described above. One of the main points of analysing Bacon from a philosophical perspective for contemporary art-practice is not to diminish, control or regulate the sensations that painting can produce, or that one could feel in relation to art. The truth of applying Deleuze to the arts lies absolutely in the opposite direction; that is, *it is to produce sensation*, and to thus extend the levels by and through which art can penetrate subjectivity. Thus, a combined Deleuze and Whitehead metaphysics of sensation points to a new thinking arts-practice, that emphasises the speculative possibilities inherent within practice, and looks for ways out of being trapped by the already-given in life and thought.

Whilst Deleuze (2003) performs considerable intellectual gymnastics, his intention is always to question the normatively pre-agreed formats that exist as part of and often due to spectator appreciation of an artist such as Bacon, to arrive at an earlier or non-aligned feeling or pre-given, intuitive perspective. In terms of the portrait of Michel Leiris, this intuitive state needs to inform any rational investigation into what the painting does to the viewer, and how we can respond. The body without organs helps with this enterprise, in that the modes of becoming of an egg are pre-organic, and therefore hold a greater level of intensity than an already cemented organ relationship with the outside world, formed, for example, when one sees something. Art-practice at the level of the pre-organic egg is parallel to Beethoven's continued composing of music after he went deaf, or the artistic writing practices of numerous experimental thinkers, such as William Burroughs (1814–1997) who used 'cut-up' to try and reach the pre-rational, aleatory level of creation (Burroughs & Gysin, 1978). However, the danger here is to create an imaginary plane of arts-practice, not connected in any way to the actual practices that are current in schools. Therefore, one must return to what is actually set up and happening now, in order to sketch possible arts curriculum, pedagogy and policy for the future.

Conventional arts-based school practice: *What can be done?*

Nicholas Bourriaud (2001) maintains that the role of contemporary artworks 'is no longer to form imaginary and utopian realities, but to actually be ways of living and models of action within the existing real' (p.13). Art becomes a moment to be lived through, opening un/limited conversations (Springgay, 2004, p.14). Thus, to open up the conversation from Deleuze's (2003) reading of the paintings of Francis Bacon, one has to relate this analysis and resultant philosophy to actual arts-practice. For example, in NSW, Australia, the arts curriculum (Board of Studies, 2006) is a framework that sets out developmental guidelines in stages, whilst not specifying exactly what the teacher has to teach. In primary schools, the arts curriculum in NSW is combined, whilst in high schools, the arts curriculum separates into the parallel syllabi of the visual arts, drama, dance, photography and visual media, visual design and music. As a framework, the NSW arts curriculum leaves the individual teacher and arts departments to decide how and to what extent to allow their students to explore the arts. Themes for content (e.g., the beach) and criteria for assessment are suggested by the curriculum (e.g. engagement with an artist's work), yet they are left as broad 'placeholders' for the teachers to interpret and use given their particular contexts. Whilst this framework does serve to present teachers with a basis for their arts-based practice, it is suggested that Deleuze's (2003) analysis of the art of Bacon could deepen and extend this practice by:

- Questioning the developmental nature of the arts curriculum. This is not to suggest that young children can suddenly become artists, or that older children might not be better at their arts practice than younger children, but that one cannot determine in advance exactly how and to what extent an arts-based curriculum might 'take off' and that artistic powers might develop exponentially given the right conditions. The key here is to have the conditions in place so that any 'take off' in arts-based practice may be properly supported, for example, by having teachers who can work with material such as Bacon's paintings and Deleuze's philosophising around them, and having the time and capacity to encourage the deep-seated engagements that this chapter has described, for example, with respect to experimentation with all the possible ways of looking at and thinking about the portrait of Michel Leiris.
- Investing in rhythm. 'Creativity' is in demand in terms of being a pre-determined requisite for and product of the arts in education (Jeanes, 2006). However, little is understood in terms of what this means and/or how to truly foster creativity. Critics of contemporary arts practice in schools such as Sir Ken Robinson have looked at the clockwork, mechanical nature of schooling that comes from the nineteenth century, and have shown how schools can act as factories for conformism, following the rules and the churning out of qualifications (Robinson, 2006). The suggestion here is to go in the opposite direction to this, and to take creativity seriously as a mode of living and becoming in line with Deleuzian vitalist philosophy by focusing on, for example, the dynamics of rhythm. However, Deleuzian philosophy is not simply a matter of opposing everything that is deemed non-creative. Indeed, one could argue that taking the Deleuzian line to enhance creativity in schools is as, if not more, rigorous than taking a conventional path. This is because, as the example of the analysis of the paintings of Bacon such as the portrait of Michel Leiris shows, the Deleuzian practice of discerning and working with the deep rhythms in and through the artwork is not a superficial or surface activity. Rather, natural, unconscious, cultural, historical and relational rhythms need to be followed and understood to enact the Deleuzian perspective on creativity.
- Working deeply with rhythms in education to produce a thoroughly inter-disciplinary approach to teaching and learning (Golding, 2009). Whilst the body, here captured and articulated through Bacon as 'the meat' and 'the body without organs', is central to understanding the effects of this reorientation to deep rhythmic learning patterns, knowledge from bodily sources is not the only kind of knowledge that is opened up through this Deleuzian approach to the arts.

Recently articulated 'new materialist' and 'post human' approaches (St. Pierre, Jackson & Mazzei, 2016) to education pointedly show us the ways in which there are material and non-human rhythms that are effective and applicable to the modes of transformation that are being advocated in this chapter. In the painting of Michel Leiris, there is a definite non-human, unworldly quality to the work, which points to going beyond the boundaries of the 'familial-human' in the creative process. There are boundless artistic opportunities to be had in extending and explicating material and non-human complexes as they appear in the world, and to extending the logic that this generates; and this expanded practice could involve, for example, the processes that lie in creatively interpreting the work of an anthill, or in performing a drama based around the dynamics of a bridge. The Deleuzian approach would be to extend and deepen arts-practice in a material, processual, metaphysical way without making it clichéd, banal or obvious.

- Teachers recognising themselves as artists involved with complex and ongoing pedagogic processes. It can always be problematic to add to the pedagogic load of a teacher, or to try and artificially extend the burden of their jobs by constantly updating their roles with new identities and new features given the latest research or trend in the field (Beijaard, Meijer & Verloop, 2004). However, one could say that the connection between Deleuze's (2003), philosophical analysis of the paintings of Bacon and real pedagogic action takes an artist's sensitivity to make sure that any obvious, representative thinking is avoided. Rather than merely taking Deleuze's ideas as a blueprint for action, or translating them literally to interpret renditions of the body as 'meat' and 'the body without organs', the higher level skill of the teacher is to articulate and see these bodily changes in the world as real. For example, these changes can be found in an analysis of old age and ageing in film, literature and real life, and could be further imbued with emotional impact and power taken from Deleuze's (2003) theory on Bacon as a means to connect outer, observational changes in the body with inner, spiritual and subjective feelings of being in the world (or the loss of being in the world, e.g. sensing one's invisibility).

- Transforming assessment practices in the arts to be in line with the revelations of 'the meat' and 'the body without organs'. This change in focus can take away the importance of concentrating on summative assessment, and requires formative, ongoing, inter-related, complex assessment practices that capture the ways in which the body, the material and the non-human buckle and transform under pressure from life. New assessments in the arts need to engage with the thinking skills necessary to articulate and analyse the ways in which matter changes over time, and therefore has to include a model of material transformation (Cole & Hager, 2010) for learning as a minimum requirement for it to function. Such a model will loop back on any investment and understanding that has been put into properly examining rhythm in and through the arts, and would manifest in, for example, in extended responses to Bacon's artworks such as the portrait of Michel Leiris.

Conclusion

The problematic for all theorists, researchers and practitioners working in the field of arts-based education and using Deleuzian concepts is the translation of the ideas to practice. On one side, one could argue, as Elizabeth St. Pierre (2016) consistently does, that the application of Deleuzian concepts, as I have attempted to do in this chapter, can lead to a thoroughgoing analysis of the foundations of one's inquiry, method or practice and this action avoids the 'rush to application' (p.111) that some may be tempted to undertake, and which may forego the deeper aspects of the analysis. On the other side of the argument, one could say that the Deleuzian concepts are already in and are an integral part of practice, even if their existence is usually not properly theorised or understood (Cole, 2008). The central role of rhythm in this chapter is a good example of the Deleuzian conundrum for practitioners and theorists, which leads to the question: *What does it really mean to understand rhythm in arts-based education?* The point here is parallel to Gert Biesta's remark on 'grown-up-ness' in education. On one side, the use of concepts such as 'grown-up-ness' can help us to delve into what we are doing in education in terms of subjectivity, relationships, development, and so on. On the other, the 'grown-up-ness' is already in education, but possibly not recognised or theorised in any way, and if it is, it can be theorised badly: 'If we think of our encounters with the material world, we may find ourselves pushing so hard that the material we want to shape and form breaks under the pressure' (Biesta, 2017, p.14). Rhythm is similarly difficult to work with, due to the sensitivity it requires, the opaque nature of its existence, and the invisibility that it hides within. The Deleuzian encounter of thought and the translation to practice is exactly in this 'in-between', where rhythms abound, where the unconscious works, and where nature has not been processed, standardised or commodified. This is the place where arts-based education needs to sit, and which is opened up through the deep engagement with profound works of art such as the portrait of Michel Leiris.

Note

1 An interview and representation of this painting can be found at: www.americansuburbx. com/2015/05/francis-bacon-discussing-photographs-painting-destructive-criticism-and-more.html

References

Anton, A., & Schmitt, R. (2007). *Toward a New Socialism*. Lanham, MD: Lexington Books.
Barker, T. (2009). Toward a Process Philosophy for Digital Aesthetics. *Proceedings of the International Symposium on Electronic Arts 09* (ISEA09), Belfast. Retrieved from: www. icinema.unsw.edu.au/assets/165/barker49.pdf
Beijaard, D., Meijer, P., & Verloop, N. (2004). Reconsidering Research on Teachers' Professional Identity. *Teaching and Teacher Education*, 20(2), 107.
Biesta, G.J.J. (2017). *The Rediscovery of Teaching*. New York: Routledge.
Board of Studies, NSW. (2006). *Creative Arts K-6 Syllabus*. Sydney: Board of Studies, NSW.

Bourriaud, N. (2001). *Relational Aesthetics*. Paris: Les Press du Réel.

Burroughs, W.S., & Gysin, B. (1978). *The Third Mind*. New York: The Viking Press.

Cole, D.R. (2008). Deleuze and the Narrative Forms of Educational Otherness. In I. Semetsky (Ed.), *Nomadic Education: Variations on a Theme by Deleuze and Guattari* (pp.17–35). Rotterdam: Sense Publishers.

Cole, D.R. (2012). Matter in Motion: The Educational Materialism of Gilles Deleuze. *Educational Philosophy and Theory*, *44*(1), 3–17.

Cole, D.R., & Hager, P. (2010). Learning-practice: The Ghosts in the Education Machine. *Education Inquiry*, *1*(1), 21–40.

Conrad, J. (1995). *Heart of Darkness*. Harmondsworth: Penguin Books (original book published 1899).

Deci, E.L., & Ryan, R.M. (2000). The 'What' and 'Why' of Goal Pursuits: Human Needs and the Self-determination of Behaviour. *Psychological Inquiry*, *11*, 227–268.

Deleuze, G. (2003). *Francis Bacon: The Logic of Sensation* (D.W. Smith, trans.). London: Continuum (original text in French, 1981).

Deleuze, G., & Guattari, F. (1983). *Anti-Oedipus: Capitalism & Schizophrenia* (R. Hurley, M. Seem & H.F. Lane, trans.). London: Athlone Press.

Golding, C. (2009). *Integrating the Disciplines: Successful Interdisciplinary Subjects*. Melbourne: Centre for the Study of Higher Education. Retrieved from: http://melbourne-cshe.unimelb.edu.au

Griaule, M., & Dieterlen, G. (1999). The Dogon. In C.D. Forde (Ed.), *African Worlds: Studies in the Cosmological Ideas and Social Values of African Peoples* (pp.76–94). Münster: LIT Verlag (first published 1954).

Jeanes, E. (2006). Resisting Creativity, Creating the New: A Deleuzian Perspective on Creativity. *Creativity and Innovation Management*, *15*(2), 127–234.

Robinson, K. (2006). Do Schools Kill Creativity? Original TED talk. Retrieved from: www.ted.com/talks/ken_robinson

Russell, F. (2015). Slave to the Rhythm: The Problem of Creative Pedagogy and the Teaching of Creativity. *Deleuze Studies*, *9*(3), 337–355.

Sherburne, D.W. (1995). Whitehead, Alfred North. In R. Audi (Ed.), *The Cambridge Dictionary of Philosophy* (pp.851–853). Cambridge: Cambridge University Press.

Sorabella, J. (2008). The Nude in Western Art and its Beginnings in Antiquity. In I. Heilbrunn (Ed.), *Timeline of Art History* (pp.211–232). New York: The Metropolitan Museum of Art. Retrieved from: www.metmuseum.org

Springgay, S. (2004). Inside the Visible: Arts-Based Educational Research as Excess. *Journal of Curriculum and Pedagogy*, *1*, 8–18, doi: 10.1080/15505170.2004.10411470

St. Pierre, E.A. (2016). The Empirical and the New Empiricisms. *Cultural Studies ↔ Critical Methodologies*, *16*(2), 111–124.

St. Pierre, E.A., Jackson, A.Y., & Mazzei, L.A. (2016). New Empiricisms and New Materialisms: Conditions for New Inquiry. *Cultural Studies ↔ Critical Methodologies*, *16*(2), 99–110.

Voss, D. (2013). The Philosophical Concepts of Meat and Flesh: Deleuze and Merleau-Ponty. *PARRHESIA*, *18*, 113–112.

Whitehead, A.N. (1929). *Process and Reality: An Essay in Cosmology*. New York: Macmillan.

Whitehead, A.N. (1967). *The Aims of Education and Other Essays*. New York: Free Press.

4

ARTISTS, PRESENCE AND THE GIFT OF BEING UNTEACHERLY

Mary Ann Hunter

> *An interruption that really interrupts always arrives unexpected, as a thief in the night*
> (Biesta, 2013a, p.52)

Introduction

In one of a series of short documentaries about artists in schools in Tasmania, multi-disciplinary artist, Selena De Carvalho, is depicted walking among the grounds of a senior college and pondering purposefully at a cafeteria table.

> The catalyst for … applying for the AIR [Artist in Residence] program … is just the opportunity to step inside an institution and bring my creative life into that space.
>
> *(De Carvalho in Mark & Tom, 2014b)*

In contrast to conventional perceptions of artists-in-residence as expert visitors charged with instructing and mentoring students, De Carvalho's intention was to both *bring* and *derive* creativity from the school environment. She describes her individual practice and motivation for working, while the visual focus remains on her connectedness with the surroundings, her artmaking and the students.

> I brought myself into that environment and at times I felt like I stuck out like a sore thumb, but it was also quite beautiful in that I was literally just connecting with students and talking to them and bringing my own personal stories and artwork.
>
> *(De Carvalho in Mark & Tom, 2014b)*

In the film, De Carvalho's persona and practice are explicitly *in place*, and reflect something of her own situating of herself and her practice in place. The relationality of the artist and her material practice to the human and non-human environment are central to the filmic framing of the value of her work. De Carvalho still appears as somewhat different from the people around her, however. Her presence, while evidently welcome by those with whom she interacts, interrupts the regulatory expectations and practices of institutional school life. She appears as a quietly disruptive and yet enabling presence. This is not artistry celebrated in its role-modelling of technique, smooth alignment with curriculum, best-practice pedagogy, or as a contribution to preconceived learning standards and outcomes – although these may have been present to various degrees during her residency. Rather, De Carvalho presents as an artist who brings an open-ended but purposeful curiosity to work and to life. She makes herself *of* the school world, but without claiming its centre of attention.

Gert Biesta's attention to the value of interruption is a reminder of the potency of present-time awareness and the sometimes bold disregard for convention required of the good educational encounter. At its most impactful, interruption heralds the arrival of new knowing without preconception and enlivens us to possibility and change. At its most embodied, such interruption can become a catalyst to act. De Carvalho's presence may not have initially seemed so significant to those around her, but her work was certainly interruptive. Without an explicit striving for preset standards or a recourse to curriculum requirements, De Carvalho's work and *whole presence* as an artist appeared to enable a unique connectedness among students. In observing her work as documented, and after gaining a sense of her intentions and interactions outside the representation of the film, I became aware of her work's interruption to my own thinking about the value of artists in schools. Instead of turning, as an evaluator might, to what the artist does for the teachers and students, and what achievements she might have enabled, I turned toward the curiosity engendered by her very presence of being. What did De Carvalho's presence ask of students, of the broader school community, and of the educational act more broadly? How might "good education" come of artists' reconceptualisation of schools as sites of "intra-action" (Barad, 2003, p.815) and "potentia" (Braidotti, 2006, p.134), rather than as institutions in need of their capital C creativity to counter regulatory practices of containment and control?

In this chapter, I open this question further to examine how school partnerships with artists may be valued differently as a necessary interruption (and therefore contribution) to our ongoing quest for what is good education within and beyond frameworks of the curriculum. In light of Biesta's reconfiguration of the educational task (Biesta, 2017, pp.7–21), I wonder how artists might quietly interrupt the assumed best practices of evidence-based, backward-aligned teaching and standards-focussed assessment with ways of working that might resonate with Biesta's notion of the "middle way" of "grown-up-ness" (Biesta, 2017, pp.7–21). I bring to this wondering my experience of evaluating a number of arts residency programmes in schools over the past eight years, including the national Australia Council Artist in Residence (AIR) initiative and the Australian Performing Rights Association APRA-AMCOS SongMakers programme. I also background this thinking with my formative early-career experiences as a travelling artist in schools and with my current research attention to discourses of creativity and curiosity that enable artist, teacher and student presence in the arts-based educational act (Hunter, 2015; Hunter & Emery, 2015; Hunter, Broad & Jeanneret, 2016). What interests me here is the ways in which some artists enter into relationships with schools not with an intention to teach, but to situate and extend their own practice in an environment not usually their own – a small but highly significant distinction when it comes to approaching work in an educational context. It is an approach which, perhaps ironically, may offer a most revelatory kind of "gift of teaching" (Biesta, 2013b, p.449). The artists to whom I refer by no means attempt to replace classroom teachers or mirror their work. As companions to classroom teachers and students, they rather offer the gift of teaching in most unteacherly ways. In exploring this, I first consider the roles that have been conventionally determined for artists working in schools, before attending to the possibilities that emerge when we let go of attempting to contain, align and measure what artists do in an effort to justify and prove their worth in schools, and instead attend to how artists be and become in school-based intra-actions and the "good" educational entanglements of matter and meaning that these afford.

From the *what* to the *how* of artists in schools

There has been extensive research conducted on the outcomes and impacts of artists working in formal and informal education settings (Bamford, 2006; Brice-Heath & Wolfe, 2005; Catterall, 2002; Deasy, 2002; Galton, 2008; Horowitz, 2004; Hunter, 2005; Imms, Jeanneret & Stevens-Ballenger, 2011; Rabkin, Reynolds, Hedberg & Shelby, 2011; Reiss & Pringle, 2003). This body of work provides clear evidence of the benefits for students in achieving personal and social learning outcomes, developing new arts skills and knowledge, and enabling positive learning dispositions that impact on their learning achievements in other subject areas. Teachers, even those who identify as artists themselves, have reported that the opportunity to work with artists improves their confidence to teach the arts, increases their arts knowledge and skills, and expands their repertoire of creative pedagogies applicable to the teaching of other subject areas (Hunter, 2011). For artists, the opportunity to give back has been strong in some programmes (Hunter, Broad & Jeanneret, 2016), as well as the chance to experience professional growth from having to articulate and reflect on their artistic processes when these might usually remain unspoken. While evaluation of artist residency programmes has tended to focus on student and teacher outcomes and benefits, large-scale research projects, such as those aligned with the United Kingdom's Creative Partnerships programme, have also engaged with artists' perceived and evidenced contributions to systemic change (Thomson, Lingard & Wrigley, 2011; Thomson, Jones & Hall, 2015) and the ways in which artists could foster more collaborative and creative learning experiences in the school context more broadly (Galton, 2008). Much of the commissioned evaluation in the field also includes attention to the processes of such partnerships, thereby offering various recommendations to practitioners, administrators and policymakers about how to plan for and conduct residencies to ensure the best outcomes possible (Burnaford, 2003; Hunter, 2011; Rabkin et al., 2011). Often these recommendations centre on *smoothing* the experience, administratively, logistically and conceptually, for the visiting artists, teachers and students. Examples include the implementation of comprehensive school induction processes, the scheduling of out of class time for teacher/artist discussion and reflection, clear role definition such as the assigning of behaviour management to teachers, and the necessity for artists' sessions to fit as seamlessly as possible within existing class timetables.

As Robert Brown (2014) attests, there has been little research attention to the specific positioning and work processes of artists themselves in such programmes. While Galton (2008), Hall, Thomson and Russell (2007), Pringle (2002), and Waldorf (2002) provide notable exceptions, their research continues a theme of attempting to identify and, again, *smooth* the interactions that artists have with students, teachers, administrative processes and the curriculum. Brown identifies some of the multiple roles of instructor, facilitator, communicator, model and activist that artists are assumed to play, commenting on Rabkin's view of artists needing to demonstrate a hybrid identity (Rabkin et al., 2011). Adopting this perspective, it may be presumed that the best artists for the school environment are those who are somewhat multidexterous and who are willing (and expected) to adapt their practice to the various contexts in which they find themselves. Brown's focus has been slightly different in studying the nexus of "artist intention and realised practice" (Brown, 2014, p.24) with children in non-school settings. But here I take Brown's work as a point of departure and refer to this nexus of intention and practice to look to a school-based residency programme in which artists are not necessarily expected to teach, facilitate or instruct, but *to be*. With such licence, we might consider the work of the artist (in their doing and being) as interruption as well as diffraction (Barad, 2007) in the school environment, guided by an ethics of positive entanglement and possibility. Drawing on the insights of feminist philosophy and science (Braidotti, 2002; Barad, 2003, 2007), we might re-imagine how artists assign themselves an alternative function in the school space, that is not about being an external independent entity, either assimilating or distancing themselves from established norms of institutionalised and standardised teaching and learning. Rather, we might reconfigure the artists' contribution as a necessary interruption, that diffracts the always already shifting relations that exist in the school environment to co-generate new knowledge. These are artists who tap into the opportunities and energies for change that educational communities are being called to aspire to and enact (Harris, 2016; Jefferson & Anderson, 2017). As yet, I'm uncertain how such a reading of the art-ist (and of the school) might best be realised or evidenced – if at all – but I con-template these ideas here having been intrigued, in my evaluation experiences, by the ways teachers and students often find it difficult to pinpoint what it is that enlivens their willingness and capacity to engage and be present when there is an artist around.

The presence of the artist

> [Laura Hindmarsh]: I always find in my practice, I have to be quite sponta-
> neous. It's me and the process of figuring it out and that kind of becomes a
> work, that's where the kind of charge is or where the accident can happen.
> Going into the school environment, I had an idea that it would be about
> drawing and gesture, but that was kind of it initially.
>
> *(Hindmarsh in Mark & Tom, 2014a)*

Like De Carvalho, Laura Hindmarsh is a Hobart artist who was engaged in the
Tasmanian Artist in Residence (AIR) programme, part of an initial $5.1 million
investment by the Australian Government to improve young people's access to
quality arts education, teachers' access to quality professional learning, and artists' professional development opportunities. The programme ran for seven years
prior to ceasing in 2016 due to a substantial government cut to arts funding
nationally. The programme in Tasmania was unique in that it was delivered solely
by the State government agency, Arts Tasmania, as part of its artist development
portfolio of programmes, and was not an education department responsibility.
The Tasmanian AIR coordinator, Wendy Morrow, a nationally recognised contemporary dance practitioner, framed the AIR programme as an opportunity for
artists to take their practice into new environments, thereby encouraging artists
to view schools not primarily as a place to teach or deliver their craft, but to
expand and gain insight into their own practice and ways of working. This meant
engaging with the "spacetimemattering" (Barad, Dolphijn & van der Tuin, 2012)
of the school context; and, I suggest, sharpened artists' perceptions of the new
configurations, subjectivities and possibilities of encounter with the human and
non-human environment that the school afforded. This attentiveness to the temporal, spatial and material dimensions of the school context not only offered a
new perspective for artists on their own practice, but enabled a different kind of
knowing about the educational task. The artists' value was not (or was not solely)
in teaching teachers to teach, or teaching students new skills, but was in offering new becomings and new beginnings, on which students and teachers could
decide to act.

> [De Carvalho:] I really did want to genuinely engage with being somewhere
> and through that, I think there's been a really beautiful exchange with stu-
> dents and teachers.
>
> I think the rewards are going to be something that slowly percolate but
> I have a feeling it's going to be quite a rich space to look back on.
>
> *(De Carvalho in Mark & Tom, 2014b)*

Of particular interest is De Carvalho's description of her experience as a "rich
space" rather than as a bounded project or achievement. The very presence of the
artist and her way of working were, in effect, the educational task: student learning

may (or may not) have come in the students' taking up her offer as an exchange. While scholarship and evaluation of artists in schools has focussed on *what* artists do to improve learning, how might we shift attention to *how* artists are in the educational encounter? What is the value of their disruptions in helping to reconfigure learning in the everyday of school?

Biesta's questioning of the purpose and task of education is salient here, particularly his conceptualisation of the responsibility of education to enable "grown-up-ness" (Biesta, 2017). Biesta is careful to distance this concept from a human development discourse; and rather defines it as an ethical and agential way of being whereby one "is able to live in the world, without occupying the centre of the world" (Biesta, 2017, p.9). I'm not suggesting here that the value of the artist is in *modelling* grown-up-ness, necessarily. There is little that is inherent in the vocation of the artist that makes it essentially "grown-up". But, as depicted in De Carvalho's and Hindmarsh's work, these artists' ways of being in the school environment showed them to be making an offer to students by their very presence. Their work as artists was a diffraction of the usually tight boundaries between teacher and learner, as well as between physical spaces for learning and for play. The artists enlivened the "timespacematter" (Barad et al., 2012, p.67) of the school environment with an acknowledgement of the always already changing relations and their positive "potentia" (Braidotti, 2006, p.134). To be grown-up in that environment is to recognise that we are not "simply located at particular places *in* the world; rather, we are part *of* the world in its ongoing intra-activity" (Barad, 2003, p.828). These artists, in their choice to be explicitly of the world of the school, materialise this valuing of the uncertain and realise the potential to change and be changed. In taking up this offer of the artist's presence, an educational exchange unfolds.

Re-roling the artist-in-residence

How might this insight into the *relationality* of the artist in the school environment – one in which grown-up-ness is important and recognised and valued – allow for a re-reading of the so-called artist-in-residence? … or rather, a *re-roling* of the artist? How might the presence of the artist necessarily and responsibly interrupt the institutionalised practices and discourses of teaching and learning, in ways that offer new possibilities and entanglements of matter and meaning: new possibilities for the educational encounter?

As has been argued by Semetsky (2006), Osberg, Biesta and Cilliers (2008), Biesta (2010) and others, people cannot be reliably *made* to change or to learn. Biesta suggests that learning only happens when change is valued and recognised as such in retrospect by the learner (2010). He cautions the diminishing value of teaching in the light of overly constructivist views of education in which teachers become little more than facilitators of learning, or handmaidens to the curriculum. In response, Biesta invites a reclaiming of teacher purpose and authority (as very distinct from authoritarianism (Biesta, 2013)), so that teachers bring something to offer to the education encounter: an offering external to the students' currently existing known world or worldview. Here Biesta approaches the notion of teaching from the perspective of "being taught", which, he emphasises, is fundamentally different from the experience of "learning from":

> While in the situation where students learn from their teachers, the teacher figures as a resource so that what is being learned from the teacher is within the control of the student, the experience of "being taught" is about those situations in which something enters our being from the outside, so to speak, as something that is fundamentally beyond the control of the "learner." To be taught—to be open to receiving the gift of teaching—thus means being able to give such interruptions a place in one's understanding and one's being.
>
> *(Biesta, 2013, p.459)*

Our interests here might turn, then, to the potential of the artist who materialises the good educational task and whose work, as interruption, we recognise as an offer. That offer, ironically, being the gift of teaching.

Interruptions and coming into presence

It might be difficult to imagine the power of interruption in a contemporary society already characterised by constant change and "permanent processes of transition, hybridization and nomadization" (Braidotti, 2002, p.2). One might expect interruption to have become an almost normative expectation. Yet many contemporary practices of schooling still maintain the claims and regimes of the modernist institution (Bauman, 2000), as well as uphold representational epistemologies that situate knowledge about the world as separate from "our knowledge itself" (Osberg, Biesta & Cilliers, 2008, p.214). This tension of conflicting worlds inside and outside the school is one that is characteristic of this contemporary educational era and is being played out in high-stakes testing and learning regimes that, for instance, value the output before the person, the standard before the student. I suggest here that artists have a role to play in enabling teachers, students and school communities to counterbalance (without necessarily rejecting) an education system that still needs to provide a degree of qualification and standardisation. As an interruption to the regulatory practices of schooling, artists' approaches to school-based work need not be monological and reactionary but can serve to ameliorate some of the more negative impacts of assessment-focussed teaching and a pre-occupation with standards, particularly for those students (and teachers) disengaged and disenfranchised with schoolings' modernist mis-endeavour. Artists' ways of being may therefore resonate well with aspirations for "grown-up-ness" in environments of necessary containment. As Hindmarsh's work shows, artists may interrupt in subtle and potentially more educative ways.

Schools should be places ripe with possibility, bursting with curiosity for the yet to be known. What artists offer is a coming into the world (Arendt, 1958) and a coming into presence (Biesta, 2016) – *or many comings into presence* – which are always already there in students and are always already dependent on how beginnings are offered and how beginnings are taken up. To return again to artist Laura Hindmarsh's description of her residency experience, recounted in further detail here:

> And so the work really came about by me trying to do an activity every day. I started doing these smaller sort of experiments – really subtle gestures like drawing my studio with my left hand, so kind of embracing this idea of being uncomfortable and then sitting out in the corridor and drawing with one eye closed or drawing with like my reading glasses on or these sort of restrained drawings that were not too precious. It was more about me being conscious of what my process was. And then there was kind of these exchanges that would happen the more I got public with those. There were about six students that seemed to be in a place I recognised in myself – wanting to do something but not knowing what. I thought it would be good to work with them a little bit almost as a mirror to myself – allowing them to explore things. So we'd do blind contour drawings of each other or encouraging them even just using a mirror, and drawing in a mirror or using a grid. And how, giving yourself these little strategies to work with just gets you going and then, within that process something else can occur. It was through doing these exercises and these restrained drawings and this tracing the inside and outside that it felt particularly right … in the end my project was moving forward conceptually in a kind of exciting way, and a really unforced way.
>
> *(Hindmarsh in Mark & Tom, 2014a)*

In this kind of description of emergent practice in a school setting, it is difficult to separate the educational encounter from understandings of emancipation and agency. For if we take from Rancière the notion that emancipation is about using one's intelligence "under the assumption of the equality of intelligence" (Biesta, 2013a, p.98), I see no better example of this than in these artists' documented work with and alongside students. And without wanting to over-determine or translate the intentions of these artists and the impacts on students, I am reminded of Barad's statement that "Agency is not held, it is not a property of persons or things; rather, agency is an enactment, a matter of possibilities for reconfiguring entanglements" (Barad et al., 2012, p.55).

As for interactions with the teacher, the idea of the artist as interruption is not about overturning an aspiration for *smooth* when it comes to the logistics of administering and maintaining artist–school partnerships; nor is it to undermine the kinds of co-mentoring among artists and educators that have been shown to be an effective means of professional learning for both. Artist residencies and school–industry partnerships create the conditions for the kinds of relational entanglements that we want of the educational task, so easing the way for those partnerships to occur by communicating what has worked for others in the past and what impacts can be made with reference to a particular policy or curriculum is relevant and important.

But to deepen our understanding of the interrelationship of art, artists and pedagogy, it is important to investigate *how* artists can *be* in schools. This raises questions that are less about *why* artists should be in schools and what they do to serve a "learnification" agenda and more about *how* their ways of being and becoming work epistemologically to help us re-imagine what matters in education. Drawing on Biesta's conceptualisation of teaching and the good educational task, the question becomes how can the offerings that artists make – the interruptions to teaching that can be, perhaps counter-intuitively, the very gift of teaching – be readily made and accepted? How can this be both an interrupting and companioning of the work of professional teachers and of school communities as they seek to address the challenges of our times?

Artistry leading reform?

The idea of the artist being a catalyst for school reform or for introducing new creative pedagogies in an ailing education system is not new. Research arising from the UK Creative Partnerships programme (Galton, 2008; Thomson, Jones, Hall & Sefton-Green, 2012; Thomson, Lingard & Wrigley, 2011) among others, provide clear evidence of the possibilities and important principles for practice. Similarly, the *TurnAround Arts Initiative* (Stoelinga, Silk, Reddy & Rahman, 2015) like other arts education reform programmes in the USA before it, has shown effectiveness in engaging students in school life and offering alternative pathways to motivating and valuing learning, particularly with young people at risk of disengaging from school altogether. But attention to *how* artists *be* in that environment offers a different perspective – one that Galton's work touches on in his investigation of artist pedagogy. When arts education partnerships are planned, delivered or evaluated, there is an aspiration to smooth the relationship among partners – teacher and artist – in an effort to pave their way to stress-free collaboration. The focus of such collaboration is often primarily focussed, and assessed on, the *what* of student learning outcomes: not even – or in some cases *especially not even* – in the arts, but in other areas of the curriculum such as English or maths, or in measures of student engagement or motivation. This is measuring how the arts contribute to student achievement. While it's important to measure that, I'm attending here to a curiosity about something else. What if we liberate our preconceptions and justifications of the artist in school, relieving her from a particular deterministic function around learning which may, ironically, uncover greater insights about the gift of teaching and "the good" of the educational task?

As I've argued elsewhere, arts curriculum offers one of the rare mandated opportunities in school life to genuinely address one of the central dilemmas of contemporary education – to acknowledge a human urge for certainty while fostering the capacities to live without it (Hunter, 2015). What Biesta's investigation about the task of education makes me curious about, is artists' capacity to bring more diffractive insights into the nature of change and the educational act, both inside and outside the curriculum as well as inside and outside the school. I'm wondering about how, in the determinism that is curriculum boundary-making in education, artistry and its *uncontainability* can be further realised: that is, its potential for interrupting. And for me, it's the "what I love" in these Tasmanian artists' approach to their work. There is an *un*knowing in their interrupting – a trust in unknowing that we need more of to counter the systematisation of the knower and the known that is taking place in our schooling practices, policies and politics. But residency programmes are so vulnerable to government funding and change, so it's fair to say we are at a point where we need to keep invested in the language of evidence, impact and achievement. There is little political will for the artistry of presence and the ways of being and becoming in the uncertain to lead school reform.

Further unfolding

There is more to unfold and refold here, but I return to "grown-up-ness" and the intention and responsibility of *all* engaged in the educational act to cultivate students' capacity to live in the world without presuming to be at its centre. This I am foregrounding as the ethical and agential act of good education. As we consider the affordances of artists in schools, it's not their *modelling* of what grown-up-ness looks like that matters, but their presence and material practice that bring light to what *should* matter – and that is presence. What artists offer are beginnings for others to come into that kind of presence. In artists' work, this is material and/or embodied – something we may identify as curiosity made real, and the virtuosic artist's tool of trade. In the school setting, it is interesting to note that it is a curiosity that is devoid of a desire to *achieve*, yet it is a great gift of teaching for those who choose to make that interruption matter.

References

Arendt, H. (1958). *The human condition*. Chicago: University of Chicago Press.

Bamford, A. (2006). *The wow factor: Global research compendium on the impact of the arts in education*. New York: Waxmann.

Barad, K. (2003). Posthumanist performativity: Toward an understanding of how matter comes to matter. *Signs: Journal of Culture and Society, 28*(3), 801–831.

Barad, K. (2007). *Meeting the universe halfway: Quantam physics and the entanglement of matter and meaning*. Durham, NC: Duke University Press.

Barad, K., Dolphijn, R., & van der Tuin, I. (2012). Matter feels, converses, suffers, desires, yearns and remembers. Interview with Karen Barad. In R. Dolphijn & I. van der Tuin (Eds.), *New materialism: Interviews and cartographies* (pp.48–70). Ann Arbor, MI: Open Humanities Press. Retrieved from: http://openhumanitiespress.org

Bauman, Z. (2000). *Liquid modernity*. Cambridge: Polity Press.

Biesta, G.J.J. (2010). Five theses on complexity reduction and its politics. In D. Osberg and G. Biesta (Eds.), *Complexity theory and the politics of education* (pp.5–13). Rotterdam: Sense Publishers.

Biesta, G.J.J. (2013a). *The beautiful risk of education*. Boulder, CO: Paradigm.

Biesta, G.J.J. (2013b). Receiving the gift of teaching: From "learning from" to "being taught by". *Studies in Philosophy of Education, 32*(5), 449–461.

Biesta, G.J.J. (2016). *Beyond learning: Democratic education for a human future*. London: Routledge.

Biesta, G.J.J. (2017). *The rediscovery of teaching*. New York: Routledge.

Braidotti, R. (2002). *Metamorphoses: Towards a feminist theory of becoming*. Cambridge: Polity Press.

Braidotti, R. (2006). The ethics of becoming imperceptible. In C. Boundas (Ed.), *Deleuze and philosophy* (pp.133–159). Edinburgh: Edinburgh University Press.

Brice Heath, S., & Wolfe, S. (2005). Focus in creative learning: Drawing on art for language development. *Literacy* (April), 35–38.

Brown, R. (2014). Portrait of the artist who works with children. (Unpublished doctoral thesis). University of Melbourne, Australia.

Burnaford, G. (2003). Language matters: Clarifying partnerships between teachers and artists. *Teaching Artist Journal*, 1, 168–171.

Catterall, J.S. (2002). The arts and the transfer of learning. In R.J. Deasy (Ed.), *Critical links: Learning in the arts and student academic and social development* (pp.162–168). Washington, DC: Arts Education Partnerships.

Deasy, R.J. (Ed.). (2002). *Critical links: Learning in the arts and student academic and social development*. Washington, DC: Arts Education Partnerships.

Galton, M. (2008). *Creative practitioners in schools and classrooms: Final report of the project: The pedagogy of creative practitioners in schools*. Cambridge: Faculty of Education, University of Cambridge and Arts Council England, Creative Partnerships.

Hall, C., Thomson, P., & Russell, L. (2007). Teaching like an artist: The pedagogic identities and practices of artists in schools. *British Journal of Sociology of Education*, *28*(5), 605–619.

Harris, A. (2016). *Creativity and education*. London: Palgrave Macmillan.

Horowitz, R. (2004). *Summary of large-scale arts partnership evaluations*. Washington, DC: Arts Education Partnerships.

Hunter, M. (2005). *Education and the arts: Research overview. A summary report prepared for the Australia Council for the Arts*. Canberra: Australian Government and Australia Council for the Arts.

Hunter, M. (2011). *Australia Council Community Partnerships Artist in Residence program evaluation 2009–2010*. Sydney: Australia Council of the Arts.

Hunter, M. (2015). Rethinking industry partnerships: Arts education and uncertainty in liquid modern life. In M. Fleming, L. Bresler & J. O'Toole (Eds.), *Routledge international handbook of the arts and education* (pp.361–370). New York: Routledge.

Hunter, M., & Emery, S. (2015). The curious schools project: Capturing nomad creativity in teacher work. *Australian Journal of Teacher Education*, *40*(10), 167–179.

Hunter, M., Broad, T., & Jeanneret, N. (2016). SongMakers: An industry-led approach to arts partnerships in education. *Arts Education Policy Review*. doi: 10.1080/10632913. 2016.1163308

Imms, W., Jeanneret, N., & Stevens-Ballenger, J. (2011). *Partnerships between schools and the professional arts sector: Evaluation of impact on student outcomes*. Melbourne: Arts Victoria.

Jefferson, M., & Anderson, M. (2017). *Transforming schools: Creativity, critical reflection, communication, collaboration*. London: Bloomsbury.

Mark & Tom (Producer). (2014a). *Laura Hindmarsh at Guilford Young College, Hobart* [video podcast]. Hobart, Tas: Arts Tasmania. Retrieved from: www.arts.tas.gov.au/industry_development/air/air_2014

Mark & Tom (Producer). (2014b). *Selena De Carvalho at Claremont College, Hobart* [video podcast]. Hobart, Tas: Arts Tasmania. Retrieved from: www.arts.tas.gov.au/industry_development/air/air_2014

Osberg, D.C., Biesta, G.J.J., & Cilliers, P. (2008). From representation to emergence: Complexity's challenge to the epistemology of schooling. *Educational Philosophy and Theory*, *40*(1), 213–227.

Pringle, E. (2002). *We did stir things up: The role of artists in sites for learning.* London: The Arts Council of England. Retrieved from: http://webarchive.nationalarchives.gov.uk

Rabkin, N., Reynolds, M., Hedberg, E., & Shelby, J. (2011). *A report on the teaching artist research project.* Chicago, IL: NORC, University of Chicago.

Reiss, V., & Pringle, E. (2003). The role of artists in sites for learning. *International Journal of Art and Design Education, 22*(2), 214–221.

Semetsky, I. (2006). *Deleuze, education and becoming.* Rotterdam: Sense Publishers.

Stoelinga, S.R., Silk, Y., Reddy, P., & Rahman, N. (2015). *Turnaround arts initiative: Final evaluation report.* Washington, DC: President's Committee on the Arts and the Humanities.

Thomson, P., Jones, K., Hall, C., & Sefton-Green, J. (2012). *The signature pedagogies project: Final report.* London: University of Nottingham and Goldsmiths College, University of London. Retrieved from: www.creativetallis.com

Thomson, P., Lingard, B., & Wrigley, T. (2011). Reimagining school change: The necessity and reasons for hope. In T. Wrigley, P. Thomson & B. Lingard (Eds.), *Changing schools: Alternative ways to make a world of difference* (pp. 1–14). London: Routledge.

Waldorf, L.A. (2002). *The professional artist as public school educator: A research report of the Chicago Arts Partnerships in Education 2000–2001.* Los Angeles, CA: UCLA Graduate School of Education and Information Studies.

5

THE IMPLICATIONS OF 'PERCEPTS, AFFECTS AND CONCEPTS' FOR ARTS EDUCATORS

Christopher Naughton

Introduction

The arts figure prominently in Deleuze and Guattari's writing, with frequent reference being made to philosophy and architecture, film, literature, dance, art and music. Their contribution to the arts and philosophy has been considerable, if not perplexing at times with the inclusion of art being thought of as 'vibration', 'sensation' or 'monument'. This reconceptualisation of art rejects the prevailing view of purely conscious rational meaning in the artwork, opening possibilities for rethinking about art and artists. This chapter will consider the implications of percepts, affects and concepts for arts education as employed by Deleuze and Guattari in their final publication *What is Philosophy?* (WP) (1994).

Deleuze, Guattari and desire

Art, for Deleuze and Guattari, emanates from 'desire', the motivation for life, a force field where the artist responds to both material and non-material properties of an artwork (Bogue, 2003). Desire, for Deleuze and Guattari, is not seen as emanating from the subject, in fact the reverse occurs, as 'desire' becomes an external life force (Butler, 2016). Desire, or that which has not yet been realised, is always there to become (Semetsky, 2009). A common understanding of the artistic process as human only in the creation of the artwork is thus removed; instead of the artist as the sole creator of the artwork, 'desire' becomes an external factor that arises in the act of making the artwork (WP, p.177).

Percepts

Percepts and affects are integral to Deleuze and Guattari's conception of the emergent artwork within which the non-human occurs in the art process. They explain that percepts are 'no longer perceptions; they are independent of a state of those who experience them' (WP, p.164). This interaction, seen as beyond man or from before man, is not a conscious response but one that prompts the artist 'to divest thinking from those habitual circuits of perceiving' (jagodzinski & Wallin, 2013, p.171). In addition, while an artist may be stimulated by a mood, place, people, feeling, in realising art, this is not necessarily a seamless process. The transition from initial desire may not relate to the actual work produced, and may not necessarily relate to the becoming conscious percept (Pearson, 2009). The act of becoming an artwork is merely a possibility that may substantiate itself differently in its realisation. The artist works with the percept being fashioned by the forces at work, leading to an unpredictable outcome where 'Sensory becoming is the action by which something or someone is ceaselessly becoming-other' (WP, p.177).

While percept does not resemble an object or represent any feeling, it is through perception that sensation occurs through the materiality of the art. This is qualified by Deleuze and Guattari as a practice over which conscious and unconscious acts are determined by the materials involved: 'As percepts, sensations are not perceptions referring to an object: if they resemble something it is with a resemblance produced with their own methods; … the smile on the canvas is made solely with colours, lines, shadow, and light' (WP, p.166). The artwork, as percept, brings to the initial desire the impulse to act, but this is without meaning at this point, owing to the artist still discovering the possible within the percept (Cook, 1998). It is in this space where also new concepts are created, that the percept transforms into some 'thing' as a becoming percept (Deleuze & Parnet, 2002).

The percept acting as a force, an energy, beyond the human, is seen as immanent to the material of the artwork: 'The material is so varied in each case (canvas support, paintbrush or equivalent agent, colour in the tube) that it is difficult to say where in fact the material ends and sensation begins' (WP, p.166). Hence the artist 'becomes' the painting, they are at one, making it difficult to say where the material and the sensation are divided. This symbiotic relationship, between the materiality and percept, liberates the artist from a subject-centred 'common sense', and affirms a life force in the artwork (Deleuze & Parnet, 2002).

As the two philosophers write, the aim of art is to take perceptions from the 'perceiving subject'. The link to the artist reveals the percept as the envelopment in the natural, the non-human world. Cezanne's landscapes 'of iridescent chaos' are percepts, as is the moor in Hardy's novels or the ocean in Melville. The landscape, for Cezanne, becomes 'in the absence of man' (WP, p.169), reflecting the percept in the artistic encounter.

The corollary between the percept and the arts educator might be seen in several ways. The process by which an educator decides on the work to be engaged in by a class is often perplexing, not least in understanding why and how choices are made. Some educators might say that it depends on experience in deciding what may work for a particular group, or what may be a best fit for a certain level, but while this may be intuitive, as recognised by Biesta (2013), intuition within the artform may take any number of guises at the outset before a teacher may present a project to a class, not knowing what the outcome may be. As the artist works with the materials, so the teacher looks for opportunities to see openings within the group to consolidate or not the direction to be taken according to the reaction of the students. The art forges itself according to what is present at the time.

Affects

Affects, for Deleuze and Guattari:

> are no longer feelings or affections; they go beyond the strength of those who undergo them. … They could be said to exist in the absence of man because man, as he is caught in stone, on the canvas, or by words, is himself a compound of percepts and affects. The work of art is a being of sensation and nothing else: it exists in itself.
>
> *(WP, p.164)*

This is the moment of transformation of percept becoming affect, as in the opening 'that draws a hidden universe out of the shadow' (WP, p.166). It is in this transformation that we 'wrest the affect from the affections as the transition from one state to another: to extract a bloc of sensations, a pure being of sensation' (WP, p.167). The artwork thus arrives as the percept and becomes affect, as the 'transition from one state to another' (WP, p.167) in which a bloc of sensation arises. The sensation is just that, the sensing part of the engagement within the artwork as the work materialises to become, where an affective description can be forthcoming.

Affect has many aspects to it though; like percepts it is dependent on the realisation of the material that may occur at the time. Affect also serves as a memory; as Claire Colebrook writes:

> They are not possibilities – what we can see as accidental or variable in what we encounter – they are affects that we can discern as having a power for all time; the red we see here has a being or potential that is perceivable in other styles, at other moments, for other observers.
>
> *(2005, p.10)*

The recognition of an affect, here being a colour – red, becomes a memory of the red as an affective response that will be called on again, in different encounters. In the role of the educator together with the students this is a recognition of affect within the scope of the art project; a combination of sounds, the impact of a colour, an image within a film text or any combination with the artform that creates an *affect*.

As an artist, sensations with the material produces art. This connection with the materiality of the artwork, as sensation, does not last however, as it is the sensation within the percept, the affect that is preserved (Deleuze, 1995). The material artwork may disappear but the sensation will 'be preserved in itself *in the eternity that coexists with this short duration*' (WP, p.166). Thus the artwork exists beyond the actual material experience, or beyond the performance, as the material and the sensation are intertwined, but the sensation remains independent of the materiality of the work. The moment sensation happens it is there as an eternal thing – the smile does not decay. This statement may seem obvious, yet deploys another way to think of the artwork that lives on in the memory.

This seeing the artwork lasting after the material has gone, Deleuze and Guattari refer to as the monument or 'fabulation', a physiological change, connected with the art event that 'goes beyond the perceptual states and the affective transitions of the lived' (WP, p.171). This '*nervous response*' forms an important part of the concept of the artwork, as percept and affect are beyond a purely thoughtful response. The depiction of art as 'monument' not as history sees the artwork's impact as fable-like or prophetic, responding to a communal validation yet to come.

If percept is the onset of the artwork, the becoming other is the affect that is observed by the artist: '*Affects are precisely these non-human becomings of man*, just as percepts are … *the nonhuman landscapes of nature*' (WP, p.169). Deleuze and Guattari cite the work of Olivier Messian (1908–1992). Natural occurrences of birdsong are percepts, the natural onset of a non-human becoming (Allan, 2013). Messian takes the birdsong and writes works for piano such as the *Catalogue d'oiseaux* (1953). As the birdsongs become piano work, the bloc of sensation occurs between percept and affect (Quaglia, 2010). Just as the artist sees the landscape and becomes the landscape in Cezanne, in Messian, the composer engages in the materiality of the birdsong; it undergoes a transformation, from one 'state' to another, as birdsong becomes piano work.

Just as the artist sees the potential within the scope of the materials, so the dancer 'typifies and allegorises the human soul as liberated from mere life' (Colebrook, 2005, p.7). Colebrook puts her case against dance as created solely by the dancer 'with a specific idea of ourselves as the agents we are' (Colebrook, 2005, p.8). Placing dance as an engagement between our potential and actual being, Colebrook does not see that we can predict the outcome: 'Dancing is crucial here in deconstructing the opposition between potentiality and actuality, where potential is (traditionally) actualized by arriving at what it ought to be' (Colebrook, 2005, p.9). Here the dancer, liberated from meaning, no longer has to produce something that answers to 'what is it for?' (Colebrook, 2005, p.8); it is dance as liberation from the need to provide a 'proper' outcome (Carlin & Wallin, 2014; Cole, 2011).

This sense of 'becoming' in dance is repeated by choreographers in relation to what can be described as Dionysian disindividuation in Nietzschean terms (see Naughton, 2009). Referring to both engagement and the loss of meaning,

Akram Khan observes how dancers lose their technical selves in the narration, no longer perceiving their work as dancers executing moves but as people realising their story:

> It's not the tools that we're showing, … it's about the actual story, the tools are just the way to tell that story, but the story is about you. I love it when I see 'people' onstage not actors or dancers.
>
> *(YouTube, 2016)*

This points to what Colebrook, referring to Deleuze and Guattari, describes as counter-actualisation:

> The body displays itself in dance both as actual (with all its present possibilities) and as counter-actual (releasing its powers that were neither determined by, nor limited to, its bodily being). An action in dance, mime, or theatre, for example, is at once the same bodily action but is also acted as a presentation of the action; the body presents what anybody could do for all time and any time, the body's virtual power.
>
> *(Colebrook, 2005, p.11)*

This overwhelming of the technical aspects of the dancer reveals dancers on two planes, that Ronald Bogue (2003) refers to as a plane of composition, subdivided between a 'technical plane' and an 'aesthetic plane'. These become two poles where 'the sensation realises itself in the material' (WP, pp.168–169). Rather than being a passive act, matter 'rises up' and becomes one so that the technical plane is 'covered up or absorbed by the aesthetic plane of composition' (WP, p.195).

Khan works in such a way that the material evolves from the interaction between choreographer and dancers. Just as the percept moves through the materiality and through its transformation creates affect, so Khan takes his material from and with the dancers, to create a problematic between his and the dancers' desire to reveal a new dance, as in the re-telling of the narrative in Giselle: 'What was really important was that I had to commit to the classical body and find my material for the language for the aesthetic within their body' (YouTube, 2016). This is not the choreographer insisting on a sequence that is preordained, but an artist working with the forces that he finds within the material, allowing the work to come from what he observes and senses as the work materialises. Just as Cezanne becomes the landscape, so the choreographer is working with the dancers to sense what may eventuate in the work.

Khan, moreover, sees dance not solely as performance, but as a political act celebrating the educative, collective nature of the enterprise, as in the fabulation: 'What makes our life so unique is because we are individuals and at the same time we can find a common mass' (YouTube, 2016). And to encapsulate the educator, Khan adds, when reflecting on the impact on the dancers of the new production: 'But more importantly for me – has it changed them?' (YouTube, 2016). This embodies a sense of democratic practice within art making, creating a middle ground for making that Biesta refers to: 'But it is ultimately *only* in the middle ground that existence is possible. The middle ground is therefore not a place of pure self-expression, but rather a place where our self-expression encounters limits, interruptions, responses' (Biesta, 2017, p.15). To create the work with the dancers becomes a middle ground where the choreographer allows his desire to meet with the affective possibilities engaged in by the dancers.

If we consider percept, affect and sensation we can see certain commonalities between these elements and pedagogical practice (Masny & Cole, 2012). The origin as a non-human starting point in nature as percept is engaged, whereby change occurs leading to affect and blocs of sensation. This might be typified in work that uses such non-human starting points as the landscape; or moods; soundscapes – such as a reverberant stairwell, a sound, or something that might be more accessible, that might be re-made in the dance or music work (Naughton & Lines, 2013). One of the most provocative aspects for the educator that arises from Deleuze and Guatarri is this interaction between the percept and the affect. The percept is seen as a point of beginning, just like Khan taking the dancers and his ideas as material to evolve a work that captures their bodily expression. It is as if he is working, not by forming something, but watching how percepts become dance. For an educator this can be a sense of working with students to negotiate openings and different kinds of engagement. This undertaking through the work of the educator and student can in turn change and alter with the materials, as in the transformation from percept to affect. Affect produces art that is not a thought response, but a '*nervous response*' where art is felt, a physiological change, that may not necessarily be recognised amongst the community until a later date.

Concepts

The implications of the concept for art educators is that this framing provides a means to re-consider the philosophy that underpins the arts curiculum, and ultimately educational practice.

The concept is seen as like art in that it brings an openness and intensity into play. Again like art, the concept arises from a plane of immanence, or plane of composition, to be followed by shifting yet sequential steps that lead to the self-conscious subject. Unlike the concept however, art does not attain the 'embodied event' (WP, pp.65–66), as it is always located in the material and blocs of sensation for Deleuze and Guttari; while the concept occupies the immaterial, the virtual, it does not need to be historically or socially grounded.

This raises the distinction between Immanuel Kant (1724–1804) and Deleuze and Guattari. Deleuze and Guattari see the concept as having no fixed point of reference or higher authority, whereas in Kant we find a system that relies on a 'subjective unity' (WP, p.46), where reason is pre-eminent. For Deleuze and Guattari, concepts have their own plane of immanence within forces of change. To explain this without going too deeply into Kantian literature, we see a split in the denotation of the concept from a system which recreates itself following a pre-scribed linear process in Kant, to an ever-changing phenomenon in Deleuze and Guattari's reading.

It is from Baruch Spinoza (1632–1677) that Deleuze and Guattari derive their principle thought on the concept. For Spinoza, God has supremacy, but there is no distinction between God and attributes. Attributes can be read as the means whereby we observe something, which might be a sense of place, a feeling, a visual depiction presented by another object. The importance of this premise is that if God has created all things, seeing God in what is presented in his creation means that we remove any hierarchy; we respond to his 'attributes'. In this two-way inter-action of recognition of God in nature, we recognise that we have an influence in how to respond to what has been termed 'expression' through the attributes.

From expression, it may not be that the plane of immanence alone produces the concept, but the pre-defined concept may also produce a plane of immanence or that our previous understanding of a concept limits how we respond. Just as we may recognise God in things that are attributes of God, so we may say that recognising the 'attributes' removes any hierarchy to arrive at a point where the experience of being and pre-determined concepts are not to be placed above one another.

This points to what we allow philosophy to become, prescribing how we respond (Naughton, 2012). The implication for the arts is that we may create a concept, a way of seeing the world, not precluded by a philosophical concept. Let us take for example the concept of art. How we configure 'art' puts us back to what our own concept of art might be and this in turn will prescribe what we do in art and perceive in art.

Taking the concept and addressing in particular the implications of the 'expression' in Deleuze and Guattari's vision, this has implications for challenging the current hierarchies in arts education. In music for example our concept is most commonly a hierarchy: pitch, duration (rhythm), dynamics and tempo. These elements are then notionally followed by timbre, texture, structure and musical notation. However, if we take it that there is no specific concept or hierarchy, this order can be changed and in turn impact on how we may regard what is music. Without the hierarchy (e.g. of colour, pattern, texture, line, shape, form and space), educators can change the hierarchy, to look at space as the fundamental in making art, and not colour. Use of space in music can be seen in the work of composers Edgar Varese (1883–1965) and Giovanni Gabrieli (1557–1612), and indeed in many other idioms, such as film music; and in art there are many sculptors who use space as a fundamental to create their work. Inverting the hierarchy typically found in curriculum documents opens the possibility of moving across subject disciplines, producing a new vitalism. Far from reducing content, this altered hierarchy may allow educators and students to engage in the discovery of affect and blocs of sensation going beyond boundaries (Lines, Naughton, Roder, Matapo, Whyte & Liao, 2014). At the tertiary level this could mean moving beyond the stylistic silos, challenging the hegemony of boundaries that only limit the process of invention and community created through common endeavour.

Conclusion

Taking the work of artists and Deleuze and Guattari's philosophy of art as presented in *What is Philosophy?*, the percept, affect, blocs of sensation and concepts create a way to re-envisage art and the possibility of re-invigorating arts practice in education. With reference to the percept it is seen how the artwork changes through the material transformation. In doing so the affective response occurs, giving rise to 'blocs of sensation'. The sense of the non-human within this presentation has been cited in dance with reference to Akram Khan realising a composition through engagement with dancers, and the materiality of the dance. In doing so the technical is overwritten by the affective, blocs of sensation arising through the making.

Affect is seen as the stage beyond the percept, where affect gives rise to the blocs of sensation. This engagement with art is where it materialises and becomes, the work existing for a time, then affect continues when the materiality of the work has ceased to be. The affects are the non-human becomings of man as the percepts are the non-human becomings of nature; a process that arrives before being produced as artwork. In terms of practice, this legitimates the change or interruption that Biesta sees as key to the education process:

> The ambition of educational interruptions is to 'turn' students towards the question whether what they desire is what they should be desiring, and much of the work of the educator is about creating time, space and forms so that students can encounter their desires, examine their desires, select and transform them.
>
> *(Biesta, 2017, pp.19–20)*

In terms of Deleuze and Guattari, new openings arise through negotiating alternative approaches to the artwork, as the materiality of the artwork is engaged from percept to affect.

In re-looking at concepts we find in Deleuze and Guattari a means to challenge hierarchies in the arts. We need no longer accept others' definitions of conceptual understanding of what art is. By seeing the origin of such a hierarchy in eighteenth-century rationalism, we can question these tenets and challenge that interpretation of the concept. If we embrace a more spontaneous and inclusive formation of the arts, different hierarchies and modes of being will emerge, presenting new opportunities and challenges for arts pedagogy.

References

Allan, J. (2013). Staged Interventions: Deleuze, Arts and Education. In I. Semetsky & D. Masny (Eds), *Deleuze and Education* (pp.36–53). Edinburgh: Edinburgh University Press.

Biesta, G.J.J. (2017). *The Rediscovery of Teaching*. London: Routledge.

Bogue, R. (2003). *Deleuze on Music, Painting and the Arts*. London: Routledge.

Butler, R. (2016). *Deleuze and Guattari's 'What is Philosophy?': A Reader's Guide*. London: Bloomsbury.

Carlin, M., & Wallin, J. (2014). *Deleuze and Guattari, Politics and Education: For a People-Yet-to-Come*. London: Bloomsbury.

Cole, D.R. (2011). *Educational Life Forms*. Rotterdam: Sense Publishers.

Colebrook, C. (2005). How Can We Tell the Dancer from the Dance? The Subject of Dance and the Subject of Philosophy. *Topoi*, *24*, 5–14.

Cook, P. (1998). Thinking the Concept Otherwise: Deleuze and Expression. *Symposium*, *2*(1), 23–25.

Deleuze, G. (1995). *Negotiations 1972–1990* (M. Joughin trans.). New York: Columbia University Press.

Deleuze, G., & Guattari, F. (1994). *What is Philosophy?* (H. Tomlinson & G. Burchell trans.), New York: Columbia University Press.

Deleuze, G., & Parnet, C. (2002). *Dialogues II*. Chichester: Columbia University Press.

jagodzinski, j. & Wallin, J. (2013) Arts-Based Research: A Critique and a Proposal. Rotterdam: Sense.

Lines, D., Naughton, C., Roder, J., Matapo, J., Whyte, M., & Liao, T. (2014). Move, Act, Play, Sing (MAPS). Teaching Learning Research Initiative (TLRI), Wellington, New Zealand.

Masny, D., & Cole, D.R. (2012). *Mapping Multiple Literacies: An Introduction to Deleuzian Literacy Studies*. London: Continuum Press.

Messian, O. (1953). *Catalogue d'Oiseaux*. Alphonse Leduc: Paris.

Naughton, C. (2009). *The Thrill of Making a Racket: Nietzsche, Heidegger and Community Samba in Schools*. Saärbrucken: VDM.

Naughton, C. (2012). 'Heidegger and Joe': Revisiting the '*Thing*' in the Context of a Student's Experience of an Online Community. *British Journal of Music Education*, *29*(3), 331–341.

Naughton, C., & Lines, D. (2013). Developing Children's Self Initiated Music Making through the Creation of a Shared Ethos in an Early Years Music Project. *Australian Journal of Music Education*, *1*, 23–33.

Pearson, K.A. (2009). *Philosophy and the Adventure of the Virtual: Bergson and the Time of Life*. London: Routledge.

Quaglia, B. (2010). Transformation and Becoming Other in the Music and Poetics of Luciano Berio. In B. Hulse & N. Nesbitt (Eds), *Sounding the Virtual: Gilles Deleuze and the Theory and Philosophy of Music* (pp. 227–248). Farnham: Ashgate.

Semetsky, I. (2009). Deleuze as a Philosopher of Education: Affective Knowledge/Effective Learning. *The European Legacy*, *14*(4), 443–456.

YouTube. (2016). The Creative Process behind Akram Khan's Giselle. [online video]. 6 October. Available from: www.youtube.com/watch?v=cs2nsC_pchw [Accessed: 8 February 2017].

6

JAZZ DEPARTURES

Sustaining a pedagogy of improvisation

David Lines

Introduction

In their seminal text *A Thousand Plateaus: Capitalism and Schizophrenia*, Deleuze and Guattari provide an interesting insight about music. They say: 'Music is a creative, active operation that consists in deterritorialising the refrain' (Deleuze & Guattari, 1987, p.300). Here, music is something that uproots and becomes a new movement away – a departure to some other place. They also suggest that music takes the refrain through a movement of becoming to a *nonmusical* form (p.309). Further, and in the same vein, they suggest that the departure can be a process of reterritorialisation, a return that falls back into a structured form. These movements away from, or back, are a concern that Deleuze and Guattari refer to as the problem of the 'labour of the refrain'; a question of whether music will travel towards a creative line 'with no end in sight' or back to something more 'sober', more formed (p.302).

Improvised jazz is one kind of musical practice that engages in these territorialising possibilities. As a member of a jazz improvisation ensemble I experience the departures and returns as the ensemble plays together in free improvisation sessions. There is a rhizomatic quality to our jazz play and the possibilities of musical exploration and creation are confronted each time a new improvised line is heard. But, there is also a *pedagogical* quality to our play. This comes through the affirmative nature of the creative work – as musicians we are always seeking something special sounding or different in the way an educator might seek out different learning experiences with students. Our play together is also a kind of apprenticeship in that we are guided by the opportunities that are available to us as we connect with different kinds of improvised sound. As Rosi Braidotti (2010, p.310) says: 'Put simply, creativity affirms the positive structure of difference'. This opening out to difference is both a pedagogical and artistic movement – a movement that I call a 'pedagogy of improvisation'.

This chapter explores improvised jazz as a pedagogy of improvisation through a mixed journey of artistic and musical articulations and philosophical positions. A broad, transdisciplinary position is taken, in the spirit of Deleuze and Guattari's writing in *A Thousand Plateaus*, which enables musical ideas to be seen as living threads with educational resonances. In the latter part of the chapter the concept of a pedagogy of improvisation is used to unsettle taken-for-granted, normalised and overcoded concepts of education that close down educative possibilities and differences. This pedagogy, in contrast, affirms a more transpersonal and material education that is sustained through a process that keeps the improvised refrain alive and enmeshed with difference.

Jazz and a pedagogy of improvisation

Early jazz arose at the beginning of the twentieth century as an expression of the African American people in the face of an oppressed and exploited way of existence in colonial America. Jazz came out of a milieu of expressions of slavery, bondage, faith and emancipation. Early blues guitarists and singers played with loose, narrative musical forms that expressed stories of sadness, longing and freedom. Within the blues they affirmed their existence and imaginaries as a soulful people who endured unimaginable difficulty and strife. Similarly, early African American gospel expressed images of faith that transcended performers' and listeners' views of their oppressive, material existence in a racially divided America. Musically, blues and gospel were sonic gestures that were reappropriated in modern jazz with recognisable features: a sense of groove, a rhythmic drive, syncopated juxtapositions of time, expansive choral-like harmonies, and 'testimonies' or improvisations taken up within a group.

Free jazz is an experimental form of jazz that developed in the 1960s as players sought new avenues of expression through the abandonment of formal structures and conventions. As a 'free jazz' player and an educator, I think of this form of jazz as a living, fluid and improvisational pedagogy. Free jazz is the embodiment of a certain way of life; an open and experimental way of approaching, playing, listening and thinking. In free jazz, there is a deliberate blurring of normal 'dialogical' lines of musical communication. For instance, the roles of composer and performer are blurred as is the role of the audience member or listener in relation to the composer/performer. In its place, all participants partake in a collective improvised experience of surprise and nuance. Similarly, free jazz may break down established genre lines. For instance, it can generate 'fusions' or hybrid forms, or follow traces of popular music forms, cultural music forms, cinematic forms, technological music forms, classical music forms, to name but a few.

Jazz in this open and changing sense is 'cultural work' (Lines, 2004) that has the potential to affect people and their material environments. It is a pedagogy that is pregnant with possibilities; a type of movement that stimulates other movements, or departures to outside possibilities. It is agile and open, a flexible way of being that offers a particular philosophy of existence that not only has artistic value, but political value, for embedded in this way of being is a political attitude too.

Jazz as a pedagogy of improvisation is not the codified genre of music found on the internet, in the music recording industry, music broadcasting, digital music technology and other contexts. In the commodified marketplace of music, jazz is a form of packaged, popular music; a stylised 'intelligent' but codified music. It conforms to the dominant cultural product that can be bought and sold as 'the jazz genre'. Jazz in this commodified sense sits alongside other 'genres' in the marketplace – such as 'Irish music', 'electronic dance music', 'soul music', 'classical music', 'classic hits of the 70s' and all the other kinds of musical identity we see associated with music products.

In contrast, a pedagogy of improvisation occurs in music playing or listening contexts where the player or listener is open to what Biesta – drawing from Heidegger – calls the 'outside' (Biesta, 2017, p.13), or what Deleuze and Guattari (1987) call the 'nonmusical' (p.309). Music in this sense finds a point of departure away from its initial soundings to something different, even to the outside of music, to the nonmusical. For example, a young child may begin her play with an improvised tune through spontaneous singing and this forms a point of departure to an imagined game with material objects. Here, the departure is sustained by the creative assemblage of the child's improvised game. Further, in another example a musical improviser may depart from normal musical sounds altogether (e.g. on conventional instruments) and begin experimenting with found sounds in the material environment. This departure is sustained by the creative assemblage of the material technological equipment at hand.

According to Braidotti, this kind of openness and receptivity to affective movement is also a decentred yet sustainable process:

> One needs to be able to sustain the impact of affectivity: to 'hold' it. But holding or capturing affectivity does not happen dialectically within a dominant mode of consciousness. Instead, it takes the form of an affective, depersonalised, highly receptive subject, which quite simply is not unified.
>
> *(Braidotti, 2010, p.310)*

Although Braidotti is speaking here of writing it is also the experience of improvised jazz, for in the process of music making, the free jazz player needs to be able to keep the improvised line sustained, lose their sense of self, and be receptive and open to the possibility of the new, and the element of surprise.

The free jazz ensemble

Throughout my years as a musician I have experienced jazz from both a performer's and listener's perspective; however, it is the performer's perspective I choose to articulate here. In around the many jazz gigs over the decades I have been a pianist in two notable recording projects (Lines et al., 2008, 2014) of free jazz improvisation involving a instrumental ensemble called the *Chris Mason Battley Group,* working with a diverse array of technological, contemporary and cultural sources.

Free jazz typically starts with players not using musical scores, rather the spontaneous sonic gestures of the musicians become the beginnings of a musical experience. In these improvisations, a player initiates a musical gesture, and other players respond through spontaneous interactions by forming a changing sonic assemblage. The choice of note selection, melody formation, harmony, rhythm, articulation and intensity becomes a transpersonal experience between the performers and their acoustic, material spaces as they enter in and out of the improvisation. In this kind of jazz, the player must 'jump' (Jarrett, Toms & Catalfo, 1997, p.81) or intentionally enter the improvised line and become part of the ensemble by adopting a sensitive disposition with it. In other words, players need to have a careful sensitivity to the unfolding play of events, to the gestures of other players, to their own gestures and a commitment to the whole sonic experience.

As a player in the ensemble, I have a 'responsibility' (Biesta, 2017, p.12) to become a part of the musical experience. What I play in each moment can be of different intensity according to each moment; it may be soft and gentle for instance, and it may unfold with the group as a sensitive and exploratory musical space. Or in contrast, I may play something more direct, assertive and explosive, as a sonic offering of more confident intent that is then taken up in a different way. But there is a loss of self in this process, an abandonment of the idea of the individual musical author. This experience can be thought in terms of what Heidegger refers to as 'thrownness' (Heidegger, 1996, p.127); no matter what space a musician finds him/herself in, they respond with the relational circumstances they find themselves in. They find themselves 'thrown' into a sonic space that determines the possibilities of their next action.

What might seem to be a rather human-centric affair, to the contrary, is quite the opposite. The circumstances of a jazz improviser's thrownness is out of their complete control – for it is relationally connected to musical memories, the changing mood of the music, the acoustic and environmental space, the technologies in use, the presence and disposition of listeners, and more besides. Even the notes chosen by the improvisers are not predetermined for they emerge as a response to their sonic embodiment. Thus the responsibility of the free jazz improvisers is an embodied response to a changing block of unforeseen elements.

As a jazz improviser then, I lose my own sphere of control. In other words these elements come from outside and I respond with them as they arise and take on a sonic form. This experience however is not a dualism of inside and outside, or of player versus other; rather is it a 'synchronic' (Lyotard, 1992, p.19) and relational experience that unfolds 'together' in real time. For instance, as a player, I am relationally connected to the acoustic and material circumstances of the room. This acoustic space has a relation with each individual and collective musical gesture and with the quality and resonance of each sound as it is produced. A music gesture offered up in an acoustic space will evoke a sonic image that changes the synchronic mood and character of the music. These outside, and unforseen elements form a relational connection with the musicians throughout the course of free jazz improvisations. 'One ventures from home on the thread of a tune' (Deleuze & Guattari, 1987, p.311).

The character of free jazz improvisation envisaged in this way tells us something about the way in which the human subject enters into an educational experience. And the way that process happens involves this connection with the outside. From a philosophical point this is posited by Lyotard (1992, p.18) who explains how the 'interior purposeiveness' of the subject (person) is not 'voluntary', or 'conceived' in the sense that it is independent of an 'outside' source; but as with the musical experience, the subject enters a synthesis that is what Lyotard calls a 'synchronic, an unmeasurable and unforestallable harmony, a harmony of the timbres of the faculties, on the occasion of a form' (p.19). In this musical and Lyotardian sense, when I improvise as part of a jazz ensemble I enter into a relational connection with the other points of departure at play. This is an experience I cannot structure in advance or write a script for. It does however require an openness, alertness and attentiveness. If this openness is present, then a pedagogy of improvisation can be realised and a more 'grown-up' (Biesta, 2017, p.7) or sustained experience is realised. This moves beyond phenomenological, humanistic conceptions of the subject (cf. Benson, 2003) to the affirmation of a broader relational existence where ongoing encounters with unforeseen elements are creatively sustained.

Overcoding and middle ground

A pedagogy of improvisation, then, is present in music wherever the creative process is kept open, and where a movement with the outside is sustained – this is the basic premise of what we might call 'grown-up jazz'. But, what happens in music making when these elements are not kept open or sustained to any degree? What happens when a more 'infantile' (Biesta, 2017, p.16) disposition is perpetuated in jazz where these conditions are not in place?

Jazz music, and other forms of music, can become overcoded to the degree that there remains little room for players to exercise openness, and indeed they can lose their awareness of openness altogether and the process becomes mechanistic in the way they approach each score or even a memorised piece. The coding or scripting that drives the process can take many forms. One kind of code is the commodity-code, and when this dominates, the music making ends up serving a financial or economic end. Another kind of code, the training-code, can appear in the jazz academy, where the training of skills becomes subject to intense micro-coding based on past performances of the 'jazz greats' like Miles Davis, Louis Armstrong, John Coltrane and Charlie Parker. Thus jazz students train by repeating a series of musical gestures, which they then mechanically reproduce. Concerns around such trends in jazz education have been critiqued by contemporary jazz theorists (Proust, 2008) who argue that many of the students coming out of jazz schools lack the ability to find new and creative forms of jazz expression. The point being that many of these players all sound the same despite their apparent virtuosity and technical ability. There is a repetition of coding and the sense of creative edge or surprise can be missing.[1] The players involved, often through no fault of their own, negate the open and sustaining conditions that continue the possibility for outside connections. They remain 'inside'.

In discussing the educational task, Biesta (2017, pp.7–9) describes the process of resistance as something that needs to mark 'middle ground'; this is seen as a space where dialogue can actually take place between different partners, a space where resistance is actioned between the poles of self-destruction and world-destruction. A middle ground can be maintained if a person is able to critically discern the dangers of these extremes and be alert, attentive and sensitive to their role and act in relation to what is happening on the 'outside'. From a jazz perspective this would mean a player finding ways to keep forms of creative openness in their musical actions all the while being attentive to the limiting tendencies of powerful blocks of 'striations' (Deleuze & Guattari, 1987, p.480) that seek to subsume all creative efforts through ongoing repetitions of the same. Such actions of resistance are political in that they work to alleviate the destructive effects of commodification, technicism and disciplinarity. This is what Adorno failed to see through his own dialectical lens informed by Critical Theory when he critiqued popular jazz solely on the grounds of its tendency to embody capitalism (Witkin, 2000).

Musical rhizomes

In free jazz an improvised line is sustained so it can find new connections, new departures to the outside. As Deleuze and Guattari (1987, pp.11–12) note:

> Music has always sent out lines of flight, like so many 'transformational multiplicities', even overturning the very codes that structure or arborify it; that is how musical form, right down to its ruptures and proliferations, is comparable to a weed, a rhizome.

The rhizome is a biological and material image of thought that draws from the concept of the rhizome grass or weed that spreads across the ground as a sporadic network of interlinking lines of organic growth.

A rhizome is characterised by connection, heterogeneity, multiplicity and rupture; it embraces difference and the ability to connect and transform into different heterogeneous becomings. But the rhizome also carries with it a sense of political power through a pedagogy of improvisation such as when the old African work songs of African American slaves blended with their new forced labour through which they underwent a process of subjectification (Deleuze & Guattari, 1987, p.137). Here, the rhizomatic expression worked to politically transform the musicians' and peoples' imaginaries as they sought to express and re-envisage their mode of existence. In this sense a rhizome is a form of agential immanent materialism; it focuses on movements away – nomadic movements – from capitalist or enslaving production or other instances of coding and capture through new, reimagined connections, juxtapositions and reversals (Cole, 2012).

The ability of the rhizome to break free of standardised form, seek heterogenous and multiple references and enact a politics of the multiple can be seen as a process that destabilises totalitarian power, translating and differentiating it into a micropolitics of possible freedoms (Marzec, 2001). In jazz, this possibility is present in a fluid setting, where the expectations of the audiences, the alertness of the musicians and the freedoms built into the setting are encouraged. An improvisation then, can be an image of thought that renders the political possible through an artistic means of departure and becoming or deterritorialisation. As Deleuze (1982, p.171) notes, art can be a stimulant for the positive 'element from which the value of values derives' by means of its potential to embody and express a will to power. Art then also holds the potential to not only offer an alternative to educational norms and values present in society, but transform them through a pedagogy of improvisation that is rhizomatic, agile and capable of re-forming and re-igniting changing expressions of desire.

A pedagogy of improvisation as educational space

A pedagogy of improvisation offers hope in an educational climate that is riddled with coded forms of existence that work to close down the possibilities of rhizomatic openness. Educational language and pedagogy is laden with normative conditions and codes (consider usage of educational words like 'learning', 'outcomes' and 'competencies' within the corporate educational landscape) that work to at best dumb down teachers into actions of compliance or at worst operate unquestioningly in an educational system that stops them thinking about images of educational space that are liberating, exciting and emancipating. A pedagogy that arises from an artistic process however can mobilise the body, and inflame and stimulate creative action.

As Nietzsche comments:

> All art exercises the power of suggestion over the muscles and senses, which in the artistic temperament are originally active … all art works tonically, increases strength, inflames desire (i.e. the feeling of strength).
>
> *(Nietzsche, 1968, #809)*

Art can work as a tonic to not only change our physical feelings and desires; it has the capacity to change our conceptions of 'theory', of what it means to think, live and act in the way of an artist. This way of thinking sees pedagogy as being informed by a transdisciplinary or post-disciplinary concept of curriculum where artistic modes like music can inform and ignite pedagogical thinking and action. Deleuze, (1994, p.xvi) notes that 'arts, science and philosophy seem to be caught up in mobile relations in which each is obliged to respond to the other but by its own means'. This suggests that arts-inspired concepts like a pedagogy of improvisation described here, can speak to educational theory and practice and find its own means and 'language' to do that. This might involve artists' accounts of their own cultural work and thinking delivered in a manner that is juxtaposed with other forms of thinking to engender rhizomatic movement – such as I have presented here in this chapter.

Educational spaces take on different forms and meanings when viewed through the lens of an expanded sense of music (Lines, 2004). 'Musical' concepts can be investigated as concepts that have a broader significance with things. Rhythms infiltrate our relational lives in many ways, such as physical movements, heart-beats, shifts in daily practices, and the natural motions of sun, moon and planets. Melodies can be seen as pulses of natural action and life, the shifting tones of voices and environmental shapes, the daily patterns of rhythms and tones. Harmonies extend to resonances between people, cultural action, nature, technology; resonances that take on various qualities of difference and ecological meaning. Dynamics are the shifts in intensities and the dramatic contrasts we encounter in daily life. Timbre, like tone, expresses the particular qualities of things, the qualities we experience as particularities in events. This kind of expansive thinking helps generate concepts that help see music worlds as extensive educational spaces that have the capacity to embody creative, rhizomatic movement. This is crucial so that a multiplicity of reference points and means of expression can be actioned in a diminished arts-informed educational landscape.

A pedagogy of improvisation gives educators and students an opportunity to work more flexibly and relationally than those who seek to comply first and foremost with the performative expectations of a commodified education. It seeks for and affirms new connections of difference and surprise. This pedagogy allows for new spaces or 'middle ground' to be opened up and sustained, recognising that the educational space is indeed a political space where opportunities are reterritorialised or denied. Because of the historical bond that ties improvisation to techniques of aesthetic and ethical power, such as the African American experience alluded to, the activity of improvisation plays a special pragmatic role; it is a tool that can be used to decode the domineering power of the individual author and coloniser.

What is markedly different from the present-day educational milieu is that a pedagogy of improvisation affirms the flexible and messy circumstances of educational work and the need to develop a sensitivity to different forms of connectedness. In a world where education processes like to be packaged and formulaic (at least as they are presented as an accountable teacher–client service) this pedagogy calls for a need for a greater thoughtfulness and alertness to the political and cultural circumstances of educational spaces and the unforeseen elements that emerge through educational processes. In this way a pedagogy of improvisation can be a creative process and an image of thought that informs educators' understandings and sense of the educational spaces they work with and hopefully transform.

Note

1 See for instance, the 2008, 4(1) issue of *Critical Studies in Improvisation* at www.critical Improv.com/public/csi/index.html

References

Benson, B. (2003). *The improvisation of musical dialogue: A phenomenology of music*. London: Cambridge University Press.

Biesta, G.J.J. (2017). *The rediscovery of teaching*. New York: Routledge.

Braidotti, R. (2010). Writing. In Adrian Parr (Ed.) *The Deleuze dictionary: Revised edition* (pp. 309–311). Edinburgh: Edinburgh University Press.

Cole, D. (2012), 'Matter in motion: The educational materialism of Gilles Deleuze', *Educational Philosophy & Theory*, *44*(1), 3–17.

Deleuze, G. (1982). *Nietzsche and philosophy* (H. Tomlinson, trans.). New York: Columbia University Press.

Deleuze, G. (1994). *Difference and repetition* (P. Patton, trans.). New York: Columbia University Press.

Deleuze, G., & Guattari, F. (1987). *A thousand plateaus: Capitalism and schizophrenia* (B. Massumi, trans.). London: University of Minneapolis Press.

Deleuze, G., & Guattari, F. (1994). *What is philosophy?* (G. Burchell & H. Thomlinson, trans.). London: Verso.

Heidegger, M. (1996). *Being and time* (J. Stambaugh, trans.). New York: State University of New York Press.

Jarrett, K., Toms, M., & Catalfo, P. (1997). The creative power of the moment. In M. Toms & R. Holland (Eds.), *The well of creativity* (pp.73–91), Carlsbad, CA: Hay House.

Lines, D. (2001). The first musical space: Articulating the music of the moment. In E. Grierson & J. Mansfield (Eds.), *Access: Critical Perspectives in Cultural Policy Studies and Education*, *20*(1), 82–89.

Lines, D. (2004). The melody of the event: Nietzsche, Heidegger and music education as cultural work. (Unpublished PhD thesis). University of Auckland, New Zealand.

Lines, D.K., Mason Battley, C., Giles, S., Garden, S., & Nunns, R. (2008). Two tides: Chris Mason Battley Group. Rattle Records: Auckland, New Zealand.

Lines, D.K., Mason Battley, C., Giles, S., Thomas, S., & Psathas, J. (2014). Dialogos: Chris Mason Battley Group. Rattle Records: Auckland, New Zealand.

Lyotard, J.F. (1992). Sensus Communis. In A. Benjamin (Ed.), *Judging Lyotard* (pp.1–25). London: Routledge.

Marzec, R. (2001). The war machine and capitalism, *Rhizomes*, *3*. www.rhizomes.net/issue3/index.html

Nietzsche, F. (1968). *The will to power*. New York: Random House.

Prouty, K. (2008). The finite art of improvisation: Pedagogy and power in jazz education. *Critical Studies in Improvisation*, *3*(2), 1–15. www.criticalImprov.com/public/csi/index.html

Witkin, R. (2000). Why did Adorno hate jazz? *Sociological Theory*, *18*(1), 145–170.

7

BODILY CONNECTEDNESS IN MOTION

A philosophy on intercorporeity and the art of dance in education

Nico de Vos

Introduction

This chapter aims to contribute to the philosophical reflection on how human beings relate to each other in dance, and what this can mean for education and to where this leads: I conclude with a new philosophical idea, namely that of *bodily connectedness in motion*. This can clearly have an *impact on educational practice*, as it amounts to a plea to give dancing and moving together a much more prominent role in the school curriculum than is the case at present. This study focuses on the significance of the relationship between human beings, specifically the relationship between bodies, in the context of the art of dance in the educational context (De Vos, 2014).

In philosophical discourse, human beings are often referred to as 'subjects'. Hence the first part of the main question becomes: how can we conceptualise the relationship between subjects? My answer to this question involves two aspects. First, there is the matter of the role of the body in a philosophical reflection on the subject. While this question is increasingly addressed in philosophies of art, a reappraisal of the human body is still urgently needed. This certainly applies to education, which continues to take much of its cue from the discourse of the humanities. Whenever thinkers wish to elaborate on the added value of art or education for society, they often tend to focus on their significance for cognitive development, mental processes or conceptual thought. But how can one think without a body? All too often, the physical, material, affective and natural aspects of human existence are neglected. When considering both sides of our existence I choose to focus on our body, the *corpus*.

The philosophy that I wish to explore finds its most fundamental point of departure, not in the lone subject but in intersubjectivity; that is, in the relationship 'between' subjects. This relationship, or this 'between', is more primordial than a subject, a singular entity. This is not then a subject-centred philosophy, but a philosophy of intersubjectivity. Put differently: what this chapter presents is a relational philosophy of the human being, or a differential relational philosophy. The first part of the question can be reformulated as follows: how can we understand, philosophically, the relationship between bodies – that is 'intercorporeity' – in the art of dance? I shall formulate an answer to this question in three steps (forming sections 2, 3 and 4).

Next we might ask how are these reflections on intercorporeity in dance relevant for education? What does such a body-centred and relational concept of the subject in the art of dance mean for how we think about and act in education? This becomes a fourth step, the last part of the chapter which looks at the 'educational task'. For an answer to what is an educational task I draw on the writings of Biesta (2017). His view serves as the basis for the proposal of a new philosophical concept and its significance for educational practice.

On the possibility of intercorporeity

It was Maurice Merleau-Ponty (1908–1961) who pioneered a relational philosophy of the human body, with particular attention to sensory perception. His work was devoted to exploring the relationship between the body and the world at a fundamental level, resulting in a relational perspective on the human body. As part of his (later) work he drew on the metaphor of two mirrors facing each other (1968, p.139), resulting in an infinite reciprocal reflection. What mattered, he realised, was not the mirrors themselves but this reciprocal reflection. For Merleau-Ponty, the relationship is primordial. This leads to two important steps in his intricate theorising.

First, Merleau-Ponty turned the philosophical ideas of René Descartes (1596–1650) regarding the 'subject' upside down. In his early main work, *Phenomenology of Perception* from 1945 (2012), Merleau-Ponty criticises Descartes' well-known dualism between *res cogitans* and *res extensa*. He attempts to offer an alternative to this traditional way of dividing reality into subject (i.e. mind, spirit) and object (i.e. body, matter, world). To emphasise that the human sensory body should already be understood as a subject, or sense-giving existence, Merleau-Ponty introduced the notion of *corps sujet*, or 'body-subject'. This body-subject he saw as inextricably tied up with reflective awareness, with consciousness. However, according to Merleau-Ponty the body already displays an intentional relationship to the world at a pre-reflective level, so preceding consciousness. This points to an interconnectedness between the human body and the world of things, which Merleau-Ponty described as an *être au monde*, or 'being-in-the-world'. We see, therefore, how Merleau-Ponty already understood the body as a subject and sought to develop a relational philosophy.

In his later, unfinished work – *The Visible and the Invisible* from 1964 (1968) – Merleau-Ponty appears to seek a deeper unity underlying the relationship between the body with the world and other bodies. Here, he points to the possibility of *intercorporéité*, or 'intercorporeity' (1968, p.141). He does so in a chapter significantly titled 'The Intertwining – The Chiasm' (chiasm is the Greek word for a cross-wise structure, coined by Merleau-Ponty as a philosophical term). In his explanation of intercorporeity, Merleau-Ponty makes clear that there is a profound interconnectedness between human beings at the bodily level: a pre-reflexive relationship based on the simultaneous perceiving and being perceived of the bodies. Our bodies are intertwined. The body is a node, or chiasm, in a network of other bodies and the world.

Merleau-Ponty goes on to provide a metaphysical underpinning for this interconnectedness. He substantiates intercorporeity in terms of 'flesh' (*chair*) and 'the Being' (*l'Être*). In his view, flesh is not matter, or spirit, or substance. Its most fundamental feature is its chiastic structure and its reversibility (*reversibilité*). This reversibility pertains to both seeing and being seen, perceiving and being perceived, but also to body and world or to bodies reciprocally. In his 'Translator's Preface' to *The Visible and the Invisible* (1968), Lingis concludes: 'The concept of flesh emerges as the ultimate notion of Merleau-Ponty's thought' (p.*liv*). To further understand flesh, Merleau-Ponty believes we need to reintroduce the ancient term of 'element' (*élément*), as was used to refer to water, air, fire and earth. As he writes, 'The flesh is in this sense an "element" of Being' (1968, p.199). According to the principal metaphor of the chapter under discussion, it is understood as the composition of threads in a network or interlacement (*entrelacs*), with a cross-wise structure (*chiasme*). These threads are not pictured physically, but understood as an 'elementary' force or movement.

Merleau-Ponty's investigation into intercorporeity reveals a profound *bodily connectedness* between human beings. On his own account, he chose to apply a metaphysical approach; that is, a philosophical interrogation that starts from 'our fundamental relation with Being' (1968, p.128). Such a metaphysical approach is committed to pursuing, yet keeping open, the question of 'what do I know?'. However, a further analysis of Being reveals three features that are philosophically contentious. First, the notion of Being can ultimately be understood only as an 'idea' (*idée*), as an expression of thought or 'the mind'. Second, Being is 'invisible' (*invisible*), beyond perceptible reality. Third, Merleau-Ponty ultimately tends towards a conception of Being as a 'unity'. In this way Merleau-Ponty's approach to intercorporeity culminates in a kind of either/or philosophy. We can identify two opposing tendencies in his reflections on the relationship between bodies, whose mutual relationship is not elaborated. In some parts of his work he dwells on the non-identical, on the difference between bodies, in their mutual relationship. Yet in other parts of Merleau-Ponty's inquiry, intercorporeity leads to a focus on unity. This latter tendency of monism furthermore seems to carry more dominance so that, in the end, the differences between bodies are insufficiently respected. In my view, however, both sides matter equally when attempting to think through the relationship between subjects.

Intercorporeity as sharing material bodies in the art of dance

We derive from Merleau-Ponty a profound bodily connectedness between subjects. However, this does pose the philosophically problematic conception of monism.

In the case of Merleau-Ponty, this pertains to the dominant tendency to consider bodies as a unity. When seeing reality as a single entity, the differences between bodies in the art of dance are insufficiently respected. Besides – and this is the underlying philosophical problem – in the end it is the thinking human being, the human mind (in this particular case, Merleau-Ponty's mind) that constructs reality as such, that captures it within a framework and hence imposes limits. As a result, the human subject remains at the centre of the universe. To me it seems the other way round: the human individual is a part of reality, and our existence can never be fully captured by thought. There is always something that eludes thinking, which philosophy must account for. This is the approach pursued by the French philosopher of *difference*, Jean-Luc Nancy (1940–).

Nancy understands our existence as 'being singular plural' (2000). This is his way of expressing three fundamental characteristics of our shared existence in their mutual interconnectedness: plurality, singularity and the being of existence. First, regarding 'being' (*être*), denoted with a lower-case letter: for Nancy, this corresponds to the 'we' (*nous*) and to 'meaning' (*sens*). He makes clear that being does not 'have' meaning, since every attempt at signification necessarily falls short. This does not mean that there 'is' no meaning at all, for in Nancy's view, we ourselves are the meaning (2000, p.1). Meaning is given to us as 'we' exist. For Nancy, being has no meaning, if that meaning is not shared (*partagé*): 'meaning is itself the sharing of being' (2000, p.2). Being can therefore not be anything other than being-together, in his view.

Understood in this way, being is both 'singular' (*singulier*) and 'plural' (*pluriel*), for the fact is that all of being is in touch with all of being. But there is another aspect, as Nancy points out: 'the law of touching is separation' (2000, p.5). The touch of meaning (*touche de sens*) therefore also calls singularity and plurality into play. In Nancy's view, being must fundamentally be conceived of as being-together. There is no being by itself, but only a being singular plural, that is to say: a 'being-with-others', a joint being or co-existence. Rather than leading to some form of monism, Nancy's thought maintains a dynamic relationship between the singularity and plurality of being.

Nancy's views on reality or existence pertain equally to how he conceives of the relationship between bodies. In other words: his ontology of 'being-with' is first of all an ontology of bodies (2000, p.84). Whenever he thinks about the body, he does so from the philosophical premise of 'being singular plural'. Hence, Nancy assumes a plurality of bodies; as he emphasises, '*the* body *is* always in the plural' (2008, p.63). His ontology of the physical concentrates on this 'world of bodies' (*monde des corps*), or, as he puts it succinctly and powerfully: 'the world = bodies = "us"' (2008, p.79).

Nancy investigates bodily existence extensively, introducing a complex vocabulary to achieve his goal. Two core concepts stand out: sharing and touching. Nancy's deliberations on the body in plurality continually return to his concept of 'sharing' (*partage*), throughout his work, also in *Corpus* (2008, pp.83–91) where he writes on 'sharing of bodies' (*partage des corps*). He chooses this word deliberately on account of its ambiguity, meaning both 'sharing with another' and 'dividing', to express that the body in plurality is shared and divided at the same time, in line with his previously mentioned ontology of being singular plural. The body is not *either* an individual entity *or* a collective entity, but both simultaneously, allowing Nancy to develop a relational philosophy of the body, but one in which 'intercorporeity' is understood as a continuous tension, between the singularity and plurality of our bodily being-together.

In Nancy's philosophy, the sharing/distribution of bodily togetherness is ultimately effected through 'touching' (*toucher*). Touching is the focal point of the relationship between bodies, but touching is not reserved for human beings only. Everything in this world is in touch with each other: humans, animals, plants, stones. Stones are just as much in touch as humans, and it is in that touch, in that contact, that the difference, the suspension and the contrast between the one and the many is realised. Touching is a core notion in Nancy's materialistic differential philosophy. He has also described his thought on this point as a quantum philosophy of nature, where in the material world, everything is connected to everything, everything touches everything else, as a perpetual dynamic reality. How Nancy thinks about reality also impacts how he thinks about the human being, as after all, the human being is part of the material world, and is him- or herself a material body. Just like Merleau-Ponty, he clearly distances himself from Cartesian thought, where the human being is equated with his or her mind alone. Intercorporeity can thus be understood as the sharing of and by material bodies through touch.

Nancy's philosophical perspective on the relationship between bodies is highly relevant to his thoughts on bodily togetherness in contemporary dance. This is clear from a number of texts that he has published jointly with choreographers (2004, 2005, 2010). I cannot discuss these here at any length, but Nancy explicates a number of concepts specific to the art of dance including 'sharing together and dividing' with respect to identical gestures and movements. Sharing the tension between the one and the many is realised, while there is also a 'rhythm' of dancers as they move together, as a specific aspect of this art form. In Nancy's view, this rhythm embodies a difference. In the rhythm of the dance, the dancing body participates in the environment and in another body. For as soon as you see another dancer, you cannot help but dance along with him or her to some extent (unless you're not really paying attention, of course). Perhaps this makes dance the purest form of *zusammensein*, of being-together, says Nancy. It is in any case indisputable, in his view, that the relationship of bodies among each other in dance is very difficult to conceptualise; but it is a good test to interrogate this relationship in general terms (2004, p.69).

Moving from Merleau-Ponty to Nancy is philosophically advantageous. The problem of a metaphysical monism has now dissipated. Nancy does not adopt the notion of 'intercorporeity' in his work, but he does write extensively about the relationship between bodies. He understands this relationship as a relationship of difference: seeing many different individual bodies *and* the single 'body' of the group, simultaneously. It is not a matter of or/or, but of and/and, without either of the paired entities dissolving into the other. It is a sharing and a distribution of the material bodies, based on an ontology of touch. This is how Nancy respects differences between bodies, while upholding the primacy of bodily being-together. However, Nancy's philosophy remains relatively sketchy on the emotional, affective aspect of the relationship between bodies. So here his philosophy deserves to be thought through more fully. I believe this is necessary, because matter *and* emotion jointly constitute 'intercorporeity'. Nancy thematises the dynamic and tense relationship between the unity and plurality of bodies among each other. In other words: the profound bodily relation can be understood philosophically as *connectedness in motion*. This pertains both to the bodily relation as demonstrated especially in dance, and more importantly, to how the relationship itself is permanently in motion. There is no static moment in the 'in between' of the individual and collective body. Think, as an example, of a swarm of birds.

Sharing material and felt bodies in the art of dance

From our discussion of Nancy's philosophy we may conclude that intercorporeity should be understood as more than just the sharing of material bodies. The emotional, affective aspect of the relationship between bodies should also be thematised more explicitly. At the most fundamental level, our bodies are found 'to be', like things among other things; but at the same time they are 'felt'. Here we may fruitfully turn to another French philosopher, Jean-François Lyotard (1924–1998).

First, to elaborate on this affective aspect in the relationship between bodies: (1) 'feeling' should be understood here in the widest sense of the word, incorporating both sensory perception and being touched by or 'feeling' what is perceived in a stricter sense; (2) it not only concerns touching/being touched, or feeling/being felt, but also seeing/being seen, hearing/being heard, smelling/being smelt, and tasting/being tasted; (3) it pertains to every and everyone's aesthetic feeling, rather than to only what a philosophy of aesthetics traditionally identifies as the beautiful or the sublime. However, I will investigate aesthetic feelings between bodies at a fundamental level, where every form of articulation fails us at the actual moment of the experience. Traditionally this applies mainly to the intense feeling of the sublime.

Lyotard introduced this concept of the sublime to philosophical discourse in the 1980s, with reference to the sublime in the world of art, and then specifically to avant-garde painting and music. In his later work, towards the end of the 1980s, he interprets the sublime as an awareness of a material event. He explores the concept in the sense of an awareness of time as an event (1991, pp.89–107). With reference to the avant-garde painter Barnett Newman, Lyotard demonstrated that the object of the sublime experience, such as a painting, is 'here and now'. The awareness of time in the work is not continuous but discontinuous: as an event, or occurrence (*événement, occurence*). Linking this sublime to matter (1991, pp.135–143) in art thus becomes a material event, where thinking always misses its mark, as it will either arrive too soon or too late. Experiencing the sublime is an intense feeling: a contradictory sense of desire and revulsion, joy and fear, ecstasy and depression, as the eighteenth-century philosopher Burke (1729–1779) already noted. That which is perceived, in nature or in a work of art, makes an immense impression, yet is found to be shocking. That is the 'terror', but at the same time, there is a sense of not being in danger personally, and that is the 'delight'.

Still later, in the 1990s, Lyotard expands his analysis beyond the sublime to include every aesthetic experience (1997, pp.235–250). He describes how the *anima minima*, or 'minimum soul', is touched or moved by sensory perception. This minimum soul is nothing other than 'being touched' (*affectabilité*), in itself. This being touched is characterised by a 'double bind', analogous to the contradictory structure of the sublime. It is a sign of a profound mutual dependency between sensation and feeling. From Lyotard's perspective, the body should be understood as nothing other than that feeling (2006). This is demonstrated clearly by the art of dance: a dancer can be touched truly and deeply by the sensory experience of another material body in motion, a shared experience of bodily interconnectedness.

This sharing is more fundamental than every person's individual experience, as is also thematised in Lyotard's last works, towards the end of the 1990s. From the various pointers in this direction, I shall briefly make one observation.

In the last paragraphs of *Soundproof Room* (2001, pp.77–105), with titles like *Stridency*, *Throat* and *Communion*, Lyotard explores the sharing of intense feelings through the profound, animal-like stridency (*stridence*) that can be emitted through our throats (*gorge*) to create a communion (*communion*). This happens under extreme circumstances. Lyotard applied the analysis to the sense of fraternity felt by soldiers fighting a war, or to a love relationship between two human beings, for example when the one partner suddenly tells the other that it's over. In such a situation, one doesn't so much hear the other's utterance with one's ears, but feel his or her sound of voice in one's own throat. Lyotard suggests that this sharing of aesthetic feelings is also possible through art. For as he writes: 'Just as we are lovers or brothers through fusion of airtight throats, the artwork places absolute solitudes in communion with each other' (2001, p.102). In other words: sharing perceived experiences can also grab us by the throat in the arts, including the art of dance.

Being touched by the sensory experience of the occurrence of other material bodies in motion can feel as if your throat is momentarily constricted. That is the contradictory sense and the shock, or the 'double bind' in which the dancer is caught. It can occur when one dancer perceives and feels the moving body of the other dancer, or when the one dancer is touched by the other. These aesthetic experiences of the dancers merge in the perceived event of each other's moving bodies, as part of the choreography. This can be a single event, or a series of events. At such a moment, the different feelings felt by the individuals and the shared feeling of the group occur simultaneously. And at such a moment in the relationship between bodies, not one but two (or more) dancers – and often the audience as well – feel grabbed by the throat. From Lyotard's perspective, 'intercorporeity' can be understood principally as the sharing of 'felt corporeality'. However, as pointed out above: feeling and matter go hand in hand. So it's about the sharing of *material and felt* bodies in the art of dance.

Significance for the educational task

The significance of this analysis, of the relationship between bodies in the art of dance, for education brings us back to the educational task. As described by Biesta (2017, p.7–21) this infers 'making the grown-up existence of another human being in and with the world possible' (p.7). For Biesta, the concept of existence refers to the subjectivity, or more specifically: 'it is the question of human *subject-ness* or of the human "condition" of *being-subject*' (p.8). As regards 'grown-up-ness', he writes: 'the grown-up way acknowledges the alterity and integrity of what and who is other' (p.8). Biesta presents his reflection on this theme in a number of ways, and we will concentrate on the first one, summarised as: 'the subject is subject!' Based on the foregoing philosophical analysis, I seek to augment and further elaborate this first step. Briefly put, my argument runs as follows: the subject is subject(ed) – *to intercorporeity*.

Biesta (2017) writes: 'The main insight I wish to highlight about the existence *of* the subject and our existence *as* subject is that, to a large degree, our subject-ness is not in our own hands' (p.10). This can even mean that it is not at all in our hands. Reflecting on this aspect of what it means to exist as a subject, Biesta finds the philosophy of Hannah Arendt (1906–1975) particularly helpful. Arendt (1958) shows clearly that the acting person is a subject in a dual sense, namely in the sense of an actor initiating an action, and in the sense of being literally subject to the consequences of that action. The latter depends entirely on how others respond to the initiated action. This line of thought brings Biesta to the idea of 'the subject is subject'.

I share the idea of the subject being subject to another (and the other), but the notion deserves further elaboration. The early work by Merleau-Ponty taught us that the body is already a subject, a 'body-subject'. In his later work, this evolves into the concept of 'intercorporeity'. At the most fundamental level of our existence, we do not find individual subjects that enter into relations with others and the other. Instead the reverse applies: the primary fact is that of the relationship 'between', the 'inter' between subjects. In other words: what we find first is intersubjectivity. We know that Merleau-Ponty first understood this in terms of our bodies, so we should say instead: 'intercorporeity'. This means that, contrary to the still fairly standard Cartesian philosophy, not just the individual (self, or 'I') and the mind matter, but certainly the relationships ('we') and the body as well. Applied to education, it suggests that we should focus more on strengthening the relationships, on developing children's social skills, and on engaging in all sorts of bodily activity. Too much emphasis on individual development on the path to grown-up-ness may be detrimental to developing the mutual interconnectedness that is already given with and through our bodies.

At the same time, we shouldn't lose sight of each and every human being, as Nancy's correction of Merleau-Ponty's philosophy makes clear. According to Nancy, 'intercorporeity' should be understood as the sharing of material bodies; that is to say, as the permanently dynamic tension between the singularity *and* plurality of our bodily being-together. The art of dance exemplifies this relationship between the individual and the group, as the various dancers swarm across the stage in permanent interaction. An important goal for education is to make this dynamic tension a substantial aspect of the child's learning and development activities.

Regarding the relationship between bodies, Lyotard's view resembles that of Nancy. He also focuses on the dynamic relationship between the individual and the group; but for Lyotard, 'intercorporeity' not only involves the sharing of our material bodies, but also and at the same time, the sharing of felt corporeality. Learning to share feelings is therefore at least as important in education and child-rearing as cognitive learning. And this is certainly not just a matter of talking about it – perhaps not at all a matter of talking about it, as it should be part and parcel of 'physical education'.

The philosophical concept that I introduce here by way of conclusion is to understand intercorporeity in the art of dance as: *bodily connectedness in motion*, in material and affective respects. This concept is relevant to the educational task in practice. It is in any case an argument in favour of giving the art of dance a more prominent role in education. And if we take a broader view, it is a recommendation to offer more physical education. I do not mean a few hours of gymnastics a week as a separate curriculum component, but physical education in a wider sense, as a counterbalance to the dominance of learning 'cerebral' skills at school. What matters is to dance and move together, in a non-competitive way. To talk less and to do more, to feel and to experience more, together. The development of mind and body, of one's subjectivity and intersubjectivity, should go hand in hand. Because: the subject is subject(ed) – to intercorporeity, which is to *bodily connectedness in motion*.

References

Arendt, H. (1958). *The Human Condition*. Chicago: The University of Chicago Press.

Biesta, G.J.J. (2017). *The Rediscovery of Teaching*. New York: Routledge.

De Vos, N. (2014). *Bodily Connectedness in Motion. A Philosophical Research on Intercorporeity in Contemporary Dance* (in Dutch, with a summary in English). Nijmegen, The Netherlands: Nico de Vos / Miranda Thoonen Graphic Design bno (PhD dissertation, Tilburg University, The Netherlands).

Lyotard, J.-F. (1991). *The Inhuman. Reflections on Time* (G. Bennington & R. Bowlby, trans.). Cambridge: Polity Press.

Lyotard, J.-F. (1997). *Postmodern Fables*. (G. Van Den Abbeele, trans.). Minneapolis: University of Minnesota Press.

Lyotard, J.-F. (2001). *Soundproof Room. Malraux's Anti-Aesthetics* (R. Harvey, trans.). Stanford, CA: Stanford University Press.

Lyotard, J.-F. (2006). The Affect-phrase (from a Supplement to *The Differend*). In K. Crome & J. Williams, *The Lyotard Reader and Guide* (pp. 104–110). Edinburgh: Edinburgh University Press.

Merleau-Ponty, M. (1968). *The Visible and the Invisible* (A. Lingis, trans.). Evanston, IL: Northwestern University Press.

Merleau-Ponty, M. (2012). *Phenomenology of Perception* (D.A. Landes, trans.). New York: Routledge.

Nancy, J.-L. (2000). *Being Singular Plural* (R.D. Richardson & A.E. O'Byrne, trans.). Stanford, CA: Stanford University Press.

Nancy, J.-L. (2004). Entretien avec Jean-Luc Nancy. (Interview Véronique Fabbri). *Rue Descartes*, *44*(2), 62–79.

Nancy, J.-L. (2005). Allitérations. In M. Monnier & J.-L. Nancy, *Allitérations. Conversation sur la danse* (pp.137–150). Paris: Galilée.

Nancy, J.-L. (2008). *Corpus* (R.A. Rand, trans.). New York: Fordham University Press.

Nancy, J.-L. (2010). Befremdliche Fremdkörper. In J.-L. Nancy, *Ausdehnung der Seele. Texte zu Körper, Kunst und Tanz* (pp.43–58). (M. Fischer, trans.). Zürich, Switzerland: Diaphanes.

8

THINKING SCHOOL CURRICULUM THROUGH COUNTRY WITH DELEUZE AND WHITEHEAD

A process-based synthesis

David R. Cole and Margaret Somerville

Introduction

Aboriginal Australian peoples have a continuous oral culture, which has changed over millennia, and continues to develop in contemporary Australia. Despite political movements towards reconciliation, and the recognition of Aboriginal cultures and rights, educational curriculum in Australia fails to engage with the *a priori* profundity and depth of living Aboriginal cultures. In order to address the profound disconnect between Western and Aboriginal philosophies, this chapter considers the arts-based Aboriginal onto-epistemology of 'thinking through Country' (Somerville, 2013) alongside a 'flat ontology' derived from Deleuze and Guattari's *A Thousand Plateaus*, and A.N. Whitehead's process philosophy. The aim is to propose ways to transform the Australian educational curriculum at the intersection of Western and Aboriginal understandings of coming to know the world.

A philosophical framework for curriculum change

The colonisation of Australia by British and other cultures since the 1600s could be framed and rethought from the perspectives of ontology and epistemology. Aboriginal peoples, who had been continuously living on the land that was called Australia by the settlers for many thousands of years, had developed a complete, living and ongoing onto-epistemology that can be understood as 'thinking through Country' in its contemporary expression (Somerville, 2013). Thinking through Country enacts ongoing relations with natural elements and forces, and is manifest in narratives and cultural practices. Previous onto-epistemological frameworks were radically disrupted by the progressive invasion and the permanent settlement of Australia by European and other immigrants. The increasing populations of settlers brought with them a rival ontology and epistemology to the resident Aboriginal Australians', which was predominantly a combination of science, Christianity and more recently, capitalism. This onto-epistemology had little or no previous connection with the natural Australian environment, and encapsulated 'human exceptionalism', with science attempting to provide a complete understanding of the world to the benefit of human kind, who, having a soul, had exclusive access to heaven. The conflict between the human exceptionalism of the white, settler culture, and Aboriginal systems of belief, has been ongoing since the initial colonial period. It is played out today within the Australian curriculum which envisages Aboriginal studies as an addition, rather than as an onto-epistemology through which being in, and knowing the world, are understood and learned.

A possible escape from the dead-end human exceptionalism in Western thought is through philosophical work that attempts to overcome the exceptionalism of the human condition. Whilst a 'flat ontology' was mentioned by Roy Bhaskar in his 1975 book, *A Realist Theory of Science*, its popularity has been augmented by Manuel DeLanda (2004, p.58) who used the term with reference to the ontology of Gilles Deleuze:

> [While] an ontology based on relations between general types and particular instances is hierarchical, each level representing a different ontological category (organism, species, genera), an approach in terms of interacting parts and emergent wholes leads to a 'flat ontology', one made exclusively of unique, singular individuals, differing in spatio-temporal scale, but not in ontological status.

DeLanda reads the 'flat ontology' of Deleuze as a realist/empiricist conception, which demarcates ontology as corresponding to the material nature of existence. However, Deleuze, who was not interested in eliminating metaphysics, attempts instead to rescue it from the thought that the material model of the universe from science negates any possible metaphysical speculation on/about the world. Deleuze's flat ontology, or immanence, is univocal (or pure response), a combination of Spinozian affect, Bergsonian *élan vital*, Nietzschian eternal return, and Marxian critique of the productive forces under capitalism (Cole, 2011). It is simultaneously an instance of disjunctive synthesis that produces a 'differential ontology'. Deleuze attempted to formulate a metaphysical notion of intensive difference through ontology that speaks to:

(1) The constitutive play of forces underlying the production of identities (human and non-human);
(2) The purely relational, that is, 'non-negational', and hence, an ontology which is not in any way subordinate to the principle of identity.

(Cisney, n.d., online)

In other words, Deleuze's ontology attempts to (re)think the conditions of and for identity (of all things), but in such a way as to not recreate the presuppositions surrounding the identity of the conditions themselves, that is, Deleuze's flat ontology attempts to think the conditions of 'real experience', or the world as it is lived through process (see framework below). In *A Thousand Plateaus* (Deleuze & Guattari, 1987), the flat ontology depends upon 'the plane of immanence', which is constructed in Plateaus at specific dates in history to join together intensive differentials as relations, a process which has been termed immanent materialism (Cole, 2013, 2014). Immanent materialism describes the task for contemporary Australian educationalists and also for this chapter, which considers the onto-epistemology of the Aboriginal Australians in relation to the contemporary curriculum and the learning that happens under its rubric.

An Aboriginal onto-epistemology through art

Chrissiejoy Marshall, an U'Alayi knowledge holder and researcher, undertook the challenging task of developing an Indigenous onto-epistemology as the basis of her doctoral research. Previous university study had left her scarred by Western knowledge frameworks, her writing was moralistic and angry, caught up in the savage binaries of Aboriginal identity politics. For the first year in the intensive doctoral residential programme with her fellow students she just listened, during the second she captivated them with a funny story about getting lost and way-finding on the long and windy road down the big hill to Kempsey. The next year, she began differently, speaking about tough doctoral conversations with her supervisor, Margaret Somerville, she said: 'Margaret challenged and extended my intellectual boundaries, she saw the need for me to divert from conventional discourse and allowed me to develop my own form and content' (C. Marshall, personal communication, June 21st, 2001).

Together they worked out that in order to make any knowledge claims at all Chrissiejoy had to 'think through Country', the specific country of the Narran Lake, where she was raised by her Noongurraburrah grandfather and uncles and her Erinbinjori grandmother, on the property of her settler-colonial father. In this sense thinking through Country does not reference a pure and idealised Aboriginal past, but emerges from a contemporary mixed-up present combining many knowledge traditions, still always essentially underpinned by a relationship to land. This is not land in general, but the specific place of Chrissiejoy's growing up.

The resulting onto-epistemology was developed using a combination of visual, oral and written forms and translations from Erinbinjori and U'Alayi languages. In performing her methodology for her fellow non-Indigenous students, Chrissiejoy presented a DVD showing a painting and an accompanying oral account, that structured and informed each cluster of meanings, or chapters of the thesis.[1] In relating her Aboriginal knowledge, she referred to herself by her Aboriginal name, Immiboagurramilbun, acknowledging her two identities, two worlds. In presenting her paintings she said:

> There is no one word in any Aboriginal language that I can find for the term 'art', which is lucky for me, who not for one moment considers herself as an artist. It is far more important that the paintings actually describe to the viewer the information that I am telling.
>
> *(Immiboagurramilbun, 2003)*

For Chrissiejoy, her paintings are a medium to express and communicate complex ideas, as much for herself as for the viewers:

> Aboriginal Art has only become Art in the last 200 years. What anthropologists described as unsophisticated art was actually Aboriginal pictorial reflections for the passing on of knowledge, so that the listener or learner could visually grasp the concept or subject matter. Similarly, that which is now described as dance, song and ceremony was the passing on of information including history, lore and laws, and not primarily a recreational pursuit. The symbols and drawings described by anthropologists constitute a complex code of interaction that reflects on Aboriginal cosmology, philosophies, spirituality, history and laws that have been used for thousands of years.
>
> *(Immiboagurramilbun, 2003)*

A mud map of Country (as flat ontology)

> Starting in the centre top of the painting this jigsaw piece is viewed as a mud map of the Noongahburrah country. The black lines are the rivers within, and marking the boundaries of this country, and the black orb in the centre represents the Narran Lake, where I was raised, and which has always been the most significant and sacred site for Noongahburrah, Murriburrah, Ngunnaburrah, and all the other peoples of the nation that spoke the U'Alayi language as well as several other nations of Aboriginal people within bordering countries.
>
> *(Immiboagurramilbun, 2003)*

The first painting is composed of the intersecting parts of a jigsaw puzzle which Chrissiejoy describes as a mud map, or conceptual framework, for the whole. She begins the narration at the top centre, a literal mud map of the Narran Lake, but the whole painting is organised around a large central piece that depicts Kurreah, the ancestral being who created the Narran Lake through the death throe thrashing of his massive tail. Chrissiejoy says of the stories she grew up with:

> They talk about Baiame who is the Creator. He was here on earth and he had two wives, and he sent his wives to go and dig yams while he went to do something else, I think it was gather honey or something, and they were to meet at this waterhole. Anyway he got to this waterhole and the wives were missing, so he figured out what had happened to them and tracked them. He

got around in front of it and it was Kurreah, he had swallowed his two wives. So he waited in ambush and killed and slit open the belly and got his wives out. He put them on an ants' nest and brought them back to life and everyone lived happily ever after but whilst he was killing the giant lizard, Kurreah swished his tail around and knocked the big hole in the ground and all the water he had swallowed flowed into that hollowed place that then became the lake. Baiame said, that in honour of Kurreah it would always refill with water and there would always be water and many birds and things there. So the birds were always there and as a resting place for them and as a place for them to come to breed, when they were going from one place to another, this was a really good place for them to stop over.

(Chrissiejoy Marshall in Somerville, 2013, p. 102)

Surrounding and interlocking with the giant ancestral lizard are other jigsaw pieces showing many different animals, birds and humans who were an integral part of their life at the Narran Lake. All living creatures and the elements that sustain them are not only inseparable and equal, but they are emergent through ongoing stories and cultural enactments within the overarching framework of Country.

Country and capitalism

The task of bringing together thinking through Country as an Aboriginal onto-epistemology with Western philosophical thought is not a straightforward one. The third item connected to Christianity and science in Western 'exceptionalist' settler culture is capitalism. The colonisation of Australia and the clash of cultures between the settlers and Aboriginal lands/communities includes the ways in which capitalism has defined and redefined relations between peoples and the world. Capitalism sets up relations of profitability and production to enable flows of capital and surplus value. The relational and objectifying (as monetary value) system of capitalism is not inherently human-centred in the way that Christianity and science can be, but provokes systems of winners and losers based on capital flows, which inherently favour capitalised positions (Marazzi, 2011).

Aboriginal Australia was characterised by a different mode of economy and exchange. Land and its resources were not considered as personal property that could be possessed and sold to accumulate capital. The division and demarcation of land in Australia by the settlers, the sedentary organisation of the settler society, and the capitalised valuation of land as property, have all worked against Aboriginal Australian communities. If the 'flat ontology' of this chapter is to work to redress the inequality that has happened to Aboriginal Australians, it must also include a critique of capitalist relationality.

It is against the triumvirate settler onto-epistemology of Christianity, science and capitalism that Aboriginal Australians have struggled to assert their rights in a country where they have been living for thousands of years. It is the thesis of this chapter that the relationship between Aboriginal and settler onto-epistemology is

changing, due in part to the recognition that the settlers have produced an unsustainable mode of being and knowing for living in a country such as Australia, and
which therefore has no future. We propose that the flat ontology of Deleuze and
Guattari (1987), supplemented and combined with the process philosophy of Alfred
North Whitehead (1929a), see framework below, has the greatest possibility for
reinvigorating and reforming the Australian curriculum to fully take into account
the onto-epistemology of Aboriginal Australians.

'Me Myself and I': ontology

Following the overview painting, the first of the chapter paintings is named 'Me Myself
and I'. It is an ontological painting on dark brown masonite with the edges cut into
multiple curves that form the ground for Immiboagurramilbun's telling of her selves.
The colour is of desert earth; it is more like a patch of country than a painting with a
series of concentric circles in the centre, each with five differently patterned petals, or
leaves, radiating outwards. When looking at these concentric circles, it is not apparent
whether the lighter ones are formed by the dark, or the darker ones are formed by the
light. Each forms and shapes the other. Immiboagurramilbun says that the five lighter
circles show the five lives that she lives; they are 'the Niddeerie [the ongoing creation story] of each one'. These lives include Yowee, inner spirit; Doowee, dream spirit;
Kungullun, secret mind; Mullowil, shadow spirit; and Mullojel, the connectiveness to
ancestors and Mulgury, which is the creative power of the universe. The darker circles
are the Niddeerie of others connected to her so that 'the whole of history is there'
(Somerville 2013 website for Immiboagurramilbun DVD excerpts and paintings).

   Through the symbols sheltering in the curves around the edges of the painting,
Immiboagurramilbun recites the Niddeerie of these others who make up her identity. The first is the swans for her mother and the Noongahburrah people of the
Narran Lake. The second symbol is the Crocodile, from her grandmother's country
of the Erinbinjori people of far North Queensland on the Gulf of Carpentaria.
The Wardook/Bohrah (kangaroo) is for the men, and the Jindi/Dinawan is in the
Mulgury of the women. The Bandabee (kookaburra) symbolises the Mulgury of
her grandmother, and the Albatross the Mulgury of her son. Each of these symbols
is linked by a trail of dots to show how they are connected to each other. The
closeness of the dots indicates the intensity of their connections to her being, an
ontological reality realised through the different countries, people and life forms
that make up those places. Through this painting, she articulates the complex system
whereby one is inextricably connected to a particular living entity through which
the multiple entanglements of being are understood:

> At the beginning all was Mulgury. Only creative power and intent. Through
> the intent and power of our Creator, Mulgury reproduces into form to carve
> the beings and shapes of the world where the water meets the sky and earth
> sings the world to life. The pattern of life is Mulgury and Mulgury is traced in
> the Niddrie [the framework of the ancient laws within Niddeerie] of Mudri

[person]. Every tracing, every rock, tree, plant, landform, the water, fish, reptile, bird, animal and Mudri is in the sacred relationship, through Niddeerie. The pattern, shape and form of Mulgury is life, and all is a continuing tracing of Mulgury.

(Ticalarnabrewillaring, 1961 translated by Immiboagurramilbun, 2003)

In elaborating the idea of Mulgury, Immiboagurramilbun begins with four black swans. The first two swans are for her mother, and the second two represent the collective of water people, the Noongahburrah, her grandfather's people. The swans are Mulgury, signalling their collective meaning as mythical creatures of the Niddeerie, as well as representing an individual's connection to a particular creature and its place. Immiboagurramilbun's mother is swan, Noongahburrah people collectively are swan. Swan belongs to the time and place of the creation of the land and people of Terewah, the home of the black swan, in the past, the present and the future. Those who carry that identity are both swan and place. Country, swan and person are together an ontological reality.

Process structure for re-thinking curriculum

In order to link this complex onto-epistemological system to Western curriculum we turn to Whitehead's process structure for re-thinking curriculum, outlined as follows:

- *Education is rhythmic.* This statement is part of the process tendency towards making things organic, entangled and inter-related, and it is a move away from linear, goal-orientated and teleological learning schemes. The non-linear, cyclic appreciation of education and learning has profound consequences for understanding the ways in which learning happens and how research can proceed in terms of determining what counts as learning. Learning, thinking and doing research 'take off' according to rhythmic conditions in time and space, and not due to the interventions of linear, often short-lived, exterior learning innovations. Learning has to be premised on collective engagement of a profound, complex, reciprocating and rhythmic nature.
- *Knowledge can become inert.* Whitehead says: '[t]his is not an easy doctrine to apply, but a very hard one. It contains within itself the problem of keeping knowledge alive, of preventing it from becoming inert, which is the central problem of all education' (1929b, p.34). In this context, modern education can become a matter of memorising vocabulary, facts and concepts in specialised knowledge areas, often of a techno-bureaucratic nature, and that is henceforth examined as recollection, and has no long-term use or impact. The flat ontology of Deleuze and Guattari (1987), and process philosophy, work in the opposing direction, making knowledge non-inert, fluid, alive and more akin to Aboriginal knowledge. Furthermore, knowledge is seen as part of the everyday working and thinking projects of the cohorts; that is, it has to be enacted

rather than only memorised and examined, and schooling needs to address these issues in terms of helping to prevent and warn against inert knowledge becoming embedded in the system as dead zones of educational practice.

- *The explicit questioning of ontology as process sets up different object–subject relations.* The 'thing-in-itself' is questioned, the objects of the curriculum change from things which are fixed to things that are always in motion. Whitehead invented different concepts to describe this process that add to those of Deleuze and Guattari (1987), but the intent is the same, to make changing processes the focus of investigation and to eliminate sedentary conceptual overlay. For example, Whitehead used the term 'prehension' to describe 'uncognitive apprehension' (Whitehead, 1967, p.69), and this is one of the bases of process thought. Prehension for education is what makes a thought a form of continually 'grasping' aspects of the world. According to process thought, connection to the world begins with a 'pre-epistemic' prehension of it, from which the processes of intentional thought are able to distil knowledge. However, knowledge is only significant as a part of the world; it does not stand in any simple one-to-one relation in or with the world. The pre-epistemic grasp of the world (prehension) is the source of our *a priori* knowledge of space, which enables us to know of the uniformities that make cosmological speculation possible, as seen in the *(Immiboagurramilbun, 2003)* narrative.
- *Prehensions can build up, until a decision or event becomes apparent.* Our collective journey along the space-time continuum as thinkers is defined by the ways in which prehension can create thoughts in the empirical as 'empirical-ideal constructs', that define future decisions and plans for action. Whitehead (1929a) called the relations between prehensions and events 'concrescence', which is a pivotal aspect of his metaphysics. The past is full of actual occasions; every actual occasion receives data from every other actual occasion by means of prehension. Whitehead called the process of integrating data by proceeding from indeterminacy to determinacy 'concrescence'. Concrescence consists of an occasion feeling the entirety of its past actual world, filtering data for relevance, and integrating and contrasting original data with novel data in stages of 'feeling' until the occasion reaches 'satisfaction' and becomes fully actual. Because this process of synthesis involves distilling the past universe into a moment of experience, Whitehead calls an actual occasion 'superject' or 'subject-superject'. After an occasion reaches satisfaction, it becomes an objective datum for future occasions. Translated into the context of this chapter, 'concrescence' avoids 'the fallacy of misplaced concreteness' (Whitehead, 1929a) that places concrete abstractions (as real) into continuums of educational flux and change, or the misplacement of Aboriginal knowledge into Western knowledge-frames.
- *The metaphysical architecture and process philosophy of Whitehead redefines the human–nature relationship*, and that is directly relevant to this chapter due to the destabilisation of human–matter agency, as seen in Aboriginal knowledges. This redefinition has been called 'panpsychism' (Chambers, 2013). Panpsychism according to Whitehead is based on his view of an 'occasion of experience' as

the ultimate particle of reality, and as possessing simultaneously both a physical pole and a mental pole. If according to process philosophy, things are nothing but occasions, and occasions are at least in part mental, then all things have a mental dimension including matter. In *Modes of Thought* (1938), in the chapter titled 'Nature Alive', Whitehead observed, 'this [traditional] sharp division between mentality and nature has no ground in our fundamental observation.... I conclude that we should conceive mental operations as among the factors which make up the constitution of nature' (p.156). Whitehead's aim is to prevent the bifurcation of nature, and any previously held positions of science, through which nature is perceived as an unlimited object that we project ourselves into. Rather, panpsychism enacts the opposite, but reciprocating process, as seen below.

'Finding and knowing place of self and others in Country': a practical methodology

An Aboriginal onto-epistemology is living knowledge within Country enacted through dance, song, music and ceremony in Country. In the painting called 'Finding and knowing place of self and others in Country' Chrissiejoy offers a contemporary form of this living knowledge as a practical methodology. It is the brightest and most energetic of all the paintings with its gaudy pinks, greens, yellows, oranges and blues. In the centre, against a background of patches of country marked by different coloured dots, a bright pink circle is outlined in blue dots with inner concentric circles of blue. The dots which make up the shapes and form of the painting shimmer and move, as if animated by the energy of the lake's waters. The concentric circles in the painting's centre are the intertwining of self and other, each shaping and forming the other through Niddeerie, the ever-present time of creation. In the epicentre of the painting, in the centre of the circles, a pale pink eye shape with a blue-lined iris gazes out at the viewer. This eye/I centre is also the blue of the Narran Lake, when the waters arrive and life returns.

Outside these circles, four pink snake-like shapes flow outwards to the four corners; at the same time, the eye is drawn towards the centre. Bright green tree-like forms also stretch out in all the directions of the painting. They are wavy childlike stems and leaves with small red and orange fruit along the stem. Around the tree leaf stems, fat shiny white bodies of witchetty grubs are scattered across this country, with the symbols of seated figures and their camps nearby. This is Chrissiejoy's practical methodology and she describes the everyday learning associated with it:

> As children we spent much time following the life cycle of the grub, as we did with all other animals, birds, insects and plant life. We would learn when they mated, how the mother prepared for her babies, we watched the young grubs grow and we knew how to know when they reached maturity. You can imagine the depth of knowledge gained from this kind of learning. It not only gave knowledge about the insect itself, but also about everything that is

connected to it, the type of conditions most favoured. We learned what happened when floods or drought hit the area, what the grub needed for survival and what other animals and birds fed on the grub itself. In addition, we were shown how it all connected to us.

(Immiboagurramilbun, 2003)

As children they learned through their everyday life of being-in-the world, but this was also enhanced by ongoing stories with deep ancestral meanings told in layers of complexity as they grew older. The lake was always a place of story and representation for Chrissiejoy, 'it wasn't only a place to supply us with food, it was this bunker of knowledge that you had'. They were told about the different parts of the lake and the events that had happened there during its creation. Some deep parts of the lake were taboo; they could never go there. The knowledge about the lake and these places of taboo was told in story. Chrissiejoy tells these oral stories and she also creates images through which to convey the ineffable meanings of the ancient stories of water:

> The first stories are almost beyond my memory. I grew up knowing the stories so I'm guessing that I was told as a very, very small child. When you first get told about the creation of the lake and Kurreah and how all that connects it's a very simplistic story, it was just simply that this huge animal was, you know, kept the kids away from the water holes because, 'look out Kurreah'll get you'. It was a story to keep you safe and then later on it gets deeper and deeper, so it's the same story but it just gets more detailed. As a tiny, tiny child you probably didn't even understand really that it was Kurreah that created the lake, it was more about he swallowed people and if you went too close to the water, the deep water, he might be still there, he might get you. Later on you get told about the creation story and then further on than that you get told about how they killed him, and how he is now called upon as the spirit to make things grow. Yeah, it was probably one of the first stories I was told.
>
> *(Immiboagurramilbun, 2003)*

For Chrissiejoy the performance of her DVD enacts the ceremony through which the lake and all of its creatures were sung into being each time the ceremony was performed. Chrissiejoy says, the lake is waiting now, waiting for all of us to sing the lake back to life. Her paintings draw on a tradition where a multiplicity of art forms including dance, song and ceremony intersect in the ongoing creation of self and Country. They draw on ancient cosmology, spirituality, history and laws, while simultaneously being contemporary. She was reflexively aware of generating knowledge in the context of a Western academic institution, and her paintings and stories emerged in an entangled space between these two knowledge traditions.

In Immiboagurramilbun's thinking through Country all knowledge is knowledge of Country and all has its origins in the Niddeerie. Niddeerie is the time when all things come into being, so is connected to the understanding of being through Mulgury. All the forms of life, Mulgury, materialise in the Niddeerie which embodies past, present and future. Through Mulgury, Niddeerie can be understood as the coming into being of all the forms of life, and of tracings, mark making, language and ideas, taking form simultaneously with Country. The creation of the world is the same process in which thinking through Country is materialised in Immiboagurramilbun's paintings, or the black marks on a white page, tracings through which we can come to know.

Conclusion(s)

The current Australian curriculum works from Western assumptions about knowledge and being that determine in advance what knowledge is and what the students can become due to its teachings (Biesta, 2017). In contrast, this chapter has positioned the Aboriginal practice of thinking through Country as a radical break from the Western mindset, instead placing the intricate and complicated processes of working with arts-based Aboriginal practices as being primary in understanding what knowledge is and how to work with it. In this context, the combined and entwined Aboriginal forces of painting, singing, dancing, story-telling, craft-making, ritual and belief work together to introduce a radically new metaphysical framework into the educative frame. The example of Chrissiejoy's onto-epistemological research narrative above, shows us some of the detail and elaboration possible when enunciating such a framework through paintings, poetry, dance and song.

It is interesting that the English intellectual, Whitehead, offers a framework for working with and including this type of practice in the curriculum, without having ever come to Australia or having sought to understand the Aboriginal mindset in any way. In contrast, Deleuze and Guattari's (1987) flat ontology was influenced and designed to work with different cultures and histories, by deliberately destabilising the hegemony and prominence of modern Western thought. Whitehead was interested in the potential of science, and in seeing this potential functioning in education. Unlike most modern Western curricula, Whitehead suggests that to improve education is to recalibrate teaching and learning along fluid thinking lines (and not to increase functionality/instrumentalism/intervention). This suggestion has been forcefully enacted by the Aboriginal Australians over millennia, and, one could argue, they have never stopped thinking in the entangled and intricate way that Whitehead proffers. Whitehead's and Deleuze's aims were to enact complex and reciprocating thought patterns that the Aboriginal Australians had never forgotten.

Note

1 A website dedicated to Immiboagurramilbun's paintings and information about her PhD journey can be found here: http://innovativeethnographies.net/water-in-a-dry-land/intimate-intensity-chrissiejoy-marshall and here: http://innovativeethnographies.net/water-in-a-dry-land/thinking-through-country

References

Bhaskar, R.A. (1997). *A Realist Theory of Science*. London:Verso.

Biesta, G.J.J. (2017). *The Rediscovery of Teaching*. New York: Routledge.

Chambers, D.J. (2013). Panpsychism and Panprotopsychism. 2013 Amherst Lecture in Philosophy. Retrieved from: http://consc.net/papers/panpsychism.pdf

Cisney, V.W. (n.d.). Differential Ontology. *Internet Encyclopaedia of Philosophy*. Retrieved from: www.iep.utm.edu/diff-ont/

Cole, D.R. (2011). *Educational Lifeforms: Deleuzian teaching and learning practice*. Rotterdam: Sense Publishers.

Cole, D.R. (2013). *Traffic Jams: Analysing everyday life using the immanent materialism of Deleuze and Guattari*. New York: Punctum Books.

Cole, D.R. (2014). *Capitalised Education: An immanent materialist account of Kate Middleton*. Winchester: Zero Books.

DeLanda, M. (2004). *Intensive Science and Virtual Philosophy*. London: Continuum.

Deleuze, G., & Guattari, F. (1987). *A Thousand Plateaus: Capitalism & Schizophrenia II* (B. Massumi, trans.). London: Athlone Press.

Immiboagurramilbun (Marshall, CJ.) (2003). *Talking up Blackfella Ways of Knowing through Whitefella Magic*. DVD produced by Young Australia Productions and presented at Doctoral School, University of New England, Armidale, New South Wales.

Marazzi, C. (2011). *The Violence of Financial Capitalism* (K. Lebedeva & J.F. McGimsey, trans.). Los Angeles: Semiotext(e).

Somerville, M. (2013). *Water in a Dry Land: Place-learning through art and story*. Innovative Ethnography Series. London: Routledge.

Whitehead, A.N. (1929a). *Process and Reality: An essay in cosmology*. New York: Macmillan.

Whitehead, A.N. (1929b). *The Aims of Education and Other Essays*. New York: Macmillan.

Whitehead, A.N. (1938). *Modes of Thought*. New York: Macmillan.

Whitehead, A.N. (1967). *Science and the Modern World*. New York: The Free Press. (originally published in 1925).

9

FROM THE ARTIST TO THE COSMIC ARTISAN

The educational task for art in anthropogenic times

jan jagodzinski

Post-truth

In his chapter 'What is the educational task?', Gert Biesta (2017, pp.7–21) explores what he takes to be the task of an educator. He maintains that such work consists of three performative teaching activities; namely, that of interruption, suspension, and sustenance. He concludes his meditative analysis in saying that these activities are a prelude to a transference of power from teacher to student. If I have understood him correctly, the teacher, who is placed in a position of power as the 'subject-who-is-supposed-to know,' to use a Lacanian presupposition, attempts to empower a student's own desires. Through such transference, this, in turn, authorizes a student towards 'being-subject.' It is a psychoanalytic model of empowerment where, in the end, the analysand (a student addressed as the 'subject-ness of a student' by the teacher in Biesta's terms) has now 'grown up' to exist in the 'world.' The teacher has, in effect, fulfilled his or her educational responsibility, and is no longer necessary as an authority figure.

In this chapter, I set up a rather different educational task, one that is framed by the geo-historical condition our species finds itself in, that of the Anthropocene. The educational task is no longer, in my view, to further 'emancipation' as it has been forwarded by such thoughtful thinkers as Paolo Freire and Jacques Rancière; I believe that time has changed the complexity of such an undertaking. If anything the basic ontological supposition of educators that we continue to focus on, a 'world-for-us' where emancipation and freedom find their most fruitful existential territory for exploration, requires a serious rethinking. Education in a capitalist world is unable to shake its dualism between neoliberal thought and its valiant and relentless rival: critical theory, or critical emancipatory theory. Both are deadlocked in a desperate struggle, like the extremes of Left and Right. Such charged terms as 'the human condition,' 'humanity,' 'race,' 'sex,' 'gender,' 'ethnicity,' are endlessly played over and over again against the backdrop of transcendental idealizations of justice, equality, and freedom—always 'to come' in a Derridean sense—in the hopes that 'progress' is being made. In the large global picture, each side—both Left and Right—claim success depending on each of their accounting systems. The World Bank and the World Economic Forum are especially good at proudly showing off their numbers.

The 'world' has changed. The Earth we live in has become a precarious place. Surely by now this widely accepted claim has been elevated to an understatement. It is the new normal. The Trump presidency of the United States secures the 'barbarism' that Isabelle Stengers (2015) had so hoped to resist just after the 2008 financial collapse. Michel Foucault's abstract and universalized 'Man' has been transubstantiated, blatantly exposed and now accepted as the Corporation made flesh through Trump where the US presidency and business interests become indistinguishable; such pretense is no longer necessary. In his ranks, oligarchy is making its comeback. Trump joins a long list of authoritarian personalities throughout the globe: Turkey's Tayyip Erdoğan, Philippine's Rodrigo Duterte, Russia's Vladimir Putin, Syria's Bashar al-Assad, Zimbabwe's Robert Mugabe, North Korea's Kim Jong-un, Israel's Benjamin Netanyahu, the Saudi regime, Hungary's Viktor Mihály Orbán, and so on. For those who argued for an 'acceler-ationist scenario,' like Alex Williams and Nick Srnicek (2015), perhaps capitalism will at this point self-destruct from its own worst excesses as the stock markets and currencies destabilize.

I begin this way to both position and 'date' myself to ask the question, fol-lowing Deleuze and Guattari's Spinozian inflexion: What can possibly be *adequate* knowledge and an *adequate* direction given this state of affairs where the 'post-truth' era of politics and persuasion (in the German, *Postfaktish*) has simply confirmed what many in Academia have articulated for some time now; that the politics of affect occur below the level of consciousness resulting in a spreading contagion of unbridled emotion, disconnected with cognition. Given this state of affairs the educational task looks quite different to me. It is perhaps best summed up by a well-known question by Gilles Deleuze: 'Can we *still* believe in the world?' An Earth that 'decentres us' from our ontological smugness is a world for itself that cannot be technologically controlled and put 'right' for our own consumptive follies; a world that we share with non-humans, more-than-humans, and inhumans (smart technologies). The educational task must grapple with the fictionalized potentials of post-anthropological and post-ontological (ontology as classically defined by our 'standard' philosophies) imaginaries.

In this chapter I explore whether 'cosmic' artisan(s) are able to make inroads to engender such an educational task; that is, a task that is capable of recogniz-ing the extent to which it means to grasp the event of the Anthropocene for the future of our species. If the educational task of such an ecological imaginary is not undertaken, there will be no future generations to 'teach.' The chapter is based on two premises: the first is that the event of the Anthopocene has already happened, and with it has emerged a two-fold ethical question that continually shapes the incorporeality of this event: what has just happened and what will happen now? These questions frame the educational task. The second premise is that our species' extinction is conceivable, and that this consequence has already happened in a probable future. While the Anthropocene is 'ironically' named, there have been other proposals to change the imaginary of this climatic shift, notably the *Chthulucene* by Donna Haraway (2015): the name has stuck, even if the body in charge, the International Union of Geological Sciences (UGS), has yet to make it official. The point to be made is the post-ontological condition that this event has now made evident; namely, the advent of a post-anthropological position. It is important to qualify these terms: 'post-anthropology' and 'post-ontology.' They signal a radical decentering of human knowledge through alliances with sophisticated computational technologies that 'crunch' big data, presenting a distribution of cognition and perception unavailable to humans. New glimpses into reality *as-it-is* become available through the employment of algorithms and technological research apparatuses that add knowledge and insight into delimited fields of reality 'as such,' requiring a redefinition of ontology as it has been historically formulated. A better term may be *onto-epistemology* following Karen Barad (2007). The dividing line between nature and culture has never existed. The subject | object divide, or 'correlationalism,' has become a rallying cry for Speculative Realists (SR) such as Quentin Meillessoux (2008) to overcome Kantian anthropological constructivism. Correlationalism has become the 'bottom line' to be questioned so that nonhuman agencies are recognized. 'Deep (geological) time' further decenters the 'anthropos' so that a renewed mathematical vigour by a strain of post-positivists can claim noumenal objectivity (i.e., Brassier, 2007). Hence, the proliferation of 'thing' philosophies generally lumped together as Object Oriented Ontology, or OOO (Harman, 2002), but there are many nuances. Such a development recognizes 'vibrant life' as articulated by Jane Bennett (2010) and company (Barad, 2007). This provides a necessary decentering of Man by recognizing a distributive subjectivity, the intra and inter-relationships between the human and the nonhuman, extended to what I would differentiate as the *inhuman*, the technologies that have their own genesis, beginning with the *eoliths* to present biomedia as charted by Eugene Thacker (2004) where biology and information are being seamlessly joined together.

The cosmic artisan

The challenge for an 'adequate' response by art and its education for such an educational task in these pressing times is already found in the philosophical work of Deleuze and Guattari with their call for a 'new earth' and a 'people-yet-to-come' (TP, pp.423, 570; WP, p.109). For Deleuze and Guattari both of these concepts do not designate a utopian world-to-come, a 'no-where' place, nor are a 'people' to be invented or to emerge at some future date; rather their call is for a perpetual potential of becoming-other that is inherent to the present and the 'now here' (WP, p.100). The potentiality of a 'new earth' and its 'people' requires a complete 'deterritoralization of the Earth' from its present capitalist stranglehold that prevents any forms of sustainability via profit and accumulated production. The links between the issues of sustainability and capitalism have been thoroughly examined by a wide range of researchers (Klein, 2014; Moore, 2016). They call on smooth spaces for this to happen, 'holey places' where change is possible; or, multiplicious utopian spaces where encounter, discussion, experimentation, and affinity can take place (Simon, 2005). The visionaries of such a potential are the cosmic artisans referred to in *Thousand Plateaus*, whom I call an '*avant-garde without authority*' (jagodzinski, 2010). These artisans are able to feel, see and hear more intensely into the inhuman and nonhuman cosmological Life that penetrates us all. They are an avant-garde in the sense that their 'work' is *untimely*, it does not fit in the past or future, nor is it 'in advance,' but addresses the 'present future' by harnessing the cosmological signs that are made manifest, providing us with a post-ontological imagination, which is the unthought of the educational task our species faces. They are 'without authority' in two very important and distinct ways, which address the political and pedagogical force of their work based on creating and producing subjectivations that are not oppositional but affirmative in their outlook (Chesters & Welsh, 2006). The first distinction is that their interventions remain *minoritarian* in Deleuze and Guattari's (1986) terms. As artisans they do not direct or determine (like an architect would) but help sharpen awareness of this precarious age as symptomologists of it. They open up the unthought in the current image of thought via smooth spaces. In this way both art and philosophy are recognized as engines of creation: "Art and philosophy converge at this point: the constitution of an earth and a people that are lacking as the correlate of creation" (WP, p.108). Thought and matter—as life itself, are the engines of such creation. The second distinction is the intensity of their 'forcework' that initiates a transformation in thinking that calls for transference of authority to those who are affected. The meaning of 'affect,' however, is quite controversial in the current literature often referred to as 'the affective turn' (Clough & Halley, 2007). Its meaning ranges from emotion to collapsing it with effect. For Deleuze and Guattari it is always connected to deterritorialization within spaces of indeterminacy. An event of 'becoming' has to occur. Art and the people it encounters address the complex of forces at work, below the level of consciousness, the material flows and forces that are 'beyond us.' The subjective 'I' as habituated contemplation can be disrupted. But, it must be compelling enough to penetrate established conventions, the habituations that Deleuze refers to as common sense, doxa and cliché (WP, p.105).

Thinking is a doing and a learning, a being-as-becoming that brings about a reconceptualization or transformation of our species-becoming in the Cosmos. A dividing lines emerges between Earth and the planet called Earth; the former is shaped by an ontology for-us (culture, Being, bios, individual life and its finitude), and marks an historical point where our species eventually differentiated or deterritorialized itself via the 'foot [paw],' 'hand [claw],' and 'mouth [fangs]' (Leroi-Gourhan, 1993), and by extension the invention of tools and technologies. The latter (Earth as a planet) is shaped by an agency without-us (Nature, zoë, free arcane life and its mysteries), which provides the importance of the planet's history, a history that is shaped by the speculative realism of science—as an ontology of the in-itself, or world-without-us.

The openness of the Earth to the cosmos makes me point to the chaosmos theory of Deleuze and Guattari where the cosmic artisan emerges as a possible candidate for such an avant-garde without authority as an adequate concept for the Anthropocene epoch. It is one direction for an adequate response to the educational task at hand. As Deleuze and Guattari write: "the earth … belongs to the Cosmos, and presents itself as the material through which human beings tap cosmic forces" (TP, p.509). The Anthropocene in effect presents a third cosmological revolution after that of Kant and Copernicus. By adding the planet's history, this collapses the history of human societies as such, given the temporal scale that is in play. As Claire Colebrook (2016) has argued, Deleuze and Guattari's stratigraphic cosmology rather worryingly posits incompossible worlds (worlds that seem paradoxical but mutually existent), each with its own coherence, having multiple strata, that are utterly incoherent and impossible in relation to one another (Deleuze, 1992, p.67). The fossil record makes this very evident as the stratigraphy of each fossil seems isolated, its context lost, placing punctuated and gradual evolutionary theories into flux.

The Anthropocene is but one imposed mode, in addition to being a racial discourse as to its consequences and whose responsibilities must shoulder its effects, where one is either for or against its anthropocentric bias (Taffel, 2017). Incompossibility challenges and provides us with 'parallel' universes, antinomies, paradoxes that place us into proliferating Deleuzian logics of the 'and': our species is doomed, and there is no such thing as a fixed essentiality to our species, *and* a planetary conscious is necessary, *and* yet we must question the very unity of this as an illusion, *and* … *and*. The educational task of the artisan requires the positing of incompossible fabulations; parallel fictions that work the smooth spaces that are already there to be explored, to provide those inroads into a post(anthropological) and post(ontological), as yet unthought, imaginary.

Why then is the concept of the cosmic artisan adequate to the event of the Anthropocene and the paradoxes of incompossibility? The above situatedness of the Earth and our species within it presents the needed backdrop to develop what Deleuze and Guattari called a 'cosmic artisan.' We can modify this to a posthuman cosmic artisan for clearly the nature|culture divide no longer exists—this state of affairs pertains to both the nonhuman (inorganic) and inhuman (technological) interactions with our species: consider for instance stem-cell research where a totipotent stem cell can differentiate into embryonic and extraembryonic cell types. Such cells can construct a complete and viable organism, making cloning possible; enzymes or proteins are also grown and harvested and form the 'building blocks' for new products. Biological engineering, GMF products, nanotechnologies, biotechnologies, neurobiology, AI—and on it goes—provide ample evidence that new strange forms of life are in the making—clones, genetically modified crops, new synthesized species, proto-cells, viruses, and bacteria. Technology, art, design, and craft have all collapsed or coalesced together when we consider these developments. This state of affairs however runs the risk of becoming a hyper-modernism where 'nature' no longer escapes human inscription in our special attempt to come to terms with the biophysical world; what this means is that *global risk* becomes part of experimentation where the contingencies and ambivalences of living with the 'failures' of control have to be accepted. One might think of that shocking scene from *Alien: Resurrection* when Ripley comes across all the failed monstrous clones of herself preserved in tube-like silos of formaldehyde. There is *always* a remainder, and this is where an *outside* is always already posited. Hence, the calls for the 'end of nature' and an 'ecology without nature' as forwarded most notably by Tim Morton (2016) are somewhat suspicious and misleading, and perhaps premature. The paradoxical claim is only comprehensible when 'nature' is understood as being an impossible excess—as infinite extension. But that said, this seems obvious enough. What is the artisan in relation to the artist in relation to such a 'beyond'?

Deleuze and Guattari distinguish three 'ages' of art in *A Thousand Plateaus*: Classicism, Romanticism, and Modernism. The classical artist was charged with the task that was God's own; he was to confront chaos and creatively organize raw and untamed matter to generate a stable relationship between form and content. In distinction, the Romantic artist, as the beautiful soul, was the privileged mediator of Nature (the Earth); the genius artist was to produce the infinite and continuous variations of form, the privilege of *adding* to Nature. But, as Deleuze and Guattari argue, the Romantics, following Kant's *Critique of Judgment*, take the sublime as the expression of 'personal longing' (*Sehnsucht*) for what is forever beyond the artist's grasp; namely, the infinity of nature and the dynamic chaos of forces that can never be comprehended. Territory and the Earth (matter and spirit) are caught up in an organic dialectic as best exemplified by Hegelian organicism. Human finitude is negated through art as a heroic and historic struggle between Human spirit and the dynamics of Nature claimed often as emancipatory praxis. 'Modern' art that followed, produced the progressive 'new,' taken to new heights by an avant-garde who were ahead of their time, projecting a future tomorrow. The postmodern variant of this was to eventually proclaim an end of art as it seemed that there had been a heterogeneity of practices that could no longer be signified under, by now, an outdated grand narrative of progress.

There is a strong sense of hylomorphism that runs throughout these three ages where form follows function in Aristotelian terms. Brute force is imposed on nature through hylocentric thinking, what is often referred to as a 'heat, beat, treat' process, which uses 96% waste and 4% product (Bernstein, 2006). Deleuze and Guattari follow the critique of hylomorphism by Georges Simondon (1980) who maintained that matter is made up of immanent intensive energetic traits, forces he called 'singularities' (Deleuze, 2004). Their differential relations determine form and maintain an inherent dynamism of form through immanent processes of 'modulation.' It is precisely in this direction that the posthuman cosmic artisan operates. Matter for Deleuze and Guattari is chaosmic. It finds a consistency—or expresses equilibrium states—through 'refrains' (*ritournelles*), repetitions of difference that produce various actualizations or individuations; these are certainly autopoietic, but with the proviso that such a becoming or actualization happens at far from equilibrium states where there is no fidelity to relations of genus or species (see Pearson, 1999, p.170). The 'modernism' promoted by Deleuze and Guattari is not the modernism of 'progress' and the 'new.'

Modernism, for them announces an age of the cosmic and the minoritarian politics of chaos. Old distinctions between creation and consumption collapse here into a single place of social production. It is a particular vitalist ontology that does away with any animistic residues. By this I mean that there is no transcendental force outside matter that gives it life (spirit). Matter is spirit (life). It is a *communist eco-politics* of art, or better still, a 'commonist eco-politics' inseparable from aesthetic processes of creative forces that do away with any state authority, but seek the 'commonwealth' that belongs to all who inhabit the Earth. It is an attempt to grasp as much inclusivity as possible in a constant deterriorialization of the Earth as it is presently structured by forces of hierarchy and transcendentalism. "We lack resistance to the present," Deleuze and Guattari claim (WP, p.108).

> [The artisan] by means of material … wrest[s] the percept from perceptions of objects and the states of a perceiving subject, to wrest the affect from affections as the transition from one state to another: to extract a bloc of sensations, a pure being of sensations.
>
> *(WP, p.167)*

The Earth as 'Nature' contains all the forces of the universe, constituting the 'deepest' levels of reality. Deleuze and Guattari assume a molecular and chaotic matter. The forces that emerge are Xpressed (jagodzinski, 2008) through the refrain (*ritournelle*), through the rhythmic repetitions of difference that compose and Xpress life; that is, matter itself. We, as a species, are the compositions of such matter, caught and captured by our own 'entanglements' and 'intra-relations' with our ecological assemblages (Barad, 2007). It is not evolutionary adaptation; rather it is *modification* of our species-being that is at stake, minimally the post-anthropological understanding that needs to be recognized. The modernist problem for Deleuze | Guattari is "how to consolidate the material, make it consistent, so that it can … capture the mute and unthinkable forces of the Cosmos (TP, p.343). It is a "molecular pantheistic Cosmos" (TP, p.327). This requires the molecularization of matter; its absolute deterritorialization, so that immanent forces of chaosmos can be harnessed in consistent, composite, and autopoietic blocs of sensation. Finite sensations are composed as refrains or 'subjectivations' that Xpress the forces of matter by constructing a chaosmic place of chaosmosis. The immanent forces of inorganic life are rendered 'visible,' as in the much heralded quote of Paul Klee's *Creative Credo* (1961): "Art does not reproduce the visible; rather it makes visible" (p.76). In this way the finite creation of art points to the infinity of the chaos(mosis), Nature, the Cosmos. Material (matter as living) is Xpressive and thus "it is indeed difficult to say where in fact the material ends and sensation begins" (WP, pp.166–167). A chaosmic, or molecularized, material makes it possible to create the blocs of sensations, made of 'inhuman' percepts and affects. Art becomes a 'passage' from finite to the infinite (WP, p.180). "From depopulation, make a cosmic people; from deterritorialization, a cosmic earth—that is the wish of the artisan-artist, here, there locally" (TP, p.346). "The cosmic artisan: [becomes] a homemade atom bomb" (TP, p.345), meaning that the potential for such immense and powerful deterritorialization rests with such a potential imaginary yet to be thought. This becomes the educational task of the cosmic-posthuman artisan. The last section addresses whether this is at all conceivable.

The contemporary posthuman artisan

Given this backdrop, can an avant-garde without authority be identified? Are they up to such an undertaking that would provide direction for 'art' education? What are the cosmic artisan experimentations of late? As Deleuze and Guattari affirm, art 'thinks,' just as much as philosophy thinks or science 'thinks': "Philosophy, art, and science come into relations of mutual resonance and exchange" (Deleuze, 1997, p.125). The 'contemporary' artisan collapses art, science (technology), and philosophy in a new "thought brain" (WP, p.210); the brain becomes a 'subject' only when it becomes 'thought,' and 'thought' only happens from the outside, when habits, opinions as doxa, and clichés are disturbed as mentioned earlier. In the era of the Anthropocene and post-truth ontology, such 'thought' might be understood in the broad sense of *post-conceptual art* where the fundamental questions revolve around *life*: its creation, its endurance, its survival, and its death. For Deleuze such concern is brilliantly and succinctly presented as *A Life*, the capital letters exemplifying its metaphysical and physical entanglements. The indefinite article *A* collapses or intertwines particularity with universalism (not generality) to provide the specificity of the finite (location or the ecology of forces at play in any assemblage), and at the same time projecting the inexhaustibility of the infinite (a new Earth to-come): physicality and metaphysics are forever in a 'disjunctive synthesis' with one another; a gap remains between them that raises issues of indeterminacy, ambiguity, contingency, paradox, and risk. It is that place of 'quantum indeterminacy' as the physicist and philosopher David Bohm referred to it.

Posthuman artisans are saddled by a seemingly inescapable capitalist entrepreneurship, the burden of a postcolonial past presses on them, and they are further caught by the difficulties of access to technologies and instrumentation that are often cost-prohibitive. They face overwhelming difficulties when it comes to fabulating a planet-yet-to-come. Those whom I would identity as belonging to such a minoritarian avant-garde appear as singularities, as outliers and anomalies that can only be gathered up via networks to form emergent bodies of thought exploring critical values aimed at the precarious state of our species; otherwise they remain in isolation outside institutional support systems, or are caught by corporate interests that continue to push for profit from the potential patents that new technologies offer, especially via the creation of new life forms. Many artisans toil in a DIY approach, relying on open-source software and a *Maker Culture* where electronic DIY becomes available, such as Massimo Banzi's *Arduino Project* (Banzi, 2008).

This state of affairs can be usefully made graspable by commenting on the two decades of curatorial work by Paola Antonelli, who is the senior curator for *MoMA*, (Museum of Modern Art in New York), in the area of science, art, and technology that its Department of Architecture and Design exhibits. Her curatorial passion is clearly aimed at the 'future.' Her three major shows: *Mutant Materials in Contemporary Design* (1995), *Design and the Elastic Mind* (2008), and an online curatorial work *Design and Violence* (2013–2015), chart a progression in her thinking from a conservative position that celebrates bio-technologism to at least the recognition that there is a dividing line, although always blurred, which can be identified in the way the posthuman artisan is addressing the state of the precarious world order and what I refer to as its commodified aestheticization under 'designer capitalism' (jagodzinski, 2010). The plus side of Antonelli's position is that she maintains an affirmative mode; there is potential for change via design technology. Pedagogically and politically she tries to promote this message through her many speaking engagements, which suits the global promotion of *MoMA*. In all cases hylomoprhic thinking has been left behind by these designers as the molecularization of matter through a 'synthetic aesthetic' (Ginsberg et al., 2014) has been fully realized. Both her *Mutant Materials* exhibit (1995)—a celebration of new synthetic materials that extend nature's own creation—and her *Elastic Mind* exhibit celebrate the faith in a technofix, a subtle technological determinism that reveals itself as digital design applications to big data crunching via computationally generated algorithms that mimic nature, nano-techological applications, bio-degradable living materials (e.g., growing Mycelium bricks), living or vibrant architecture (Armstrong, 2015), biomimesis (Benyus, 2002; Baumeister, 2015), and the release of designed organisms with functional lifespans into established ecologies to re-establish damaged ecosystems. This last initiative, forwarded broadly under the label of 'synthetic aesthetics' (Ginsberg, 2011) relies on venture capitalist investment and military support for its applications, pervaded by the twin worries of 'bioerror' and 'bioterror.' In general, the message of biomimesis or 'bioneers' is generally harmony, holism, and biophilic 'love' with Nature couched most often in capitalist green economy with an emphasis on sustainability. There is a strong theme of the control of nature through symbiosis at the molecular level by scientists and designers working together to gain control of information-based evolutionary processes of a self-organizing complex system at every scale as life's 'operating manual': molecular structure of DNA, growth potential of cells, computational algorithms that mimic natural processes, animated three-dimensionally printed models and robots, like empathetic telenoids, are celebrated as the future, with *MoMA* bringing this news to the masses via exhibits. This is the political and pedagogical role that Antonelli's Research and Development department has set up.

The dividing line that I would present in relation to this entanglement is the grasp of life as a disjunctive synthesis that constantly presents our species with the dilemmas of an ethico-political aesthetic that can never go away but should be recognized through a *speculative design problematic*, which is the role of the *avant-garde without authority* that I would advocate. Their role is to play with the place of entanglement to raise the 'flights out' that provide the incompossible worlds needed for that post(anthropological) and post(ontological) imagination within education. It is the virtual dimensions of bio-art as *proto-types* that need exploration (see Kacs, 2007). That might be one such 'flight.' *[The entanglement is in the indeterminate space between life as matter and matter as life; the emphasis on the first—life as matter—is metaphysical, nonhuman and always in excess of what can be controlled—an infinite vitalism is available, subject to multiplier effects in energy gains when harnessed. It is 'cosmological' in the truest sense of chaosmosis. The second—matter as life—is inhuman, technological, animistic, and controllable to a probable level.]* The transition from one to the other never escapes a *risk* factor that cannot be weighed in economic computational terms (profit) but struggled with against the backdrop of the Anthropocene. It is only in the indeterminate space of this entanglement that a minoritarian fabulation emerges, where art and design become blurred, or in terms of the historical avant-garde of the twentieth century, art becoming life and life becoming art are grappled with. This is the moment when a left glove turns into a right glove through topological stretching and mutation, when a 'true' problematic emerges: true in the sense that there are only questions that demand action. Vitalism (as zoë) and animism (as bios) become blurred at this point; the 'uncanny valley,' for instance, disappears and a *Blade Runner* world emerges where the fabulated science fiction obliges us to hesitate and 'to think.' Media (as in communication) and medium (as in biology) become indistinguishable. In the mid-nineties, the Cybernetic Culture Research Unit (CCRU) at the University of Warwick coined this development 'hyperstition.'

The developments in bio-art (Kacs, 2007), especially as articulated by the pioneers of tissue culture, Oron Catts and Ionat Zurr (2002) of SymbioticA fame, provide one such instance as exemplified by their signature work: *Victimless Leather: A Prototype of a Stitch-less Jacket Grown in a Technoscientific 'Body'* (2004). Such a bio-art experiment first appears as if Catts and Zurr are presenting an alternative possibility for growing synthetic food, thereby overcoming cruelty to animals. However, on closer examination their synthetic 'leather' plays an ambivalent role: is it an ironical ploy that it takes more energy to produce and grow in vitro 'meat' than at first assumed? The ecological footprint includes the 'costs' of running their lab. Animal blood plasma is required as a nutrient for these 'semi-live' objects, so there is no 'victimless' existence: victims still exist but are pushed further away. All kinds of contradictions continue to stack up when this bio-experiment is critically examined, including the issue of life and death as the project further problematizes the distinction between the living and the machine. These 'semi-living things' highlight again the absurdities inherent in technological solutions and efficiencies, recalling once more the semi-living replicants of *Blade Runner*. Here the semi-living 'thing' raises the specter of zoë, and can be contrasted to any synthetic object whose functionality is in place to 'heal' a damaged ecology or is produced to make our life easier.

The projects of *The Tissue Culture and Art Project* (TC&A) present the very dilemma we face without 'solution.' This is the dilemma of an avant-garde *without authority*: it can only illustrate and bring to the brink the problematic of the age; it makes the educational task that much more difficult, for such creativity is not ubiquitous, which is the usual rhetoric in both industry and schooling. This is not the same *irony* that flooded postmodernism. As Deleuze (1990, p.138) argues, irony is not a critical response, for such a gesture seems to play into mastery of the author-artist. Here there is no 'authority.' We have the 'bald' problematic actualized. TC&A are exemplars of 'speculative design,' as are (perhaps) the work of Revital Cohen and Tuur van Balen (2013) who problematize 'embodied energy,' the finity of bios in this case, where the human intrinsic and extrinsic bodily energies are being constantly harnessed by capitalism for productive (profitable) labour in the capitalist machine, and most recently ergonomically quantified to flood the market with all sorts of smart technologies that measure and report back the body's expenditure—from heart rate monitors to electronic brainwave feedback devices. Formal subsumption of the labour process has now become real; it has penetrated all aspects of our lives (Read, 2013). Cohen and van Balen's *75 Watts: Production Line Poetics* (2013) presents a performative video-sound installation of Chinese assemblage line factory workers putting together a mass produced *useless* object as designed by the artists and the choreographer, Alexander Witley, choreographing their movements intermittently into dance routines. *75 watts* is precisely the amount of energy an average worker can sustain throughout an eight hour long day on an assembly line. Playing in the indeterminate zone between zoë (the poetics of dance) and bios (the production of labour) Revital Cohen and Tuur van Balen present the problematic of posthumanist Taylorism, updating Charlie Chaplin's *Modern Times*. The 'object' on their assembly line now becomes a 'thing'; it finds itself in a zone of indeterminacy: commodified functionless junk.

It is to the credit of Paola Antonelli's most recent online exhibit: *Design and Violence* (2013–2015) that this indeterminate, contingent, risk-oriented dimension of human productivity is exposed by questioning the products that are being synthetically produced—from new synthetic materials to proto cells. Our species playing 'god' becomes the question for all 'global citizens' as to where we are headed as a species through our own design: to the hell of extinction or a new earth of affirmation. This is never resolved. We need an education in design and art to orientate students to such a post-anthropology and a post-ontology. This I maintain to be the current task of education. Some maintain that this requires a reawakening of curiosity and wisdom, but few question the capitalist schizophrenia that makes these very values impossible to fulfill to begin with. All educators toil within global capitalism's accounting system. The cosmic artisan fabulates virtual lines of flight with the 'want' of an incompossible New Earth. Whether one such flight is actualized is another matter. But our survival depends on it.

References

Armstrong, R. (2015). *Vibrant architecture: Matter as a co-designer of living systems.* Warsaw: De Gruyter Open Ltd.

Banzi, M. (2008). *Getting started with Arduino.* Sebastopol, CA: Make: Books.

Barad, K. (2007). *Meeting the universe halfway: Quantum physics and the entanglement of matter and meaning*. Durham, NC: Duke University Press.

Baumeister, D. (2015). Biomimicry: Life operating manual. Bioneers. TED Talk. Available on YouTube at www.youtube.com/watch?v=yl2s7yI6eDI

Bennett, J. (2010). *Vibrant matter: A political ecology of things*. Durham, NC: Duke University Press.

Benyus, J. (2002). *Biomimicry: Innovation inspired by nature*. New York: William Morrow.

Bernstein, A. (2006). Janine Benyus: The Thought Leader Interview. *strategy+business, 44*. Retrieved from: www.strategy-business.com/article/06310?gko=8fe46

Biesta, G.J.J. (2017). *The rediscovery of teaching*. New York: Routledge.

Brassier, R. (2007). *Nihil unbound: Enlightenment and extinction*. Houndmills, UK: Palgrave Macmillan.

Catts, O. & Zurr, I. (2002). Growing semi-living sculptures: The tissue culture and art project. *Leonardo, 35*(4), 365–370.

Chesters, G. & Welsh, I. (2006). *Complexity and social movements: Multitudes at the edge of chaos*. New York: Routledge.

Clough, P. & Halley, J. (Eds.) (2007). *The affective turn: Theorizing the social*. Durham, NC: Duke University Press.

Cohen, R. & Van Balen, T. (2013) *75 Watts: Production line poetics*. Retrieved from https://vimeo.com/66263206

Colebrook, C. (2016). 'A grandiose time of coexistence': Stratigraphy of the Anthropocene. *Deleuze Studies, 10*(4), 440–454.

Deleuze, G. (1990). *The logic of sense* (M. Lester trans.). New York: Columbia University Press.

Deleuze, G. (1992). *The fold: Leibnitz and the Baroque* (T. Conley trans.). Minneapolis: University of Minnesota Press.

Deleuze, G. (1997). *Negotiations 1972–1990* (M. Joughin trans.). New York: Columbia University Press.

Deleuze, G. (2004). On Gilbert Simondon. In G. Deleuze & D. Lapoujade (Eds.) *Desert islands and other texts, 1953–1974* (M. Taormina trans). (pp.86–89). New York: Semiotext(e).

Deleuze, G. & Guattari, F. (1986). *Toward a minor literature* (D. Polan & R. Bensmaïa trans.). Minneapolis: University of Minnesota Press.

Deleuze, G. & Guattari, F. (1987). *A thousand plateaus: Capitalism and schizophrenia*, Vol. 2 (B. Massumi trans.). London: University of Minnesota Press.

Deleuze, G. & Guattari, F. (1994). *What is philosophy?* (H. Tomlinson & G. Burchell trans.). New York: Columbia University Press.

Dukes, H. (2016). Assembling the Mechanosphere: Mondo, Althusser, Deleuze and Guattari. *Deleuze Studies, 10*(4), 514–530.

Ginsberg, A. (2011). Synthetic aesthetics. TED Talk. Available from YouTube at www.youtube.com/watch?v=9i3kXyQ8qSI

Ginsberg, A.D., Calvert, J., Schyfter, P., Elfick, A. & Endy, D. (Eds.) (2014). *Synthetic aesthetics: Investigating synthetic biology's designs on nature*. Cambridge, MA: MIT Press.

Goh, I. (2008). 'Strange Ecology' in Deleuze-Guattari's *A thousand plateaus*. In B. Herzogenrath (Ed.), *An [un]likely alliance: Thinking environment[s] with Deleuze | Guattari* (pp. 196–215). Newcastle upon Tyne, UK: Cambridge Scholars Publishing.

Haraway, D. (2015). Anthropocene, Capitalocene, Plantationocene, Chthulucene: Making kin. *Environmental Humanities, 6*, 159–165.

Harman, G. (2002). *Tool-being: Heidegger and the metaphysics of objects*. Peru, IL: Open Court.

Hayles, N.K. (2012). *How we think: Digital media and contemporary technogenesis*. Chicago, IL: Chicago University Press.

Ingold, T. (2010). Bringing things to life: Entanglements in a world of materials. NCRM Working Paper. Realities, Morgan Centre, University of Manchester. Retrieved from http://eprints.ncrm.ac.uk/1306/

jagodzinski, j. (2008). *Youth and television culture: Televised paranoia*. New York: Palgrave Macmillan.

jagodzinski, j. (2010). *Visual art and education in an era of designer capitalism*. London: Palgrave Macmillan.

Kacs, E. (Ed.). (2007). *Signs of life: Bio art and beyond*. London: MIT Press.

Klee, P. (1961). *Notebooks, volume 1: The thinking eye* (J. Spiller Ed.). London: Lund Humphries.

Klein, N. (2014). *This changes everything: Capitalism vs. the climate*. New York: Simon & Schuster.

Laruelle, F. (2013). *Principles of non-philosophy* (N. Rubchak & A.P. Smith trans.). London: Bloomsbury Academic.

Latour, B. (1991). *We have never been modern* (C. Porter trans.). Cambridge, MA: Harvard University Press.

Leroi-Gourhan, A. (1993). *Gesture and speech* (R. White trans.). London: MIT Press.

Maturana, H. & Varela, F. (1980). *Autopoiesis and cognition: The realization of the living*. Dordrecht, Holland: D. Reidel Publishing Company.

Meillassoux, Q. (2008). *After finitude: An essay on the necessity of contingency*. London: Bloomsbury Publishing.

Moore, J. (Ed.). (2016). *Anthropocene or capitaloscene? Nature, history, and the crisis of capitalism*. Oakland, CA: PM Press.

Morton, T. (2016). *Dark ecology: The logic of future coexistence*. New York: University of Columbia Press.

Novak, M. (2002). Eversion: Brushing against avatars, aliens and angels. In B. Clarke & L. Dalrymple (Eds.), *From energy to information: Representation on science and technology, art, and literature* (pp. 309–323). Stanford, CA: Stanford University Press.

Pearson, K.A. (1999). *Germinal life: The difference and repetition of Deleuze*. New York: Routledge.

Read, J. (2013). *The micro-politics of capital: Marx and the prehistory of the present*. New York: SUNY Press.

Saldanha, A. (2015). Mechanosphere: Man, earth, capital. In J. Rolffe & H. Stark (Eds.), *Deleuze and the non/human* (pp. 197–216). Houndmills, UK: Palgrave Macmillan.

Simon, T. (2005). From utopian world to utopian spaces: Reflections on the contemporary radical imaginary and the social forum process. *ephemera: theory, politics and organization, 52*(2), 394–408.

Simondon, G. (1980). *On the mode of existence of technical objects* (N. Mellamphy trans.). London: University of Western Ontario Press. Retrieved from chrome extension://oemmndcbld-boiebfnladdacbdfmadadm/http://dephasage.ocular witness.com/pdf/SimondonGilbert. OnTheModeOfExistence.pdf

Stengers, I. (2015). *In catastrophic time: Resisting the coming barbarism* (A. Geoffrey trans.). New York: Open Humanities Press.

Taffel, S. (2017). Mapping the Anthropocene. In N. Holm & S. Taffel (Eds.), *Ecological entanglements in the Anthropocene: Working with nature* (pp. 219–240*)*. Lanham, NC: Lexington Books.

Thacker, E. (2004). *Biomedia*. Minneapolis: University of Minnesota Press.

Williams, A. & Srnicek, N. (2015). *Inventing the future: Postcapitalism and a world without work*. London: Verso.

10

TOWARDS 'GROWN-UP-NESS IN THE WORLD' THROUGH THE ARTS AS CRITICAL, QUALITY PEDAGOGY

Robyn Ann Ewing and John Nicholas Saunders

> *It is a rare moment indeed when a young person can not only explore and express their own reality but also act upon it to make an intervention into the world around them.*
>
> *(Prentki, 2014, p.5)*

Introduction

Many western education systems are currently in crisis, providing an increasingly technical approach to classroom learning and assessment (Darling-Hammond, 2009). Perhaps one of the reasons stems from a longstanding tendency in educational policy to polarise children's social and emotional wellbeing and intellectual needs (Brunker, 2012). A second factor may relate to the privileging of a never-ending quest to improve measurable academic outcomes by governments and policymakers. Alongside this reductive view of teaching and learning, a growing body of international research demonstrates the important role that arts-rich pedagogies and experiences can and should play across our lifespan in helping us make sense of the world. The Arts as critical, quality pedagogy has the potential to transform the competitive academic school curriculum (Connell, 1994; Ewing, 2010a) to ensure that learning is transformative (O'Sullivan, 1999), relevant and engaging for all (Wyn, 2009).

This chapter focuses on how engagement in two artforms, literature and drama, can enable teachers, children and young people to learn in transformative ways. O'Sullivan (1999) defines transformative learning as involving the questioning and experiencing of our understandings, feelings, ideas or actions that result in a shift in our consciousness, our way of relating to others and the natural world and our sense of the need for social justice. By imagining different realities from others' perspectives and exploring what it means to approach the world, educational or process drama can realise the 'grown-up-ness' Biesta (2017) envisions. We also draw on the philosophy of Maxine Greene (1995) and the poetic and social imagination.

In addition, this chapter draws on the research findings emerging from a contemporary Australian teacher professional learning programme, *School Drama*™ (Ewing & Saunders, 2016). This co-mentoring programme was developed through a partnership between Sydney Theatre Company and the University of Sydney. Through suspending disbelief and working in fictional contexts using a range of process drama devices, students explore real problems, dilemmas and issues about their relationships with others and the environment to develop deep understandings about the need for a moral imagination (Greene, 1995). Two exemplars drawn from the *School Drama* research case studies are included, to demonstrate how the enactment and embodiment at the core of process drama can interrupt our stereotypes and saturated consciousness to make the familiar strange and enable the educational moment to emerge inside the resulting artistic 'work'.

Approaching the world in a 'grown-up' way … towards empathy

While acknowledging that 'grown-up-ness' is a slightly misleading term, Biesta (2017, p.8) argues that this concept is at the very heart of envisaging a mature way of being-in-the-world. Grown-up-ness involves assuming responsibility to appreciate 'the alterity and integrity of what and who is the other' (Biesta, 2017, p.8) and our place in the world. Biesta asserts that it is important for individuals to stay in 'the middle ground' to enable dialogue with the other. Interestingly, Biesta cites the following educational challenges:

- to engender and sustain the students' desire to engage with the other outside their preferred comfort zones;
- to open up and provide literal and metaphorical spaces and schedule sufficient time to play with these external relationships;
- to provide the time and space for difficult but powerful questions and conversations to continue.

These challenges or interruptions to traditional conceptions of the educational tasks resonate with Maxine Greene's (1995) advocacy of 'wide-awakeness' in fostering the development of a poetic and social imagination.

Wide-awakeness and the poetic and social imagination

> *Imagination … is the capacity to break with the ordinary, the given, the taken-for-granted and open doors to possibility.*

> *(Greene, 2007, p.1)*

Maxine Greene suggests that in order to see the world through another's eyes (poetic imagination), we must enter into their world and understand how it looks. She suggests that we need to be 'wide-awake' to activate our imaginations, to really see 'the abandoned ones, the homeless ones, the broken windows, the redesigned museum, what is absent, what is realized' (p.1). Only then can we also re-imagine an alternative reality – envisage what might be possible (social imagination) and hopefully bring about change as we become more aware of others. Greene acknowledges the pivotal role that the Arts can play in fostering such understanding.

The potential role of the Arts in learning

The Arts remain an under-used component of early childhood and primary curricula despite unequivocal evidence that quality arts experiences and processes are important for human social and emotional wellbeing. Embedding the Arts in learning experiences 'can enhance students' imaginative and creative capacities whilst improving their overall learning outcomes in other curriculum areas' (Gibson & Ewing, 2011, p.2). Meaningful engagement in quality arts processes and experiences has the potential to enhance student academic and affective learning (e.g., Fiske, 1999; Deasy, 2002; Bamford, 2006; Catterall, 2009; Ewing, 2010b; Gibson & Ewing, 2011; Martin et al., 2013; Winner et al., 2013). According to Arnold Aprill et al. (2001), 'an arts-rich curriculum can help transform a school into a dynamic learning community in which educators and students are more likely to think critically, express themselves creatively, and respect diverse opinions' (p.2). All artforms are disciplines with distinctive knowledges, skills and understandings and all are different ways of making meaning. It is our contention, however, that because each artform involves play, design, experimentation, exploration, provocation, metaphor, expression or representation, communication and the artistic or aesthetic shaping of the body or other media (Ewing, 2010), they can play an important role in fostering our creativity. The following section explores the concept of drama as critical, quality pedagogy.

Drama as critical, quality pedagogy

> We must recognise the absolute centrality of drama in giving a sense of what it is to be other than ourselves in a world where otherness and difference is often something to be feared and punished.
>
> *(O'Connor, 2008, p.29)*

Vygotsky (2004) theorised that creative or 'pretend' play is the first outward indicator of a child's imagination and that dramatic play usually emerges seamlessly from other forms of play as children make sense of their experiences and build an understanding of their place in the world. From an early age they employ all kinds of objects to aid their exploration and are prepared to take risks with what they know to explore possibilities, reenact stories and problem solve. Dramatic play is not about acting as someone else: it's about suspending your own situation and *being* someone else.

Building on this in early childhood and primary classrooms, educational or process drama emphasises bending time and space to engage with story, embody feelings and concepts and walk in the shoes of others to understand their perspectives, new thoughts or approaches. Engaging in stories that lead to 'as if' experiences can nurture children's imagination, encourage them to try out their ideas and build confidence in who they are – and who they would like to become.

Educational or process drama builds on Deweyan notions that drama can help us explore/rehearse a range of possibilities and alternative perspectives. Moral imagination, argues Fesmire (2003), can be conceptualised as an aesthetic process or artistry. Critical and creative thinking, collaboration, communication and compassion, 'the four C's' (NEA, 2013), can be nurtured through opportunities for dramatic play that encourage the embodiment or enactment of the experiences of others. Focusing on the use of faces, gestures and bodies through mime and movement helps us understand how powerful non-verbal communication can be in meaning-making. Learning to communicate questions, thoughts and dilemmas clearly, helps students to better convey how they are feeling. While there is strong research evidence that demonstrates the effectiveness of educational drama as critical, quality pedagogy, particularly in English, literacy, expressive language (e.g., Baldwin & Fleming, 2003; Miller & Saxton, 2004; O'Toole, Stinson & Moore, 2009; Ewing & Saunders, 2016) many teachers report feeling constrained to focus on the teaching of literacy and numeracy skills through standardised tests. As a result, the Arts more generally, and drama in particular, are often undervalued and underused in classrooms, and engagement in quality literature is often postponed until after decoding of contrived texts has been mastered.

The concept of 'grown-up-ness' aligns with empathy and compassion for others but such attributes are not easily measured by testing regimes. According to Daniel Goleman (2006), empathy is not fully realised until we are motivated to act. Similarly Miller and Saxton (2016) remind us that thinking and feeling as another is not enough; empathy requires that we respond with some kind of action. To stand with another – even in fictional circumstances – is to *practise* compassion. Drama educator Jonathan Neelands (2010) asserts that nothing happens in drama unless we take action: we make decisions to take on roles, and then must carry through with the choices made. He argues that if we can begin to see and understand our own agency through taking on roles in imagined worlds, then we can start to realise that we can act to bring about change in our own real contexts. The embedding of educational drama in the English curriculum can then act as an 'interruption' by enabling both the teacher and students to interrogate their learning, own it and make connections amongst, between and beyond themselves.

The *School Drama* teacher professional learning programme focuses on developing primary teachers' confidence and expertise to use the artform of drama to further explore the artform of literature.

The *School Drama* programme: a brief outline

Despite the growing body of research documenting the potential of the Arts to transform the learning process, ongoing cuts in pre-service and in-service arts education in Australia has resulted in many early childhood and primary teachers expressing a lack of confidence in and expertise to embed the Arts in what is an already overcrowded curriculum.

Since 2009, Sydney Theatre Company's *School Drama* programme, in partnership with the University of Sydney, has worked with primary teachers keen to embed drama in their classrooms. Initially all participating teachers are involved in professional learning workshops. A professional actor or teaching artist then works alongside the class teacher throughout a school term, to plan, model and explore quality literature using drama to focus on English and literacy skills (for example, in oracy, description, narrative writing and inferential comprehension). Participant teachers report that using one artform (drama) to delve more deeply into another artform (literature) has contributed to their students' development as confident, creative, engaged literacy learners. Findings emerging from a long-term evaluation (Gibson 2011; Gibson & Smith, 2013) demonstrate the pedagogic robustness of the *School Drama* programme, and the benefits that emerged for teachers, students and teaching artists. A number of case studies (Robertson, 2010; Sze, 2013; Smith, 2014; Saunders, 2015) have also demonstrated that not only do students' academic outcomes improve, teachers report children's improved confidence and self-efficacy across the curriculum along with shifts in respect for each other and more empathy for the other. Teachers also see the possibilities for authentic integration of teaching and learning experiences to overcome the difficulties of an overcrowded curriculum.

Since its inception the programme has expanded across greater Sydney, reaching hundreds of teachers and thousands of children. It is currently making exciting expansions into other Australian states and regional New South Wales. In 2017 alone the programme will include more than 150 teachers and over 3700 children in over 50 schools. The following exemplars are drawn from the body of research about the programme.

Exemplar: *The Duck and the Darkling* (Millard and King, 2014)

> In literature we find the best expression of the human imagination and the most useful means by which we come to grips with our ideas about who and what we are.
>
> *(Chambers, 1985, p.16)*

One of the underlying tenets of the *School Drama* programme is the selection of quality literary texts to explore challenging themes or dilemmas or characters. *The Duck and the Darkling* is a beautiful picture book that in our opinion has huge symbolic significance for children (and adults) of all ages. A unit of work, *Hope in Dark*

Times, was developed (Ewing & Saunders, 2016) and piloted as part of the *School Drama* programme with 46 Year One children in a suburban Sydney school in 2015. The story is set in the Kingdom of Dark, which can be seen as a metaphor for the current tough times being experienced by many in today's war-torn countries. The class teachers were interviewed before the unit was taught, and asked to share their goals for the unit and the literary outcomes they wished to focus upon. At the conclusion of the unit both the children and the teachers were asked to reflect on their learning journey. The children drew and wrote in role and provided suggestions for the unit's improvement in a class discussion.

A brief snapshot of some of the drama strategies used to explore the text is provided below. The emphasis throughout the unit was on creating spaces and places for the children to explore new possibilities and perspectives, and investigate the hope that transformed the relationships between the main characters, Peterboy, his Grandpapa and Idaduck, as well as the potential for a changed Kingdom. More details about the unit itself and the drama devices employed can be found in Ewing and Saunders (2016).

Scraps of wonderfulness
At the beginning of the unit the children were asked to write down something wonderful (a memorable experience or a special person or place rather than a thing). These 'scraps of wonderfulness' were shared over time.

Trust walk
Because the unit aimed to explore the concepts of trust, courage and hope, the children also engaged in a trust walk. One child was blindfolded and another led them around the obstacles in the room. Afterwards they reflected on the experience from both perspectives.

Wonder
After sharing the initial pages of the story, children worked in pairs to imagine how what was once a bright and beautiful world had become the sorry and spoiled Kingdom of Dark. They depicted this process through frozen images, represented these possibilities through drawings and later wrote about their hypotheses (for example: pollution completely blocking the sun to make the kingdom so dark; greed and hatred spoiling the outside beauty of the world; a nasty witch casting a spell to make the world dark).

A duck with hope
Searching for a scrap of wonderfulness to put the light back into his grandfather's eyes, Peterboy found a duck who, although seriously injured, had hope beating within. Children sculpted this critical moment, engaged in conversations between Grandpapa and Peterboy about the pros and cons of keeping Idaduck and used conscience alley to reflect on whether Grandpapa should allow the duck to stay with them until she was healed.

The children found spaces in the text to dialogue about relationship entanglements and appreciate other points of view – in Biesta's terms, they were finding a middle ground. The classroom teachers commented during debriefings after each workshop and at the post-unit interview that the students had enthusiastically connected with the book and approached both the drama sessions and follow-up activities with excitement. They noted the growing mutual respect and empathy that grew between individuals, evidenced by increasing collaboration in classroom activities. The children moved beyond their own identities to appreciate the other. They were transforming many of their ideas and understandings and learning to work together, building on each others' ideas. Interestingly the sharing of 'scraps of wonderfulness' that had begun the unit endured for many more iterations as the children really enjoyed listening to the things that gave each other joy.

Exemplar: *The Burnt Stick* (Hill, 1994): the development of empathy

Saunders (2015) chose to research Year Six students in northern Sydney to explore the development of their academic and non-academic outcomes over a seven-week timeframe. His case study documents his work as both teaching artist and researcher alongside the classroom teacher, Linda O'Connor (pseudonym). The pre-text selected for this *School Drama* experience was *The Burnt Stick* (Hill, 1994), which traces the experience of an Aboriginal child, John Jagamurra, as he is taken from his mother and placed at a mission.

Over the seven weeks, Saunders recorded the drama sessions, undertook short debriefing conversations with O'Connor and led focus group discussions with students. Some excerpts from these reflective interviews and focus groups are used below to illustrate the co-mentoring and co-learning model between the artist and teacher.

> Early in the unit O'Connor and Saunders asked the students to lie on the floor, close their eyes and listen to and visualise the story as they were reading the first section of the book. This was followed by a visualisation activity where the students were asked to imagine themselves in the two places the story is set. They then shared what they could see, hear or feel with their peers before drawing them. Teacher learning about the text and about her own learning is encapsulated in O'Connor's comment:
>
> *I was surprised by just the depth of their thinking and again their thoughts and things that I hadn't even considered when I analysed the text. … And sometimes the connections that they make are surprising as well. So I just think that also means that as a teacher, you can learn from your students as well. I suppose … and I'm quite happy to learn from them and I think that contributes to creating a supportive environment.*

Saunders (2015) found that over the seven weeks of the programme, the participant class demonstrated, through pre-programme and post-programme benchmarking, positive shifts in inferential comprehension and descriptive language.

> Dan: *There are some moments and you don't know how to describe it and then someone thinks of a word that you might not have learnt before and then you can use that word in stuff that you do.*

Interestingly, the students who were achieving at a mid to low level in the pre-programme literacy tests had the strongest increases in literacy. Perhaps even more important, however, were the positive shifts in empathy, motivation and engagement in the Year Six students. The students articulated how they observed how the drama work contributed to their own learning and engagement:

> Eamon: *Especially with the hot-seating, because we got to talk about, we got to ask the characters questions that we wanted to know in the story, that weren't in the story, especially with Mr Grainger, like 'what was going through your head when you told the Big Man about John Jagamarra's trick?' And that it doesn't say in the [text], so you can ask the character hand to hand questions …*

They commented about how embodying the characters helped them empathise with them:

> Sandro: *In some books you just read about the characters and you don't really feel what they are feeling. But since you actually act it out you actually know what they are going through and you feel for them …*
>
> Joshua: *And putting yourself in the character's shoes, it's like, when you are in character you feel a better prediction of what could happen next … because you've been through what they have been through … kind of …*
>
> Gia: *'Cos we get to do frozen moments and like we do step by step with what's happening in the story. So you can choose who you are going to be like and compare that to you and put yourself in their shoes and like what they would do.*

Others attempted to define how the process was both a different and an enjoyable way of learning:

> Zac: *When we first met you [John] and we had to do the writing task, I thought you were going to be really boring because we had to do writing, but then the next week and all these other ones, it's actually been a lot more fun because you haven't made us do writing, we've done all these fun activities. So it was a good way to learn about the Stolen Generations and how life was back then. Yeah, because we didn't have to do any writing or research, we just got to learn it our way. A fun way. Yeah.*

Conclusion

> *For me, the child is a veritable image of becoming, of possibility, poised to reach towards what is not yet, towards a growing that cannot be predetermined or prescribed. I see her and I fill the space with others like her, risking, straining, wanting to find out, to ask their own questions, to experience a world that is shared.*
>
> *(Greene, 1987)*

Imaginative and dramatic play opportunities in both contexts allowed students to learn how to better work in groups, to share, to negotiate, to resolve conflicts, and to learn empathy. Children as co-creators along with teachers can develop decision-making skills, move learning experiences at their own pace, discover their own areas of interest, and ultimately engage fully in the action. Making art through drama and literary texts enables children to move into a transformative space in which they can play with possibilities that take them beyond their own perspectives to encourage openness and mindfulness towards the others who share their worlds.

If we truly want to develop children's communicative, collaborative and problem solving skills and help them become resilient and productive individuals, we must put creative pedagogy at the heart of the classroom experience. Drama can help students develop a broad and inclusive worldview that includes an understanding of the vast diversity of cultures and approaches to living.

References

Aprill, A., Burnaford, G., & Weiss, C. (2001). *Renaissance in the classroom: Arts integration and meaningful learning*. Mahwah, NJ: Lawrence Erlbaum Associates.

Baldwin, P., & Fleming, K. (2003). *Teaching literacy through drama: Creative approaches*. London: Routledge Falmer.

Bamford, A. (2006). *The wow factor: Global research compendium on the impact of the arts in education*. Berlin: Waxmann Verlag.

Biesta, G.J.J. (2014). *The beautiful risk of education*. London: Paradigm.

Biesta, G.J.J. (2017). *The rediscovery of teaching*. New York: Routledge.

Brunker, N. (2012). Conceptualising children's social and emotional wellbeing: Portraits of lived meanings in primary schooling. (Unpublished PhD). Sydney, University of Sydney.

Catterall, J. (2009). *Doing well and doing good by doing art: The long-term effects of sustained involvement in the visual and performing arts during high school*. Los Angeles, CA: Los Angeles Imagination Group.

Chambers, A. (1985) *Booktalk*. Gloucester: Thimble Press.

Connell, R. (1994). Poverty and education. *Harvard Educational Review, 64*(2), 125–149.

Darling-Hammond, L. (2009). President Obama and education: The possibility for dramatic improvements in teaching and learning. *Harvard Educational Review, 79*(2), 210–223.

Deasy, R.J. (Ed.) (2002). *Critical links: Learning in the arts and student academic and social development*. Washington, DC: Arts Education Partnership.

Ewing, R. (2010a). *The Arts and Australian education: Realising potential*. Australian Education Review number 58. Australian Council for Educational Research, Victoria.

Ewing, R. (2010b). Literacy and the arts. In F. Christie, & A. Simpson (Eds.), *Literacy and social responsibility: Multiple perspectives* (pp. 56–70). London: Equinox.

Ewing, R., & Saunders, J. (2016). *School drama: Drama, literature and literacy in the creative class-room*. Sydney, NSW: Currency Press Pty Ltd.

Ewing, R., Simons, J., Hertzberg, M., & Campbell, V. (2016). *Beyond the script: Take three*. 3rd edn. Newtown, NSW: Primary English Teaching Association Australia.

Fesmire, S. (2003). *John Dewey and moral imagination*. Bloomington: University of Indiana Press.

Fiske, E. (Ed.). (1999). *Champions of change: The impact of arts on learning*. Washington, DC: Arts Education Partnerships/President's Committee on the Arts and Humanities.

Gibson, R. (2011). *Evaluation of school drama 2010*. Sydney, NSW: University of Sydney.

Gibson, R., & Ewing, R. (2011). *Transforming the curriculum through the Arts*. Melbourne: Palgrave Macmillan.

Gibson, R., & Smith, D. (2013). *Meta-evaluation of school drama 2009 to 2012*. Sydney, NSW: University of Sydney.

Goleman, D. (2006). *Emotional intelligence*. New York: Bantam.

Greene, M. (1987). Bank Street College commencement address. Retrieved from https://socialimagination.wikischolars.columbia.edu/quotes

Greene, M. (1995). *Releasing the imagination: Essays on education, the arts and social change*. San Francisco, CA: Jossey Bass.

Greene, M. (2007). *Imagination and the healing arts*. Maxine Greene Center. Retrieved from https://maxinegreene.org/uploads/library/imagination_ha.pdf

Hill, A. (1994). *The Burnt Stick*. Sydney: Penguin/Viking.

Martin, A.J., Mansour, M., Anderson, M., Gibson, R., & Leim, G.A.D. (2013). The role of arts participation in students' academic and nonacademic outcomes: A longitudinal study of school, home, and community factors. *Journal of Educational Psychology*, *105*(3), 709–727.

Millard, G., & King, S. (2014). *The duck and the darkling*. Sydney: Scholastic.

Miller, C., & Saxton, J. (2004). *Into the story: Language in action through drama*. Portsmouth, NH: Heinmann.

Miller, C., & Saxton, J. (2016). *Into the story 2: More stories, more drama*. Bristol, UK: Intellect.

National Education Association. (2013). *An educator's guide to the four C's. Preparing 21st century students for a global society*. Retrieved from www.nea.org/tools/52217.htm

Neelands, J. (2010). Mirror, dynamo or lens? Drama, children and social change. In P. O'Connor (Ed.), *Creating democratic citizenship through drama education: The writings of Jonothan Neelands* (pp.143–158). Stoke on Trent: Trentham Books.

O'Connor, P. (2008). Drama for inclusion: A pedagogy of hope. In M. Anderson, J. Hughes & J. Manuel (Eds.), *Drama and English teaching: Imagination, action and engagement* (pp.136–149). Melbourne: Oxford University Press.

O'Sullivan, E. (1999) *Transformative learning: Educational vision for the 21st century*. Toronto, Canada: University of Toronto Press.

O'Toole, J., Stinson, M., & Moore, T. (2009). *Drama and curriculum: A giant at the door*. Dordrecht: Springer.

Prentki, T. (2014). *Banking on drama education*. Drama Australia Monograph no.7. Stafford, Qld: Drama Australia.

Robertson, A. (2010). The School Drama experience: A case study of learning in and through the art of drama. (Unpublished Honours dissertation). Sydney, The University of Sydney.

Saunders, J. (2015). School Drama: A case study of student academic and non-academic achievement. (Unpublished Masters (Research)). Sydney: University of Sydney.

Smith, D. (2014). *School Drama program sustainability case study*. Sydney: The University of Sydney.

Sze, E. (2013). Sustainable professional development: A case study on quality Arts partnerships in the primary classroom. (Unpublished Hons dissertation). Sydney, The University of Sydney.

Vygotsky, S.L. (2004). Imagination and creativity in childhood. *Journal of Russian and East European Psychology*, 1(42), 7–97.

Winner, E., Goldstein, T.R., & Vincent-Lancrin, S. (2013). *Arts for art's sake?* Overview, OECD Publishing.

Wyn, J. (2009). Touching the future: Building skills for life and work. *Australian Education Review*, No. 55, 42–55. Melbourne: Australian Council for Educational Research Press.

11

AUTHENTIC TEACHING ASSESSMENT IN GRADUATE TEACHER EDUCATION

Becomings of pedagogical artistry and leadership

Julianne Moss and Anne-Marie Morrissey

Introduction

This chapter explores questions of identity and subjectivity raised through Biesta's recent conceptual framing of the educational task (*pedagogiske*). In this chapter we focus on the 'becomings' (Britzman, 2003, p.70) of pedagogical artistry in Australian graduate teacher education by developing an argument that criss-crosses the issues of identity and subjectivity in graduate teacher education. The question 'how I am?' raised by Biesta is central to the hermeneutics of the educational 'task'. As noted by curriculum scholar Slattery, hermeneutics, at its most basic level, is 'an approach to understanding the meaning of texts, laws, language, historical artifacts, and pedagogy' (Slattery, 2006, p.115).

Teacher education and its task

When read in English, as Biesta states, the use of the term 'task' is far from ideal (Biesta, 2017 p.7). He goes on to explain that language use in Germanic and Dutch gives us a much broader and potentially deeper understanding of both reflexive value and utilitarian purposes of the educational task. '*Aufgabe*' (the German equivalent for task) implies the educational task carries with it 'a particular responsibility, a particular imperative' (Biesta, 2017, p.7). Biesta highlights 'grown-up-ness' (which he describes as 'a slightly awkward term' (Biesta, 2017 p.8)), and the overall significance of 'the relationship between my existence and the existence of the world' (Biesta, 2017, p.8). How can this be achieved in a world of global and performative teacher education practices? A world where the perceived loss of pedagogical artistry is accompanied by external mantras such as professional standards of teacher quality and 'bad teachers', distorting what it means to be a teacher educator and a graduating teacher (Kumashiro, 2012; Kirkby, Moss & Godinho, 2017). Under these conditions, questions surface that relate to the networks of power in policy and practice discourses. As Biesta observes, 'the promise of liberation has all too often turned into an exercise of power' (Biesta, 2017, p.9). Pedagogically, these words are also an echo of feminist poststructuralist researcher Patti Lather, who citing Elizabeth Ellsworth notes:

> (t)oo often such pedagogies [liberatory pedagogies] fail to probe the degree to which 'empowerment' becomes something done 'by' liberated pedagogies 'to' or 'for' the as-yet unliberated the 'other', the object upon which is directed the 'emancipatory' actions (Ellsworth 1989).
>
> *(Lather, 1991, p.16)*

Teacher education pedagogy is not exempt, as we have seen, from such constraints and power structures. For example, making practice the core of teachers' professional preparation is cited as a major issue for teacher education course design (Ball & Forzani, 2009). 'Authentic' teacher performance assessments are praised for the innovative ways of assessing teacher knowledge and skills and for the potential to promote teacher learning and reflective teaching (Chung, 2008; Allard, Mayer & Moss, 2014). Equally, 'authentic' assessment has been misconstrued as measures of effectiveness and 'classroom ready teachers' (Teacher Education Ministerial Advisory Group, 2014).

In constructing this chapter, central to our arguments of authenticity are the take up and theorising of identity and subjectivity work of the graduating teacher. As both curriculum designers and researchers, we aim to foreground, entangle and disrupt the often heard retort that the relationship between self/subject in 'becoming' (Britzman, 2003, p.70)[1] teacher education graduates is so obvious that it needs no further discussion (Doy, 2005). Over the last three decades the theorisation of identity and subjectivity has shifted considerably (Deleuze & Guattari, 1987; Butler, 1997; Foucault, 1997; McLeod & Yates, 2006). *Subjectivity* is explained by McLeod and Yates (2006, p.38) as being a preferred construct to *identity* as:

> subjectivity alerts us not so much to the idiosyncrasies of the individual (though this is, of course, relevant), as to how 'subjects' are formed – the range of influences, practices, experiences, and relations that combine to produce a young person and young people.

As Foucault points out, in the history of subjectivity it is the '"relations with oneself", with their technical armature and their knowledge effects' (1997, p.84) that matter.

The case of one authentic teaching assessment

This chapter draws upon the curation of an authentic teaching assessment (ATA). In Australia, the development of the ATA often draws from the Performance

Assessment of California Teachers (PACT) initiative. Internationally, ATAs now form an accepted part of the curriculum and assessment practices of teacher education. Elsewhere they are also viewed as the window to practice that many claim can dissolve the theory/practice binary that is so often raised as one of the key problems that teacher education must overcome. A report for the Queensland College of Teachers, the teacher regulatory authority in that state, suggests that:

> Authentic assessment makes the core aspects of teaching visible and measurable against a set of agreed standards. … Authentic assessment, therefore, requires preservice teachers to be explicit about their thinking and decision-making in designing teaching episodes, to reference the sources and rationale for their ideas, and to reflect upon the actual teaching experience and plans for revising and redesigning the teaching episodes. This dissolves the division between theory and practice and creates a system of reflective practice that adds to the professional knowledge of teaching.
>
> *(Queensland College of Teachers, 2012, p.25)*

The ATA that is discussed and analysed in this chapter was curated in 2014 by Georgina who is now successfully teaching in an early years setting in Australia. As teacher educators we maintain that Georgina's document remains one of the most outstanding examples that has been produced by an early year's candidate. Georgina completed a dual strand primary and early childhood qualification. As a preservice teacher in a graduate programme, she gained her entry into the programme on the basis of her first degree in graphic design. When we commenced the analysis of Georgina's work, we were unaware of this disciplinary base. Her disciplinary formation may explain her mastery of the arts-based teaching and learning sequences she developed with her group of four-to-five year olds. However as will be revealed in the following section of the chapter, she developed a capacity to foreground the negotiation of pedagogical artistry, by attending to the formation of 'desires' (Biesta, 2017, p.19) and multiple selves, in dialogue with the young learners whom she names as being the curriculum leaders.

Foregrounding negotiation in pedagogical artistry

Excerpts from Georgina's ATA provide an overview of the key task that is central to illustrating how her pedagogical moves developed in the process of demonstrating that she was 'ready to teach', the language of use in course accreditation requirements that she was undertaking. Within her selected sequence of lessons and reflective journal notes, a theoretical and pedagogical framework is ever present. The understanding of differences, children's worlds and children as curriculum makers and leaders are explained in her teaching and learning ratio-nale. As Georgina wrote:

> The differences in children should be recognised and cultivated for the rich-ness they offer, enabling every child to grow and assert full and competent individuality (journal, 21 August, 2014). To do this I needed to have an aware-ness of what was happening to each child in their lives as they individually strive to understand the world around them and master it.
>
> Being curious and in awe of their environments, the children naturally showed an eagerness and enthusiasm to construct their own learning path-ways. I therefore considered the children as leaders of the curriculum, with the teacher-student relationship being that of a mentor or a guide that facili-tates learning environments that extend from children's interests, and engage them in active, collaborative and independent practices, in the discovery of their own learning.
>
> Processes of planning took a three-fold approach, i.e. designing activities based on children's interests. The intent of using such a holistic approach was to offer the children an open framework to experiment expressing and communicating their ideas and emotions through a myriad of mediums, i.e. verbal, visual and gestural, in essence, to support and educate them in a way that their own innate and unique qualities may come to greater fulfilment.

The description of how the learning activities were designed further illustrates her personal confidence as an art maker, someone who qualified as a graphic designer and as an emerging professional, who has the confidence to defray the power of her mentor teacher. As Georgina continues:

> When introducing the art discipline of 'still life' painting, instead of getting the children to colour in a picture outline of a fruit bowl, which was what my supervising teacher had originally organised for them to do, I decided to pre-sent children with a blank sheet of paper, different colour inks and a real-life fruit bowl consisting of an array of different coloured, shaped and textured fruits. Designing the activity in this way challenged the children to observe the colours, lines, shapes and compositional structure of the fruit bowl's arrange-ment. Features that may have otherwise been unnoticed became demystified through acute observation and visual inquiry, 'I didn't know those dots on strawberries were actually seeds', 'Look, orange skins have dints all over them'. Discovery of new colours, shades, textures, shapes, patterns, forms of natural and manmade objects emerged through this process, helping the children to develop a deeper awareness and appreciation for their environments.

Georgina in our analysis evolved a position that recognises a nuanced sense of respon-sibility and subjectivity for all young learners. Equally these qualities apply to her emergent professional self. As a soon to be newly graduating professional she writes:

Teaching is not just about having the theoretical knowledge base and practical skills, in fact it is about having the ability to evaluate who you are as a person and understand how your own identity shapes the quality of your practice (Palmer, 1990; journal, 25 September, 2014). In deference to my original view, I now understand that my endeavour to become a teacher must begin introspectively … and … over time I became aware that meaningful learning could only truly take place once teacher-student relationships based on positivity, trust, care, fairness, support and authenticity were formed (Groundwater-Smith et al., 2006; Bowman et al., 2001, in Arthur et al., 2012). I am now aware that my teacher identity is not a separate body of knowledge to acquire and be affixed to my own identity; rather my methodologies should be drawn from and remain faithful to my own identity.

In concluding her final reflections on planning for teaching and learning she states:

I have observed that some children feel more confident expressing themselves in certain ways. By providing embodied pedagogies that offer multiple avenues for children to communicate their ideas though a myriad of mediums, I believe this has contributed to children's heightened sense of autonomy and agency in learning, as well as a deeper awareness of the self (journal, 22 September, 2014).

Georgina's capacity to go it alone in developing the art making, rather than being caught up in the power of her own learning-to-teach relationship was instrumental in the opening up of the pedagogical artistry for herself and her young learners. Doy (2005) in her explanation of subjectivity, which she has drawn between the fields of psychoanalysis and Marxism, questions that the 'relationship between self/subject and art is so obvious that it needs no further discussion' (Doy, 2005, p.6). Like many theorists who locate their work in the field of visual culture she also conveys that subjectivity is full of contradictions and tensions. She further contends that ideas of the self 'continue to evolve ways of representing subjectivity, whether … digitally merged or with the "selves" of others' (Doy, 2005, p.5).

The words of Doy are important if we are to engage with significant questions for arts education and what Biesta poses as the educational principle of '*suspension* – a suspension in time and space, so we might say – that provides opportunities for establishing relationships with our desires, make them visible, perceivable, so that we can work on them' (Biesta, 2017, p.18). Critical scholars such as Butler have long recognised that the 'legitimization of [children's] knowledge affirms their lived experience and encourages their power to examine the world' (1998, p.108). In the foregrounding of pedagogical artistry, the question, 'how I am?' encapsulates the recognition that graduating teacher subjectivities are formed through emergent rather than either/or positions and supported by viewers and voices of learners, who in this case are four-to-five year olds. Thus the becoming teacher and the learner, each in an encounter, is granted access to their desires as a living question and embodiment of the educational task.

Biesta points out:

> As long as the educator decides for the child or student which of their desires
> are desirable, the child and student remain objects of the educator's intentions
> and activities. The key educational challenge, therefore, is not simply to tell
> the child or student which of their desires are desirable, but for this question
> to become a living question in the life of the child or student.
>
> *(2017, p.18)*

For Georgina the curation of her authentic teaching assessment further illustrates
how desire has a presence in an educational task that is formatively generated and
is enabling of the co-construction of pedagogical understanding.

In times of the teacher education standards and discourses of teacher quality,
questions of identity and subjectivity and their centrality to the design of teacher
education are considered barriers to predictors of teaching performance. In this
chapter we have evidenced the experience of one preservice teacher and the
steps taken in the production of an authentic teaching assessment, a compulsory
core requirement for a graduate teacher education programme and regulatory
requirements in the large Australian state of Victoria. Drawing its theoretical
inspiration from the field of visual culture, the chapter has opened up the theoretical spaces of identity and subjectivity as both experienced and lived through
the juxtapositions of self and others. Understanding and theorising 'how am I?'
unsettles the concept of the educational task and foregrounds the significance of
subjectivity in pedagogical artistry. Authentic teaching assessments are enacted
by the self but also demonstrate the self as work in process. In the context of
learning to teach, representations of teaching subjectivities live inside a task
such as an authentic teaching assessment through the assemblage of documents,
reflections and images. Recent reports and accreditation requirements have
moved quickly to position such tasks as the window to competence. However
another interpretation is that the practice of authentic assessment forms the
openings of pedagogical artistry where the traces of future pedagogical leadership come into sight.

Acknowledgement

This chapter arose through our engagement as teacher educators with the work of
Georgina Shepherd. Georgina is currently a full-time educator practising in a long
day care centre in Victoria, Australia. She leads the learning of a two-to-three year
old room. The text in this chapter has been read and revised and approved in collaboration with her. We extend our deep appreciation to her and acknowledge that
throughout the process of both teaching and assessing her work and writing this
chapter we have established the significance of a focus on pedagogical artistry in the
becoming of graduate teachers.

Note

1 Britzman (2003) states that she uses the term 'becoming' to convey the simultaneity of time, place, events and the meanings we give them. She further states that 'the sense we make of the chronology depends on the discourses we take up' (p.70).

References

Allard, A., Mayer, D., & Moss, J. (2014). Authentically assessing graduate teaching: Outside and beyond neo-liberal constructs. *Australian Educational Researcher*, *41*(4), 425–443.

Arthur, L., Beecher, B., Death, E., Dockett, S., & Farmer, S. (2012). *Programming and planning in early childhood settings*. 5th ed. Melbourne: Cengage Learning.

Ball, D.L., & Forzani, F.M. (2009). The work of teaching and the challenge for teacher education. *Journal of Teacher Education*, *60*(5), 497–511.

Biesta, G.J.J. (2017). *The rediscovery of teaching*. New York: Routledge.

Bowman, B.T., Donovan, M.S., & Burns, M.S. (Eds.) (2001). *Eager to learn: Educating our preschoolers*. Washington, DC: National Academy Press.

Britzman, D. (2003). *Practice makes practice: A critical study of learning to teach*. 2nd ed. New York: State University of New York Press.

Butler, J. (1997). *The psychic life of power: Theories in subjection*. Stanford, CA: Stanford University Press.

Butler, M.A. (1998). Negotiating place: The importance of children's realities. In S.R. Steinberg & J.L. Kincheloe (Eds.), *Students as researchers: Creating classrooms that matter* (pp.94–112). London: Falmer Press.

Chung, R.R. (2008). Beyond assessment: Performance assessments in teacher education. *Teacher Education Quarterly*, *35*(1), 8–28.

Deleuze, G., & Guattari, F. (1987). *A thousand plateaus: Capitalism and schizophrenia* (B. Massumi trans.). London: University of Minnesota Press.

Doy, M.G. (2005). *Picturing the self: Changing views of the subject in visual culture*. London: I.B. Tauris.

Ellsworth, E. (1989). Why doesn't this feel empowering? Working through the repressive myths of critical pedagogy. *Harvard Educational Review*, *59*(3), 297–325.

Foucault, M. (1997). *Ethics, subjectivity and truth* (P. Rainbow ed.; R. Hurley & others trans.). London: Allen Lane, Penguin Press.

Groundwater-Smith, S., Ewing, R., & Le Cornu, R. (2006). Behaving ethically. In S. Groundwater-Smith, R. Ewing & R. Le Cornu (eds.), *Teaching: challenges and dilemmas* (pp.331–345). Melbourne: Thompson Learning.

Kirkby, J., Moss, J., & Godinho, S. (2017). The devil is in the detail: Bourdieu and teachers' early career learning. *International Journal of Mentoring and Coaching in Education*, *6*(1), 19–33.

Kumashiro, K. (2012). *Bad teacher! How blaming teachers distorts the bigger picture*. New York: Teachers College Press.

Lather, P. (1991). *Getting smart: Feminist research with/in the postmodern*. New York: Routledge.

McLeod, J., & Yates, L. (2006). *Making modern lives: Subjectivity, schooling, and social change*. New York: State University of New York Press.

Palmer, P. (1990). *The courage to teach: Exploring the inner landscape of a teacher's life*. San Francisco: Jossey-Bass.

Performance Assessment of California Teachers – PACT. Retrieved from https://scale.stanford.edu/teaching/pact. Accessed 14/2/2017.

Queensland College of Teachers. (2012). *An investigation of best practice in evidence-based assessment within preservice teacher education programs and other professions*. Brisbane: Queensland College of Teachers.

Slattery, P. (2006). *Curriculum development in the postmodern era*. 2nd ed. New York: Routledge.

Teacher Education Ministerial Advisory Group – TEMAG. (2014). *Action now: Classroom ready teachers*. Canberra: Australian Government.

12

BEYOND BELIEF

Visionary cinema, becoming imperceptible and pedagogical resistance

Jessie L. Beier and Jason J. Wallin

Introduction

Deleuze (1989, 1995) writes that what we lack most in the contemporary moment is *belief in the world*, or rather, the means by which new ways of believing in the world might be created. Deleuze's provocation references the problem of an all-too-human mode of *cinematic* thinking, or rather, a mode of thinking based on the privileged assumption that the world is *always-already* given to thought and phenomenological experience such that belief in the world becomes belief in its *a priori* correlation to established patterns of representation by which it is rendered 'sensible' (Deleuze, 1989). This mode of thinking marks a more general schism that has come to mark our contemporary existence, that is, a rupture between the human and the world, an interval that has reduced our worldly connections to those that can always-already be recuperated into pre-established modes of sensing, thinking and existing in the world (Lambert, 2000, p.279).

This correlationist mode of thinking whereby the future is made to reflect in the past-present symptomizes a creeping inertia or particular 'stuckness' in terms of thinking how pedagogical life *might* be thought anew. For their ostensible openness, most pedagogical inquiries seem to be situated in a readymade field of possible, if not definitive, responses. Future-focussed policy developments and curriculum reforms, for instance, hinge on the dominant discourses, reified ideologies, and limited subjective resources produced and maintained in relation to what has been considered acceptable or necessary in the past-present. While the rhetoric of education's orientation to the future has become commonplace, the future presumed by this aim is one largely indistinguishable from the continuation of present political and economic orders. In turn, belief in the world has become founded upon a particular philosophy of access, that affirms the material limits of thought and cognition by which today we have the impression of having *seen it all before* (Flaxman, 2012, p.392). This is to say that the poverty of contemporary educational thought is in part born from the presupposition that the world is *always-already* given to thought, and more pointedly, to the thought of an all-too-human present of which the future is a mere perpetuation. That belief in the world has come to entail the affirmation of what *everybody already knows*, not only presumes a world submitted to established thought, but worse, a world given in adequation to the concepts and fashions of a perpetual present, that in turn suffocate difference (Culp, 2016).

While educational standardization constitutes an obvious culprit of the world's narrowing, this suffocation of belief is as much an effect of the ostensible inescapability of the alignment between *being* and *world* through which the world is made to appear *for us* (Thacker, 2011). Beyond the usual suspects of educational standardization and the Fordian adequation of education to a world modeled in the image of the factory, the alignment of *being* and *world* implicates an array of educational approaches nascently presumed to constitute direct access and commentary on reality. The assumed givenness of the world, to habitual interpretive schemas, the submission of reality to the time and experience of the human subject, and the presupposition that reality correlates to our thinking it, each conspire in the narrowing of belief. Generally, such narrowing might be said to preserve a longstanding educational fidelity to anthropocentric (centrism of the human agent) and anthropomorphic (centrism of human representation) thought, in that each passively rely on a philosophy of access that presupposes the givenness of reality to human thought and cognition in which it is so often made to reflect.

The aim of this chapter is to obliquely rejoin Biesta's (2017) challenge that education ought to be rethought as the task of dilating the subject's perceptual corridors and further, that the educational event should, in its most mature instantiation, produce a recognition of alterity by which new forms of existence might be produced. Between 'world-destruction,' wherein we enforce our all-too-human intentions in spite of our worldly connections and 'self-destruction,' wherein we withdraw from worldly problematics, Biesta (2017, p.13) calls for us to take the 'middle ground,' or rather, to recognize and embrace existential forms wherein our encounters with the unexpected limits and untimely interruptions of the world might: "wake us from drowsy states of being" (p.15). The task Biesta sets for education is as much an affirmation of escape from the perpetuation of hatred, violence, and supremacist thinking—*the way things are*—as it inadvertently advances a horrific speculation that might challenge approaches to education based in all-too-human coherences and familiarities. The flattened ontological world suggested by Biesta entails a recognition of inhuman, non-human, and more-than-human relations as remote nodes of knowledge and encounter that might produce new ways of believing and acting, aimed at overturning the reified organization of the senses and thought conditioned through the orthodox practices of schooling.

The visionary power of cinema

We would like to posit a rather unconventional 'answer' to Biesta's (2017) question of what education should take as its task by contorting the problematics of anthropocentrism and anthropomorphism along the revolutionary vectors of cinema, or rather, its potential creation of new perceptual vantages that assume neither the primacy of the human organism nor its phenomenological experience of the world. As Deleuze (1989) writes in *Cinema 2: The Time Image*: "the link between man and the world is broken" (p.172), that is, we no longer possess the resources or will for thinking a world out-of-sync with its given image. Hence, for Deleuze, what we require most in the contemporary moment are new "reasons to believe in this world" (p.172). Deleuze goes on to say that modern cinema ("when it is not bad") has the potential to do this. The function of cinema, for Deleuze, is not one of reflecting reality, but one of envisioning new images of it. Such *visionary* cinema is characterized as one capable of inducing passages from ordinary sensorial habits and experiences—*the way things are*—to those encounters that push toward the edges of what can be perceived in the first place. Visionary cinema aims at exposing 'the unbearable' nature of experience and an 'outside' that exceeds our state of ordinariness, in turn producing modes of discordance that are capable of generating new ways of believing in the world (Deleuze, 1989). In other words, cinema holds the power to actualize ways of seeing beyond ordinary or habitual vision by producing new perceptual circuits between humans and the world, in turn suggesting that *something else is possible*. In this way, Deleuze's visionary cinema can be likened to that which does *violence to thought*, or that which produces a 'strangeness' that is able to cross the bounds of commonsense relations and habitual organizations (Rajchman, 2000, p.10), in turn dilating what is possible to think in the first place.

Science fiction cinema, for instance, constructs fabulations and speculative extrapolations that go beyond overly limited assumptions about *the way things are*, compelling viewers to respond vicariously to incompossible situations that extend beyond habitual modes of interpretation (Shaviro, 2015). As Steven Shaviro (2015) asserts: "even the most reductionist SF stories still work, not just to explain, but also to entangle us within their grim scenarios" (p.15). When, in films such as Villeneuve's (2016) *Arrival* or Glazer's (2013) *Under the Skin*, cinematic characters make contact with extraterrestrial beings, for instance, we are not only confronted with counterintuitive scenarios about weird life in the universe, but also new hypotheses about the limits of our own human existence that can then be put to the test, to see whether they 'work' or not, and what consequences follow from them (Shaviro, 2015, p.11). If confronted with an alien entity, for instance, how might one communicate? And in asking this question, what assumptions, desires, and modes of existence must we challenge in the process? Approached in this way, cinema is not only capable of dilating the all-too-human sensorium in favor of new images of thought, but is also a force of destruction that refuses and frustrates understandings of the world based on outdated diagnostics and historical exemplifications.

Beyond its confrontation with the rapidly expanding orthodoxies of thought and their reification within the educational habitus, cinema might be thought as a mode for rethinking the world—albeit not necessarily a human one.

In response to both Biesta's question—*what is the educational task?*—and Deleuze's notion of a *visionary* cinema, it is therefore crucial that we speculate on the power of cinema to model discordant and dissident vectors of potentiality for re-thinking the educational task as one capable of producing new belief in the world. Working alongside Biesta's (2017, p.17) call for the particular educational 'work' of inter-ruption, suspension, sustenance, and metamorphosis, we question how one might approach the educational task as one in which learners struggle to exist in and with the world without thinking of themselves as central to it. This chapter will bring together examples from contemporary cinema and speculative philosophy to, firstly, explore how we might dilate perceptual modes in order to (re)think sub-jectivity along discordant vectors, secondly, to learn to "say 'no' to those who tell us to take the world as it is" (Culp, 2016, p.17), and thirdly, to develop alternative ethico-aesthetic modes that might open up new potentials for believing, and ulti-mately existing, in the world. Through this exploration our aim is to not only chal-lenge and disrupt educational approaches that have become stuck within diminished conditions of possibility and postures of fatalistic passivity towards the world, but to fabulate the educational task as something that is capable of producing more livable futures for both the human and non-human entities with whom we share the planet.

Dissident subjective vectors

In a climactic scene from Marvel's (2015) *Ant-Man*, Ant-Man, aka Scott Lang, pushes the limits of his suit to shrink into the quantum fabric of reality. Receding into an imperceptible world of crystalline intricacy, the camera creates, but briefly, a transcendental virtual cosmos without reference to the space-time of the human organism or the representational constants of the *given world*. Much like his species counterpart in Deleuze's *The Incredible Shrinking Man* (1957), *Ant-Man* palpates a perception of the imperceptible, or rather, of perceptual thresholds far finer than the sensory limits of the individual human organism. In its momentary exploration of scales eclipsing those of phenomenal existence, *Ant-Man* fabulates a condition for thinking and believing in a world in which anthropic reference is dismantled through its dilation of both temporal and spatial scales. Put otherwise, the scene of Lang's descent contorts the very notion of reality's *givenness* to the ordering metrics of human life, or human subjectivity, by envisioning new conditions for believing in the world—or rather, believing in the difference of the world and the human subject corollary to it. In this instance, the camera engenders a virtual subject by taking a position that humans cannot, removing the sense of a totalizing human or 'rational' perspective in favor of that which cannot be experienced directly. In brief, in its deterritorialization of anthropocentric perception, this visionary scene submits the viewer to noncognitive vantages out of joint with human phenome-nological experience.

The visionary potential of cinema is, of course, nothing particularly novel. For its displacement of the human eye and sensori-motor apparatus, modern cinema has long conspired as a mode of post-human, or even inhuman, thought. Vertov's cinematic production of the 1920s, for instance, already demonstrates an affirmation of the camera over the human eye, most notably in *Man With A Movie Camera* (1929), wherein the camera is utilized to capture a dramatic array of inhuman vantages and perceptions achieved through the displacement of the eye from 'sensori-motor' expectation. Such vantages take flight from popular conceptualizations of cinema modeled in the structure of theatrical stage-plays of the time, fabulating instead a world charged by new durations and (dis)cognitions; Vertov's average shot length of 2.3 seconds resisted the 11.2 second industry standard, and his revolutionary use of the camera actualized vantages that frustrated the spatio-temporal consistency of theater optics, in which most films were modeled at the time. In his break from literary and theatrical models, Vertov fabulates a new potential for cinematic thought—one founded in neither the familiar vantage of a perceiving subject nor regulation in the organizing metrics of narratological continuity, but in what Deleuze (1989) refers to as *gaseous vision*—that is, a vision before, and we presume, *after* the vision of man and the adaptation of reality to its perceptual and sensory habits. Vertov's camera composes an image of 'thinking' that actualizes the *plasticity* of the cinema to eclipse the *given world*, or rather, the world organized from and given to the vantage of the human subject.

Inhering this capacity to fabulate a style of thinking that transversally intersects our familiar existential presuppositions, cinema might be thought as obliquely enjoined to the educational question of how perception, and in turn subjectivity, might be contorted so as to *interrupt* ordinary sensations in order to create a more dilated vantage of reality. In the case of *Ant-Man*, Lang's descent into the infinite complexity and unfathomability of the quantum field actualizes scales of existence non-uniform to 'sensori-motor' organismic perception or the phenomenological *givenness* of experience.[1] Herein, the viewer is confronted with the emergence of alternative coherences among the faculties, that is, what the viewer sees, hears, and senses is no longer characterized by that which adheres to individual interpretive schemas, but rather, that which refuses and counteracts all-too-human modes of temporal coherence and perception. Operating beyond simple metaphor, such cinematic examples "escape the body, presenting something it cannot perceive on its own—not different worlds but realities that exist in the present (though not currently lived) that confirm reality by weakening it" (Culp, 2016, p.63). It is such contortion that might intersect with the highly patterned presuppositions of anthropocentric human centrality, and the anthropomorphic obsession with the representation of the *world as it is for us* (Thacker, 2011). As a general extrapolation, then, cinema's visionary power is intimate to its capacity to flee such representations through the fabulation of new conditions for believing in the world. It is in the cultivation of such new beliefs that our relationship with the world might not only be tactically relaunched, but populated by modes of sensing, thinking, and existing that are unanticipated by the present order of things.

Refusal and pedagogical resistance at the end of a world

Through its dilation of sensory circuits that move beyond ordinary subjective experience, visionary cinema fabulates a mode of perceiving and thus existing in and with the world that *refuses* to nominate all-too-human knowledge as the medium through which worldly connections are made. Transposed to educational thought, we might look to this operation of refusal as a necessary mode of (re)thinking processes of teaching and learning as those that move beyond what has been considered 'good' in the past, towards more *desirable* approaches for the future. Desire, in this sense, is not based on the fulfillment of some subjective lack decided by the educator, but rather, the *suspension* of a time-space wherein learners "can establish a relationship with their desires" (Biesta, 2017, p.18), a perspective on their desires, so that (grown-up) relationships in which the child can emerge as subject become possible. As Biesta (2017) writes, one of the key educational challenges of our time is "not simply to tell the child or student which of their desires are desirable, but for this question to become a 'living' question in the life of a child or student" (p.16). It is through this principle of *suspension*, a site of abeyance where we might question desiring-flows, that both teachers and students might learn to "say 'no' to those who tell us to take the world as it is," in turn restoring belief in the world as an *active* kind of ethics that is capable of affirming that *something else* is possible (Culp, 2016, p.17).

This mode of suspension is especially important in light of the broken connection between humans and the world that has come to characterize our contemporary moment, a new epoch that some have dubbed *the Anthropocene* (Crutzen, 2002; Crutzen & Steffen, 2003). Signaling the geological age since the industrial revolution, where, through its activities and its growing population, the human species has emerged as a geological force now altering the planet's climate and environment, the Anthropocene underscores the manner by which the Earth has been conflated with a human-centered 'world,' one divided, categorized, and made disparate through all-too-human regimes of representation. In addition to highlighting the commonsense ways in which we, as humans, have come to relate to our world, that is, how we have come to think of ourselves as free agents separate from and contending with the rest of so-called 'nature,' the Anthropocene also sheds new light on the possibility of our own species extinction. At the same time that the term Anthropocene provides a naming device that might help to unfold the way in which we have recuperated the world under narrowing modes of thinking, it has also exposed the important, if difficult, acknowledgment that in the face of human extinction, life will indeed survive without us.

Despite its reliance on apocalyptic clichés, contemporary cinema is a primary site within which the acknowledgment of our potential extinction has raised new provocations for what it means to live in anthropocenic times. In a scenario horrific to the presumption of human continuation, for instance, Bong Joon-ho's (2013) apocalyptic film *Snowpiercer* composes an image of the future in which the very idea of continuation and development teeter on the brink of extinction. Outside the highly patterned social order reproduced aboard the luxury-liner *Snowpiercer*, Joon-ho composes the image of a post-anthropocene ice-age withdrawn from the orthodoxies of human will and desire and anthropocentric ordering of things. Likewise, Lars von Trier's (2011) *Melancholia* fabulates a world marked by the impending annihilation of the human species, leaving the viewer to ask what it might mean to live at the end-of-*a*-world. In the opening scene of the film, we witness a surreal vision of the world coming to an end: a planetary collision between Earth and the fictional planet of Melancholia causes a slowing of time, a re-organization of insides and outsides, and the subsequent obliteration of human life. *Melancholia* breaks from dominant apocalyptic narratives by turning its focus away from the chaos and destruction that is most often depicted in end-of-the-world scenarios, towards the micro-political movements, desiring-flows, and intimate moments between two sisters. Although varied in their aesthetic and narrative approach, each of these examples presents an image of human extinction that refuses and frustrates interpretive analyses based in moral origins and/or judgment and critique. The overarching narrative in each of these films is not concerned with how to 'save' the human species when confronted with extinction, but rather how *life*, writ large, might endure *in spite of* human will and desire.

In this example, the cinematic reorientation to the prospect of our own species' extinction rejoins Claire Colebrook's (2014) sombre elicitation that "what we are is not something essential" (p.13). Similar to Anthropocene discourse more generally, what these films make apparent is that "there was a time, and there will be a time without humans" (p.32). It is within this confrontation with the limits of our own species' continuation that the educational task takes on a very different character. If every decision to teach and/or learn involves some sort of commitment to the future, how does one go about teaching *at the end of a world*? Where education is founded in linear and uncomplicated correlations between past, present, and future, the educational task is reduced to the habitual and instrumental reinforcement and perpetuation of the narratives and techniques for living that are required to contain the inherent unpredictably of times to come. The problem for contemporary pedagogy is thus how to deal with the expectation that education should provide future opportunities, what some might call *hope*, given the challenges raised by the growing acknowledgment that the world as we know it is undergoing significant and uncertain transformations. In these cinematic examples, the viewer is forced to engage with the difficult notion that our commonsense ideas of linear and unlimited progress and human exceptionalism are, indeed, themselves fictions. Taking seriously the pressing challenges raised by the threat of our own species' extinction, then, the educational task must be capable of experimenting with how to produce belief in a world that is indifferent to our own continuation.

Endurance, sustainability, and becoming-imperceptible

For Deleuze (1989), visionary cinema is not only capable of broadening the scope of human perception by interrupting all-too-human temporal and spatial coherences, but also holds the potential to reformulate conceptions of subjectivity that move beyond limiting models of anthropocentric essentialism towards thinking the subject as that which is able to *endure* and *transform* in relation to worldly problematics. As Deleuze (1989) writes, "the question is no longer what we see behind an image but rather, how we can *endure* what we see in it already" (p.230, added emphasis). It is through this mode of endurance that we might rejoin with Biesta's questions of *sustenance* and *metamorphosis*, that is, how the educational task might support positions that take the 'middle ground,' in turn permitting both students and teachers a space to continuously ask what one does when faced with worldly interruptions.

Enjoining these 'principles' of sustenance and metamorphosis to the power of cinema, we assert that in order for visionary cinema to dilate subjectivity in favor of encounters with more dynamic and hitherto occulted forces and intensities, the subject must be able to *endure*, in a sustainable fashion, that which one encounters in the world. As *Ant-Man* demonstrates, there persists a threshold through which the very coordinates of perception and assuredness of existence are rendered perilous and insecure. While Lang was able to encounter a space-time that pushed his own perceptual bounds beyond those of the human (or even the ant), this mode of existing was ultimately not sustainable. The survival of 'Scott Lang' as a molar entity required counteracting his line of absolute deterritorialization. Any question of endurance and transformation, or in Biesta's words sustenance and metamorphosis, should therefore address how we might move towards more ecological *and* sustainable modes of existence that have the capacity to take pain, exhaustion, and even extinction into account as not only obstacles to but a fulcrum for an ethics of change and transformation (Braidotti, 2006, p.1). Such modes of existence have the potential to raise important questions about how the field of education might become more *adequate* to the pressing challenges facing both teachers and students today. The threat of our own extinction, for instance, has raised new questions about the continuation of life on this planet we call Home, and thus any educational task must be capable of addressing how we, as teachers and educational researchers, might re-imagine a radical subjectivity that is capable of forming dynamic and uncertain connections with the world, while *enduring* the problematics raised by such connections.

As Braidotti (2006) asserts: "processes of change and transformation are so important and ever so vital and necessary, that they have to be handled with care" (p.1). Braidotti therefore calls for the need to develop concepts of ethical sustainability. We need to conceptualize the radical subject as that which "endures through sets of discontinuous variations, while remaining extra-ordinarily faithful to itself" (Braidotti, 2006, p.4). The use of faith here is not meant to signal some sort of psychological or sentimental reference to a transcendent identity, a faithfulness to some essential 'I,' but rather a mode of constructing an understanding of oneself predicated on "mutual sets of inter-dependence and inter-connections, that is to say, sets of relations and encounters" (Braidotti, 2006, p.4). Put otherwise, this 'multi-layered subjectivity' is one that is both sustainable, in that it lasts in time and space, *and* transformative, in that it is capable of de-centering anthropocentric and unitary visions of the subject through its own continuous and immanent becomings. Positioning the subject in this way poses new ethico-aesthetic problematics, ones that might help us reforge connections with the world that have hitherto been broken or otherwise scarcely fathomed. That is, such an ethics does not prescribe how one *ought* to relate to the world, but rather, marks a process of confronting and re-working the pain and exhaustion one experiences through ongoing experimentation and connections. This ethical mode therefore necessitates adequate assemblages of interaction, that is, one has to *actively* create encounters with, as Biesta (2017) writes, *resistance*:

> The encounter with resistance, that is, the encounter with the fact that something or someone resists our initiatives, is a tremendously important experience as it shows that the world is not just a construction of our mind or desires, but actually has an existence and hence an integrity of its own.
>
> *(p. 14)*

We might think of this encounter with resistance as a mode of *becoming-imperceptible*, that is, "the point of fusion between the self and his/her habitat, [or with] the cosmos as a whole" (Braidotti, 2006, p.25). As Deleuze writes, all processes of becoming aim at becoming-imperceptible (Deleuze & Guattari, 1987); however, in order to trigger this process one must endure quite a transformation in terms of what we have come to think of as the self. Such a transformation might be found in films such as Shane Caruth's (2013) unconventional science fiction film *Upstream Color*, a story of intertwined lives and behaviors that are unknowingly affected by an obscure parasite. In Caruth's tale of a man and woman mysteriously drawn together by the entangled life cycle of a parasitic organism, the notion of a stable self, bound by unitary identifications is exposed as a complete illusion as the characters try to reassemble the ruins of their collapsed identities. As the lovers struggle to understand their own connections with one another and their environment, they push against the thresholds of their own subjective sustainability, that is, they must actively experiment with alternative attunements to relationships and ecologies that have otherwise been ignored. Operating at the limit of their own experience, which needless to say, creates various levels of pain and exhaustion, Caruth's protagonists are nonetheless able to endure; they are not only able to last in time and space, but also *endure* the pain of confronting life, in all its complexity, confusion, and violence, "cracking, but holding it, still" (Braidotti, 2006, p.xx).

Through its central characters, *Upstream Color* fabulates modes of becoming-imperceptible, wherein individual identities and seemingly stable subject-positions disappear into a pulsing nexus of "multiple inter-connections that empower not the self, but the collective, not identity, but affirmative subjectivity, not consciousness, but affirmative inter-connections" (Braidotti, 2006, p.25). Such processes of affirmation not only dilate potential becomings in and with the world, but also hold the capacity to short-circuit *the way things are*, plunging us into impossible, noncommutative and entangled modes of sensing, thinking, and existing in the world. That is, beyond operating as yet another form of transcendent productivism wherein thought is founded in linear ties between past, present, and future, "becoming-imperceptible is the event for which there is no immediate representation" and thus it is capable of short-circuiting linear time and all-too-human modes of thinking. In this way, becoming-imperceptible takes on the double, or compossible operation of both affirmation—affirming that something else is possible—and destruction, where we might "learn to hate the world" in order to fend off the "here and now" so as to think the difference of the world (Culp, 2016, p.24).

Coda: unthought futures

As outlined above, we are now facing a plethora of challenges in relation to the degradation of our planet, to which there has been inadequate, if any, political, economic, and by extension, educational response. Instead, we are witnessing a reconstitution of conventional reference points and new and ever-more violent articulations of power in the face of continuous failures in social, political, and economic realms. As evidenced by recent American political events, such responses, or lack thereof, have re-ignited a powerful, if illusory, reliance upon past images of thought that are somehow reconstituted as the ideal. Likewise, in the field of education, postures defined by adaptation, maintenance, and ultimately *survival* mirror our worldly anxieties and disconnections. Symptoms of this anxiety are growing in both frequency and impact: growing job precarity, ever-increasing focus on quantity over quality, and the slippery corporatization of educational domains position schools among the many institutions that work to produce and maintain visions of the future undergirded by the world *as it is given*, that is, a world defined by the limited purview of the past-present. At the same time, however, there remains a pressure to position education as that holy space of possibility, a space where hope is born and optimism prevails. This comforting narrative, however, does not adequately address the real, material conditions of our contemporary existence, thus leaving us with very little in which to *believe*.

In order to address this worldly precarity and the profound loss of belief it has enabled, the educational task must be capable of actualizing new and unthought images of the future, which in turn might provide new belief for how pedagogical life might go. As education scholars in the area of 'future studies' have pointed out, thinking of the future of education requires an exploration of the range of alternatives at play, which in turn has the potential to activate more thoughtful and responsible action in the present (Hicks, 2001, 2004, 2006). In this way, educational discourses are not only guided by images of the future, but also have the potential to create *new images of the future* (Toffler, 1974). As outlined above, perhaps visionary cinema has the potential to produce such unthought futures in the way that it exposes the 'unbearable' dimensions that exceed ordinary experience and, through such excess, forces us to think differently (Deleuze, 1989). In its capacity to dilate the sensorium, thus exposing otherwise occluded forms of becoming—becoming-ant, becoming-extinct, becoming-imperceptible—visionary cinema mobilizes operations of interruption, suspension, sustenance, and metamorphosis that are required to re-imagine the educational task beyond belief in *the way things are*. In this task, visionary cinema might be linked to two crucial tasks for expanding educational thought—short-circuiting the sensori-motor apparatus that founds an expectation that the world will repeat in the image of the present so as to prepare new conditions for believing that something 'else,' or rather, that new dispositions for thought and action beyond the human-all-too-human character of the present might be possible.

Note

1 Similarly, in films such as *Edge of Tomorrow* (2014) and *Source Code* (2011), both of which plunge their characters into *video game* or *digital time*, real time is not marked by linear duration, but by what we might think of as the historical time of our contemporary existence—the Anthropocene—where the human is confronted with the spatio-temporal limits it has itself created (Wark, 2014).

References

Arnold, J. (Director). (1957) *The Incredible Shrinking Man* [Motion picture]. United States: Universal International.

Biesta, G.J.J. (2017). *The rediscovery of teaching.* New York: Routledge.

Braidotti, R. (2006). The ethics of becoming imperceptible. In C. Boundas (Ed.), *Deleuze and philosophy* (pp.133–159). Edinburgh: Edinburgh University Press.

Caruth, S. (Director). (2013). *Upstream Color* [Motion picture]. USA: ERBP.

Colebrook, C. (2014). *Death of the posthuman.* Ann Arbor: Open Humanities Press.

Crutzen, P.J. (2002). The 'Anthropocene.' *Journal de Physique IV (Proceedings), 12*(10), 1–5.

Crutzen, P.J., & Steffen, W. (2003). How long have we been in the Anthropocene era? *Climatic Change, 61*(3), 251–257.

Culp, A. (2016). *Dark Deleuze.* Minneapolis: University of Minnesota Press.

Deleuze, G. (1989). *Cinema 2: The time image* (H. Tomlinson & B. Habberjam trans.). Minneapolis: University of Minnesota Press.

Deleuze, G. (1995). *Negotiations 1972–1990* (M. Joughin, trans.). New York: Columbia University Press.

Deleuze, G., & Guattari, F. (1987). *A thousand plateaus: Capitalism and schizophrenia* (B. Massumi, trans.). Minneapolis: University of Minnesota Press.

Flaxman, G. (2012). *Gilles Deleuze and the fabulation of philosophy.* Minneapolis: University of Minnesota Press.

Glazer, J. (Director). (2013). *Under the Skin* [Motion Picture]. UK/USA/Switzerland: Studio Canal.

Hicks, D. (2001). *Citizenship for the future: A practical classroom guide.* Godalming, UK: World Wide Fund for Nature UK.

Hicks, D. (2004). Teaching for tomorrow: How can futures studies contribute to peace education? *Journal of Peace Education, 1*(2), 165–178.

Hicks, D. (2006). *Lessons for the future: The missing dimension in education.* Victoria, BC: Trafford Publishing.

Jones, D. (Director). (2011). *Source Code.* [Motion picture]. United States/France: Summit Entertainment

Joon-ho, B. (Director). (2013) *Snowpiercer* [Motion picture]. South Korea/Czech Republic: CJ Entertainment.

Lambert, G. (2000). Cinema and the outside. In Flaxman, G. (Ed.). *The brain is the screen: Deleuze and the philosophy of cinema* (pp.253–292). Minneapolis: University of Minnesota Press.

Liman, D. (Director). (2014). *Edge of Tomorrow* [Motion picture]. United States: Warner Bros. Pictures.

Rajchman, J. (2000). *The Deleuze connections*. Cambridge, MA: The MIT Press.

Reed, P. (Director). (2015). *Ant-Man* [Motion picture]. United States: Walt Disney Studios Motion Pictures.

Shaviro, S. (2015). *Discognition*. London: Repeater Books.

Thacker, E. (2011). *In the dust of this planet: Horror of philosophy*, vol. 1. Ropley, UK: Zero Books.

Toffler, A. (1974). *Learning for tomorrow: The role of the future in education*. New York: Vintage Books.

Vertov, D. (1997). *Man with a Movie Camera* (Chelovek s kinoapparatom). DVD. United States: Kino International Corporation. (Original music composed and performed by the Alloy Orchestra. 1929.)

Villeneuve, D. (Director). (2016). *Arrival* [Motion picture]. United States: Paramount Pictures.

Von Trier, L. (Director). (2011). *Melancholia* [Motion picture]. Denmark/Sweden/France/Germany: Nordisk Film.

Wark, M. (2014). Edge of tomorrow: Cinema of the Anthropocene. Retrieved from www.publicseminar.org/2014/06/edge-of-tomorrow-cinema-of-the-anthropocene/#.WG_dnLYrKV7

13

FLIGHT FROM FLIGHT

Composing a pedagogy of affect

John Roder and Sean Sturm

One

"Let it go! It's all about 'letting go'", said two of the early childhood teachers, reflecting on their role as teachers after a year of arts-based encounters involving community artists in their centres. Exactly what was being let go of, I (John) wondered. *What* they had let go of seemed less significant than *that* they had let go of it. Their talk seemed infused with a sense of inquiry as becoming, such that becoming became the *sine qua non* of teaching – and learning (their students' and their own). The event of which I was part was a MAPS (Move, Act, Play, Sing) research cluster day. MAPS was a two-year TLRI (Teaching and Learning Research Initiative)-funded project that involved a dancer, storyteller and musician exploring forms of collective practice cum action research alongside teachers, children and their families from the early childhood centres. On this day, the teachers were sharing their journeys as practitioner-researchers. They were reflecting on the expectations of the participating adults when they took up a teaching role. They seemed to believe that they had let go of control: of their personal power in the classroom, and of the institutional power that was vested in their practice – and this process as a significant, perhaps necessary, interruption, or even disruption, of their teaching practice.

We (John and Sean) would argue that, for many teachers, the realisation that they can let go of control of their classroom is an epiphany to them: a teachable moment for them as "teacher-learners." However, to paraphrase Deleuze and Guattari in *Anti-Oedipus* (1983, p.28), teaching that cultivates desire for its own sake would be a malfunctioning machine (apparatus), apparatuses being defined by the connections they make with other such machines. And we ask at this point: what would Gert Biesta, the arch-critic of *learnification*, say about this moment?

Biesta would likely see this epiphany as an instance of learnification: "the reduction of all that matters educationally to learning" (Biesta, 2012, p.36). In *Against*

Learning, Biesta argues that this reduction "allows for a re-description of the process of education in terms of an economic transaction" (Biesta, 2005, p.58), as a consumer relation, with the learner – and the teacher reconceived as teacher-learner – as consumer. This places responsibility for education onto the learners, who may not know what they need: "the underlying assumption that learners come to education with a clear understanding of what their needs are … forgets that a major reason for engaging in education is precisely to find out what it is that one actually needs" (Biesta, 2005, p.59). Biesta argues that education requires that the teacher "expose students, learners, to otherness and difference, and … challenge them to respond" (Biesta, 2005, p.64). Learning becomes "responding to what is other or different, to what challenges, irritates and disturbs us, rather than as the acquisition of something that we want to possess" (Biesta, 2005, p.62). And, "if teaching is about … asking difficult questions, then … the first responsibility of the teacher is a responsibility … for that which allows the student to be a unique, singular being" (Biesta, 2005, p.63), for "the way in which they respond to the other, to the question of the other, to the other as question" (Biesta, 2005, p.62). It goes without saying that, for Biesta, this task would be impossible for those who are self-taught, like teacher-learners.

We ask, what does this "difficult task" (Biesta, 2005, p.64) of teaching responsibility to the other have to do with desire(s)? In *The Rediscovery of Teaching* (2017), Biesta offers an answer. He writes: "the educational task consists in arousing the desire in another human being for wanting to exist in and with the world in a grown-up way, that is, *as subject*" (Biesta, 2017, p.7). In an echo of *Against Learning*, he argues that subject-ness, or grown-up existence, "acknowledges the alterity [otherness] and integrity [singularity] of what and who is other" (Biesta, 2017, p.8). More than that, it "asks the question whether what we desire is desirable for our own lives and the lives we live with others," which "always poses itself as an *interruption* of our desires" (Biesta, 2017, p.16).

Biesta (2017, p.18) sees the task of the teacher as to interrupt the student's desires and "open up literal and metaphorical spaces where they can establish a relationship with their desires". Education becomes, in a phrase that Biesta borrows from Gayatri Spivak, the "uncoercive rearrangement of desires" (Biesta, 2017, p.18, citing Spivak, 2004, p.526). In this way, Biesta counters "the multiplication of our desires" (Biesta, 2017, p.17), the unleashing of desire that characterises capitalism, with the consumer relation that exemplifies it.

Two

In order to escape the impasse of desire(s), Biesta suggests that a teacher must interrupt the student's desires so that they can establish a relationship with – and perhaps rearrange – their desires. Interruption involves what he calls "suspension" and "sustenance". We quote him at length:

> The key educational challenge … is not simply to tell the … student which of
> their desires are desirable, but for this question to become a living question in

the life of the … student. This requires … opening up literal and metaphorical spaces where the … student can establish a relationship with their desires. … The educational principle here is that of *suspension* – a suspension in time and space … – that provides opportunities for establishing relationships with our desires, make them visible, perceivable, so that we can work on them. … Supporting the student with staying in this difficult middle ground … involves providing *sustenance* … so that the student can endure the difficulty of existing in and with the world.

(Biesta, 2017, p.18)

This passage opens up a number of possibilities. What is the nature of the suspension, what is it to "open up literal and metaphorical spaces" for students? And what is the nature of the sustenance, to "support the student with staying in the difficult middle ground"? And what if subject-ness, or subjectification, were not individual, but collective? To answer these questions, we must actualise these possibilities.

As sometime Deleuzians, we ask: what would Gilles Deleuze, the arch-emancipator, say about Biesta's reading of the educational task – and our suggestive re-reading of it? It is often said that while Deleuze took an interest in numerous disciplines and fields, everything from "mathematics, biology, psychology, political science and anthropology to logic, ethics, painting, literature, metallurgy and the decorative arts" (Bogue, 2007, p.53), he has surprisingly little to say about education or pedagogy. Deleuzians have not been as reticent. The editors of *Deleuze and Education* (2013), Inna Semetsky and Diana Masny, suggest that their volume should be read as a "transversal line of flight along which in Deleuze's spirit, a multiplicity of new concepts are created – concepts that will give us a new sense of teaching *and* learning" (our emphasis: Semetsky & Masny, 2013, p.1). For Deleuze, students must work for their insight, must work with concepts as a creative endeavour, transversally – as readers must do with his works. They must suspend the desire to explain, and *explicate* (unfold) instead (as Biesta would no doubt agree). This unfolding (and the enfolding that is its complement) is not just something that students must do in the classroom through concept-creation; they must work to do it in life as subjects, as Semetsky and Masny suggest:

Deleuze conceptualised the fold as the inside *of* the outside. Education is to be understood broadly as both formal – inside of a classroom – and informal – outside the walls of a typical classroom but inside "a" life, explicated in experience and culture.

(Semetsky & Masny, 2013, p.1; see Deleuze, 1988)

What is the role of the teacher in this process of subjectivisation, of unfolding and enfolding? We know that Deleuze, as a teacher, suspended the desire to explain. He did not directly answer questions asked in lectures. He would pause, then move on without contradicting the questioner, perhaps, offering a slow affirmative *yes*, which acted not as an affirmation of a truth, but as a moment of "exaggerated suspension … And, in that moment of suspension, you suddenly saw all the possibilities of thought surge forth, light and free like birds, liberated from ponderous habits and mediocre objections" (Mengue, 2000, cited in Bogue, 2013, p.25). Although Deleuze chose to lecture rather than workshop concepts, the effect of his *cours magestral* (seminar series) was to give time for concept creation to work through "slow absorption" (Semetsky & Masny, 2013, p.4). A seminar became like a concert, with Deleuze "like a soloist 'accompanied' by everyone else" (Deleuze, 1995, p.86). He would "model the process of thought as an experience, a singular event", claiming that he was unprepared, then he would "pose questions to himself and offer tentative responses. Only after that would he gradually reveal a line of thought leading to a fully fledged conceptual apparatus" (Semetsky & Masny, 2013, p.3). In *Difference and Repetition*, Deleuze sums up the role of the teacher:

> We learn nothing from those who say: "Do as I do." Our only teachers are those who tell us to "do with me," and are able to emit signs to be developed in heterogeneity rather than propose gestures for us to reproduce.
>
> *(Deleuze, 1994, p.23)*

How do we take up the role of the teacher who says "do with me"? What is it to "emit signs to be developed in heterogeneity" (Deleuze, 1994, p.23)? It is to open up spaces for concept-creation through "counter-actualization" (see Deleuze, 1990, pp.150–152), sometimes translated as "vice-diction" (see Deleuze, 1994, pp.189–191). Bogue offers a concise definition: "Vice-diction is the process whereby one identifies and engages the virtual events immanent within one's present world, whereby one 'counter-actualizes' the virtual" (2007, p. 9). Virtuality consists in possibilities that continue to exist even once actualised. Counter-actualisation takes two forms: "the specification of adjunct fields", or the exploration of existing connections to better understand them; and "the condensation of singularities", or experimentation with new connections to transform existing ones (Deleuze, 1994, p.190). Both forms involve a moment of disequilibrium, an unsettling event, in which we sense the virtual and its possibilities, and, as Biesta would say, are able to "acknowledge the alterity and integrity of what and who is other" (Biesta, 2017, p.8). In section three we undertake a collective experiment in counter-actualisation.

Three

It is maybe the third or fourth visit by Adrian Smith, the dancer, to Awhi Whanau, a Māori-medium early childhood centre taking part in the MAPS project. The setting for the encounter is a sunken circular pit, amphitheatre-like, five metres in diameter and slightly off-centre in the main room of Awhi Whanau. The visit begins with a settling in period, its *kaupapa* (ritual) involving *karakia* (prayer), *waiata* (song), *korero* (talking and stories) and other ways of communing. This allows the *tamariki* (children) to get used to Adrian and him to get used to the rhythms of life in the centre: he is becoming less a *manuhiri* (visitor) and more one of the *tangata whenua* (people of the place). New corporate bodies materialise. An emergent curriculum comes into being: imaginative play in corners, in sandpits; collective problem-solving in games, where rules are fleshed out and announced in timely fashion; pictures in print, paint and story – children "becoming-curriculum" (Sellers, 2013). This is no assigned dance class, just a semi-regular exploration open to whomever feels the provocation: wandering-wondering expeditions are undertaken into the far reaches of the garden, and searching experiments in movement appear when *tamariki* come together in the pit, with Adrian and one another, called to shared inquiry.

What follows is a reading of a video clip just over a minute and a half long, from an encounter lasting well over an hour. The clip shows three children with Adrian, towards the end of the session as two children move in and out of the action. They are aged from three to almost five. Adrian leads off, but the lead shifts quickly to and fro between Adrian and the children, as they take up each other's questioning gestures in a dance that is at once careless and careful: a subtle "art of dosages" (Deleuze & Guattari, 1987, p.177). The left column of the table describes the events as they unfold; the column on the right, our thought process. The table is a flow momentarily suspended. It is offered as a testament to the shared inquiry that is our encounter with the video clip.

Creating teaching: moving, dancing, learning, producing *desiring-stutters* …

beginning in the middle

the children begin by watching, standing …

… or have hesitated, standing-paused, watching.
[*a* beginning, an *interruption*-disruption?]

swirling circular movement takes off

it starts flowing when Adrian spins 180°:
new directions

trading flows
responsiveness
mutual play
little talk
messy emergence … dialogue
or
non-verbal dialogue

a tipping point
[literally, as the group splits, the desiring energy *fractures*]

another pause:
Adrian sits down *to wait* …
watchful waiting …

duty to the Other

[**skilful neglect** *opens a space*]

a girl in a red t-shirt leads a new circumnavigation of the space: body leaning
inwards … body following arms, hands, stretched in front
moving in an echo … adapting

trading flows
responsiveness
mutual play
little talk

messy emergence … dialogue
or
non-verbal dialogue

leading/transversal leadership distributed temporally and in
relation to intensities in the assemblage

path-making
going with flows
swinging
exploring the limits of the floor space
AND carpet, toes, feet, air moving: vertical assemblages
AND closeness of body-carpet …
horizontal, close contact

a child goes with his own *desires*
[remembers dance activity from previous session exploring a giraffe story]
… animals in pairs … he *plays* the tail, in imagination

stable/unstable *assemblages*

a *rhythm*: bodies affecting each other …
bodies of all kinds – visible and invisible

the feeling of textures

a child goes with his own *desires*

intensities; tipping points

Dance makes visible the social drama

other children release turbulent flows,
drawing upon repertoires from everyday life:
jogging,
     jumping,
          leaning,
               swinging-out,
                    breakdancing …

a mimicking of sleeping, while moving in figure 8s

… centrifugal forces in play as the children lean into the flow and work the space

      … pushing boundaries – the limits of the body.

duty to the Other

     … a minor politics of alterity & integrity

[@ 60% point …]
the lead is taken up by one of the girls stopping and
creating a foot-planted star stretch,

     lunging forward … Adrian picks it up
a moment or two later … the mood shifts to stationary stances
and feet-planted movements: stretching, reaching …

collectivity:
collective agency
a group subject

     a *group* subject
collective agency

collective subjectification

now bodies are upside down, as Adrian
picks up on eye
contact made with a child

     more breakdancing: a circular movement
with one arm as a pivot and
body horizontally leaning, feet moving,
creating a circular machine

curiosity on the part of
those who've been lurking … now joining in …

between bodies,
under and around and moving through, now between …

the legs of Adrian …
one child transfixed
… joining in … more playful responses.

[materials!] string: for our
boy-becoming-swinging-tail-becoming-tethered-rope …
moving vertical structures

the feeling of textures
assembling lines, *escaping*
lines of flight

a headstand from Adrian …
slow collisions … structure eventually pulled down by "tail": at first, turning
the conjunction of bodies; then, pulling it further outwards to the point of
toppling …

intensities; tipping points
literal and metaphorical spaces
literal and metaphorical *lines*

child mimics headstand *adapts*

difference repeated differently
production of *desiring-stutters*

collectivity:
collective agency
a group subject

a *group* subject
collective agency
collectivity

d e s i r i n g – s t u t t e r s
c o l l e c t i v e s u b j e c t i f i c a t i o n

Four

We began this chapter with a reading of an event in which teachers testified that they had let go of control of their personal and institutional power in a necessary disruption of their teaching practice. But we questioned whether this disruption, this learning experience for them as teacher-learners, was really an interruption in Biesta's sense, an "uncoercive rearrangement of [their] desires" (Biesta, 2017, p.18). By way of contrast, we shared an encounter at Awhi Whanau that prompted shared emergent inquiry that did indeed represent a genuine interruption in Biesta's sense. The teacher in that case did not shift pedagogical responsibility onto the children, he opened up a "literal and metaphorical space" (Biesta, 2017, p.18) for the children to effect an inquiry into their subjectivity. There was thus letting go, not only of teacherly control, and the traditional aligned curriculum, and even the dance canon. However, there was no letting go of the responsibility to suspend time and space, and to sustain students (plural) in the "middle ground" (Biesta, 2017, p.18). What emerged in the artist-teacher teacher-artist experimentation – and in the MAPS project as a whole – were "desiring-stutters" (Matapo & Roder, in press), or figural "glitches" (see O'Sullivan, 2009), that is, transversal co-created movements in a collective body made possible by a "pedagogy of affect" (Albrecht-Crane & Slack, 2003):

> We know nothing about a body until we know what it can do, in other words, what its affects are, how they can or cannot enter into composition with other affects, with the affects of another body, either to destroy that body or to be destroyed by it, either to exchange actions and passions with it or to join with it in composing a more powerful body.
>
> *(Deleuze & Guattari, 1987, p.256)*

This dance of affective composition was a playful, bodily, collective, disciplined and respectful encounter, rich in transversal movements, unfolding and enfolding, counter-actualising the pedagogical moment, producing new subjectivities, immanent in the assemblage of the spatial, temporal and material conditions of the setting.

Deleuze and Guattari caution those who risk "flight from flight" (Deleuze & Guattari, 1987, p.227, citing Blanchot, 1971, p.232), where everything opens up and becomes experiment that can be quickly captured once more by controlling desires operating in ourselves and in institutions. Letting go is just the first step in interrupting and more importantly in acknowledging other ways of existing, creating and ordering worlds, thinking differently of one's relations both to oneself and others.

Acknowledgement

We would like to thank the staff and children of Awhi Whanau Early Childhood Centre, along with members of the MAPS team, including Adrian Smith community dance artist, and researchers Christopher Naughton, David Lines and Jacoba Matapo.

References

Albrecht-Crane, C., & Slack, J. D. (2003). Towards a pedagogy of affect. In J. D. Slack (Ed.), *Animations (of Deleuze and Guattari)* (pp.191–216). New York: Peter Lang.

Biesta, G. J. J. (2005). Against learning. *Nordisk Pedagogik, 24*(1), 70–82.

Biesta, G. J. J. (2012). Giving teaching back to education: Responding to the disappearance of the teacher. *Phenomenology & Practice, 6*(2), 35–49.

Biesta, G. J. J. (2017). *The rediscovery of teaching*. New York: Routledge.

Blanchot, M. (1971). *L'amitie*. Paris: Gallimard.

Bogue, R. (2007). *Deleuze's way: Essays in transverse ethics and aesthetics*. London: Ashgate.

Bogue, R. (2013). *Deleuze on cinema*. New York: Routledge.

Deleuze, G. (1983). *Anti-Oedipus: Capitalism and schizophrenia* (R. Hurley, M. Seem & H. R. Lane, trans.). Minneapolis: University of Minnesota Press.

Deleuze, G. (1988). Foldings, or the inside of thought (subjectivation). In G. Deleuze, (S. Hand, trans.), *Foucault* (pp.94–123). Minneapolis: University of Minnesota Press.

Deleuze, G. (1990). *The logic of sense* (C. V. Boundas, ed.; M. Lester, C. Stivale, trans.). New York: Continuum Press.

Deleuze, G. (1994). *Difference and repetition* (P. Patton, trans.). New York: Columbia University Press.

Deleuze, G. (1995). *Negotiations 1972–1990* (M. Joughin, trans.). New York: Columbia University Press.

Deleuze, G., & Guattari, F. (1987). *A thousand plateaus: Capitalism and schizophrenia* (B. Massumi, trans.). Minneapolis: University of Minnesota Press.

Matapo, J., & Roder, J. (in press). Affective pedagogy, affective research, affect and becoming arts-based-education research(er). In L. Knight & L. Cutcher (Eds.), *Arts, research, education: Connections and directions*. London: Springer.

Mengue, P. (2000). 'En homage a Gilles Deleuze: Vincennes, une voix, un personage proustien…' In Y. Beaubatie (Ed.), *Tombeau de Gilles Deleuze* (pp.49–56). Tulle: Mille Sources.

O'Sullivan, S. (2009). From stuttering and stammering to the diagram: Deleuze, Bacon and contemporary art practice. *Deleuze Studies, 3*(2), 247–258.

Sellers, M. (2013). *Young children becoming curriculum: Deleuze, Te Whāriki and curricular understandings*. Abingdon: Routledge.

Semetsky, I., & Masny, D. (2013). Introduction: Unfolding Deleuze. In I. Semetsky & D. Masny (Eds.), *Deleuze and education* (pp.1–17). Edinburgh: Edinburgh University Press.

Spivak, G. C. (2004). Righting wrongs. *The South Atlantic Quarterly, 103*(2), 523–581.

14

WEAK SUBJECTS

On art's art of forgetting—an interview with John Baldacchino by Gert Biesta

John Baldacchino and Gert Biesta

GB: Perhaps we can start with a central and innovative concept in your work, that of unlearning. Could you explain what this concept is about— and perhaps also what it is not about, so that readers can grasp what is distinctive about it and what kind of distinction you want to make with it?

JB: Dewey once said that "he is lucky who does not find that in order to make progress, in order to go ahead intellectually, he does not have to unlearn much of what he learned in school" (Dewey, 1997, p.47). Nietzsche said something similar, arguing that "the philosopher in Germany has more and more to unlearn how to be 'pure science': and it is to precisely that end that Schopenhauer as a human being can serve as an example" (Nietzsche, 1997, p.137).

The whole idea of unlearning is neither a quip against schooling nor a dismissal of disciplines and their boundaries. In Dewey's case this comes from his preoccupation with the debate on schooling which was then emerging when he wrote *Experience and Education* in 1938. In Nietzsche, we find a slightly more elaborate way of going about the educational value of philosophy, which to him has to start from giving autonomy to philosophy itself in order to begin to engage with it. Then he was a young man and pretty skeptical about his own education.

Both philosophers, in their different contexts, are suggesting that we unlearn what has often been deemed to be a heteronomous imperative by which the school or a discipline would be adhered to. More so, they are suggesting that we cut loose from what has often been assumed to have enough canonical power by which it sets an order of knowledge without which we could neither learn, nor do philosophy.

GB: Would you say that this is still an "issue" in our times?

JB: Yes. Without regurgitating what Dewey and Nietzsche said, I would indeed argue that the context in which they are suggesting forms of unlearning is one that should be familiar to us. This is especially so in terms of the recurring argument between those who see education as a foundational process that operates on canonical lines, and those whose approach to education is open to emergent needs. In the latter case, human experience cannot be simply ignored.

Dewey would not come out clearly on one formula or another. As a pragmatist, he kept his approach open, where plasticity and disposition offered a way for humans to grasp what life throws at them. This emerged from his approach to Darwin, where survival is not sourced in brutal power, but in a disposition to adapt and creatively find those exploratory and experimental skills by which we take risks, learn, and unlearn the ways of survival as a form of creativity (see Dewey 1958; Baldacchino 2014).

I find clear parallels with Nietzsche's appreciation of Schopenhauer and how he, like Dewey, appreciated the contingent nature of life. Through the example of art in its tragic form, Nietzsche urges us to take ownership of adaptability and survival. He stresses a sense of autonomy which he calls a will to power, with power understood as one's ability to assert one's freedom and intelligence creatively.

GB: What would unlearning look like pedagogically?

JB: Pedagogically, unlearning implies that students first accept the notion of mistake and error, as they embrace accident as an opportunity to break into the unknown. Secondly unlearning is crucial in how representation takes an artistic form by which students unlearn what they come with into the studio—that is, their presumed image of things and what they should be—so that they would then understand what is in front of them. The crucial point of unlearning is how this process of *representation* (which is very different from *imitation*) allows students to critique and articulate what they see, so that reality becomes something they *make*.

Unavoidably, unlearning presents us with a paradox. It directs us to two opposite paths. One path is that of the pedagogy of unlearning *in* art. This makes *another* case for *education through the arts*. It advocates for the arts in schools.

However, I would also argue that the case for art as unlearning must move away from a schooled pedagogical dimension. From art's intrinsic dimension— what some might call art's immanence—unlearning makes a case for a distinction between art and education. Thus, while it makes a case for art in schools, the case for unlearning also roots for art's autonomy, often taking the opposite direction.

Yet the paradox of unlearning runs on the same horizon. Both directions are moved by the need for art's autonomy. However, while unlearning as a case for art education would warrant a dialectical take on the School, from within art's autonomous perspective, unlearning as it is engaged artistically, moves outside the jurisdiction of the School and what is often camouflaged under the pretext of *learning*. Outside the jurisdiction of learning, art expresses what it does best: claim autonomy so it could function in a heteronomous world—which is where we go back to make a case for unlearning as a case for art education.

GB: There are two other concepts that are important in your thinking as well: the notions of weakness and reality. Again, can you explain what these concepts are about and what their relationship to the idea of unlearning is?

JB: I would begin with the triangulation of reality and weakness with illusion. This requires an arts perspective where many (including myself) often refer to art as a "making." The identification of art with making follows on from the notion of *poiein* (in Ancient Greek, to make, produce) that gave us *poiesis*, artistic poetry. A number of art theorists and arts educators still insist on emphasizing the process of art making. They argue that to regard a work of art as an end-product would ignore aspects of learning, development, and creativity. Yet to identify art with making is not immune from backfiring on instrumentalist grounds. When art is entered into the realms of learning, development, and creativity, there is a good chance of reducing it to *process* as a measureable instrument.

As I have argued in *Art's Way Out* (Baldacchino, 2012, p.89), art cannot be misconstrued as an act of learning. This equivalence would essentialize art and learning as constructs of a foundational reality. More so, it upholds reality as a ground, as an *a priori* foundation, sustaining the myth that without a strong reality, there would be no meaning in the world.

Far from being equivalent to learning, art must be understood from where the ground gives way to a horizon, as Laclau (2005) has put it. On this horizon, we engage with the infinite diversity of interpretations that the arts give. Through art's hermeneutic power, we engage with the world interpretively. This in turn provides us with an approach to what I am here calling a *weak reality*—that is, a reality that recedes in the background of the multiplicity of possibilities that make it.

Reality and illusion come in this triangulation from the need to recognize art's paradox; more precisely, to recognize art's *aporia*. As an aporia, art signals directions that both confront but also run away from each other. This is how an aporia works. This inherent plurality of dispositions in art's nature enables human beings to engage in the dialectic between what is existent and what is real.

In the arts, we talk about beauty. Though we know that beauty is real, one never meets beauty strolling down the main street on a Sunday morning. Rather, one comes across beautiful weather, highlighting a beautiful sense of living, alongside beautiful things and beautiful people listening to beautiful sounds and responding to beautiful objects. This is where philosophers come in. They ask whether one needs to extrapolate beauty as *the reality* of how we feel about what we are or have. But this leads to other questions: Do we need to extrapolate the real from what we experience in our existence? Aren't the real and existence philosophical constructs that explain what, in effect, comes from human history and experience?

How one answers these questions determines how one orders the reality and/ or existence of everything. This is a very important question. When we talk about learning we often remain stuck within the notion of a Platonic idea, where we assume that we could extrapolate learning from a foundational construction of reality. We also know that art is very susceptible to this approach.

However, in art we find a way out of this quandary as in both the process of making art (that "art" that makes an object) and in what we call "art" (the object itself); the real is qualified by our aesthetic capacity to engage in illusions that would in turn allow us to transcend what we experience. This transcendence, this suspension of what is certain, provides us with a way of critiquing the world, by which we unlearn those certainties beyond which we could see other possibilities.

GB: What kind of notion of "weakness" would follow from that?

JB: As I have explained in *Art's Way Out* and papers that followed, weakness does not pertain to power as understood politically or anthropologically. The claim for weakness comes from the conclusion that neither reality nor thought could be assumed as strong *a priori* foundations. In asserting "strong" realities we relay our freedom and intelligence to the ideological certainty of the School, the Church, the Party, the Corporation, or the State.

To summarize, I would say that as I make an argument for reality (as a horizon of diverse possibilities) and illusion (as art's critical transcendence), I am qualifying reality as *weak reality* (see Baldacchino, 2012, pp. 92ff). In a weak reality, I seek possibilities from the multiplicity by which art allows us to lay claim to truth by means of the infinitely diverse forms of expression and interpretation that art brings. In the constant flow of art as an occurrence, we understand how we can cope in a world that is unpredictable and where far from being universal, reality emerges in the particular and singular aspects of what we do and live.

Turning to education, my question is: Are we in any way allowing our students to engage with reality by regarding the role of thought as being weak, diverse, kenotic, and ultimately open? Or are we educating generations of students who are expected to be certain in what they do, and where they always have to give us "correct" answers, because to doubt, err, let alone fail, is considered unacceptable by the School and the State that sustains it?

GB: I read your work as a critique of a particular conception and practice of education. Can you say a bit more about the conception and practice of education that you are critical of and what the main thrust of your criticism is?

JB: In itself, education must not be expected to give us a conscience—social or otherwise. If it were to do so, education would immediately trap the person into a supposition of a strong foundational reality. Likewise, if we are to make education a tool for liberation, we must find a way of turning education onto itself in order to negate its own moral and social precepts. This is because to claim to liberate with an equally strong assertion of thought and action would leave no space for the multiplicity of interpretations that are the prerequisite for a broad education.

Those who offer a wider view of education by keeping away from social developmental and constructivist views remind us that education cannot be reduced to a teleological project. I can mention a few, starting with your own work (Biesta 2006 and 2014) as well as the work of Jacques Rancière (1991) and Maxine Greene (1973 and 1988). In these works I find an honest and clear rejection of the questions that are still assumed to be canonical in educational theory and philosophy.

Speaking from the perspective of the relationship between art and education, I would also cite those arts practitioners who dwell on education, and who have argued that education is seriously compromised and could ultimately become a non-question when posed on assumptions which, *a priori,* already frame the educational act as either moral or social (see amongst others, Charles Garoian, 2013; Dennis Atkinson, 2011; jan jagodzinski et al., 2017; and again Maxine Greene, 2001).

Education remains and retains a central position in what, over many years, has become a priority in the machinations of the State. People forget that while education was for a long time considered as an offshoot of other disciplines, it spent many years in colleges of teacher training, and while we seem to think that education was always on politicians' minds, the position of Secretary of State for Education in the United States, to take one example, is a very recent addition (the first was appointed in 1979 by Jimmy Carter).

Likewise, what education is, and what it was a few decades ago is worth looking at, in terms of how it gained centrality now that the School has reached the apex of its institutionalized history. We now need to acknowledge that when we make a case for education we need to distinguish between the discipline of education, and what society has *learned* to accept as the institution of education.

My qualm is not with education as such, but with how the educative, that which we engage with as a human way of living and growing, has become embroiled in what Dewey wanted to avert us from: an illiberal world that finds itself stuck in the promise of certainty while we are slowly being deprived from our inability to unlearn what was ingrained in us within and around a schooled society.

GB: It is one thing to be against something, but it is another thing to be for something. You have already explained the key concepts of your thinking—unlearning, weakness, and reality. What kind of view or conception of education do you endorse and can you indicate why you do so, why this conception is important?

JB: Someone could object and tell me that we have long resolved Descartes's dualistic world of mind and body, and yet here I am still talking about reality and existence. Others would say that we tried Open Schools and a myriad of other models, and yet here we are still stuck with the School as the only place where we effectively teach our children, whether this happens in a building that is socially or privately owned, or whether this is done with siblings at home or with strangers in the classroom.

So, a question that would supplement yours beautifully would be whether indeed there could be an alternative and if so why aren't we speaking of it? And indeed, if there is no alternative, then why are we still doubting the very foundation of what characterizes modern society—schooling for all, entrenched in law and celebrated as a revolutionary concept?

The case for education is more often than not made as a way of asserting the certainties and the strength of foundational principles which, depending on the person, they would either find their satisfaction in ethical values of family, state, and faith; or indeed in the opposite argument for a liberal approach where the space for diversity will secure an ethical order which still preserves what we have.

Yet this betrays a failure in education itself. Upon insisting on learning—whether didactically or experimentally—the School insists on teaching us *how* to learn. This teleological form of teaching is what taught learning is all about. On the other hand, to teach unlearning is anathema. To unlearn has no "how," as otherwise it becomes learnt and therefore it neuters itself. This is what often happens in settings that claim to be critical and child-centered: as they grew, children chose to forget because at school their interest was simply aroused by forms of taught learning but were never placed within the realms of what happens.

GB: So perhaps education has progressed less than is often claimed?

JB: I do indeed believe that beyond the pedagogical advances that we have gained through schooling, we are still stuck in a Platonic assumption of recollecting specks from a foundational reality (see Baldacchino, 2015a, 2015b, and 2017). Many would contend that this is an exaggeration. Yet when I look at how teaching has evolved, I still find that it has not resolved Meno's paradox.

In the *Meno* (Plato, 2002) Socrates claims to help a slave-child remember what his eternal soul (all-knowing intelligence) always knew. Yet it is very evident that Socrates is teaching the slave-child how to learn. Socrates, in other words, is teaching a child to remember. The child seems to be at the center of this process, but we know that when Socrates misleads the child, the child falters. The child is expected to learn from the mistake and recall what he forgot. Yet the error is procedural, in that the child is always led to "realize" and follow a taught process. In defense of Socrates one could argue that it is the process that matters, rather than the result. Yet the point is that Socrates is teaching one how to learn, and that goes against the premise of his argument for anamnesis, which radically goes against a pedagogy of learning.

Contrary to a taught process, unlearning reasserts a willed form of forgetfulness that is twice removed from the Platonic assumption of anamnesis, just as it needs to move twice away from the developmental-constructivist assumption of "discovery" which we often pose in schools as a liberal counter argument for didacticism (see Baldacchino, 2013 and 2015a). It is important to clarify that when it comes to unlearning, this cannot be taught as a way of relearning. Rather, unlearning rejects a strong reality whose ground is supposed to be critically discovered, socially learnt, or methodically accepted by the School.

So, you may well ask: Is this your alternative to schooling? My answer is that to speak of an alternative to schooling is to re-assert education as it is. We need a degree of methodological suspension, where we begin to look at education in a different way—just as Ivan Illich and Jacques Rancière have done.

Speaking of Rancière, I agree with you and Charles Bingham when in your *Jacques Rancière: Education, truth, emancipation* (Bingham & Biesta, 2010), you critique the confusion of Jacotot's ignorant schoolmaster with a child-centered approach, not to mention those who read *The Ignorant Schoolmaster* (Rancière, 1991) as a Rancièrian approach to critical pedagogy that is somehow aligned with Paulo Freire's. This approach is not only wrong in terms of theoretical confusion (as you rightly demonstrate, for example in Biesta, 2017) but I see it as a confirmation that education theory has become excessively canonical, especially in its liberal and progressive claims.

Beyond an alternative that mirrors what we have, we need to think outside the parameters that we have received as education has become increasingly institutionalized while society has become more and more schooled. Yet as I say this, Illich (2000) has long confirmed that the real need is not to counter schooling with another form of schooling. In many ways, what we need at this stage is a shift which cannot offer an alternative, but which seeks something totally different, almost unrelated to education as we know it. But as yet, I am not seeing this anywhere, not even in technology.

GB: We have explored questions of education and unlearning in a more general sense, but the real focus of your work is on the arts. How do you see the connection(s) between your views on education and the arts? Does this also amount to a theory of art education, or would you say that your actual interest is in the educative "force"—if we might use that word—of art itself?

JB: My initial approach to unlearning did not come from philosophy. As in many other things related to education and philosophy, I came to this concept from art practice in the studio, and the practice of teaching art in the classroom.

As an arts practitioner, I dislike the artificial hierarchy that educational policy makers and curricular engineers often construct along the line of experience, learning, education, and schooling. While this is often presented as the rational way by which we get an education, everyone knows it to be problematic. Its assumptions—starting with experience and learning—are often tied to a developmental certainty that fails both in terms of its own measure, and more so in terms of experience, where in later life, we find ourselves in need of unlearning what the School taught us as younger persons.

But there is another aspect of unlearning which emerged in my own experience of teaching art. In art lessons, both where the objective is to engage children with forms of creativity beyond number and word, but also in higher levels of education where art is taught as a discipline, the idea of unlearning became central to my pedagogical approach. This came to me as an epiphany when I realized how, wrongly, child art is viewed as a programmed succession that is somehow followed in the history of art itself.

You will find many theorists and also many teachers who attribute, or try to find, parallels between naïve forms of art that emerged throughout human history and child art. I have come across theories of development which almost always relate this growth in an individual to a sequence that seems to find parallels in history.

Yet if we turn this upside down, and instead look at art history as a reflection of how human beings approach the world in their daily yet complex ways, we find that far from a preordained developmental pattern (let alone a romanticized view of "diverse intelligences"), art history reveals something which I would call a "mannerist" approach, a mannerist pedagogy.

This mannerist approach comes across like a form of willed forgetting, in that it rejects the canon, its influence and progress. Instead, we come across artists who do not seek progression. Their art suspends the meaning of past, present, and future. This suspension is sought for a reason. It is prompted by a need to find other forms of renewal that would render progression irrelevant.

GB: Bringing art and education into the here and now then?

JB: Indeed. To seek new ways of thinking the present in a context that is alien to the immediate is a method by which we could make sense of what we currently do, and through which we realize that what we have learnt from the foundational strong realities that were imposed on us, must be broken back by a sense of appropriation.

Those who appropriate the present are us. We have suspended the imperatives of influence, the anxieties that they bring to us in a future that is still unknown, and instead we seek to regain our place within art's promise. I would argue that the same is done with regards to the loss of the anticipation of being, where as we become accustomed to new technology, we use it to seek what came before it through the tools that we use and create (see Illich, 2001).

To use what appears as a simplistic example, is how we have now gone back to analog sound and somehow became tired of digital. To my mind, the value of analog is very close to that of the manner by which in art we suspend history, progress, and influence, and instead we claim to roam back and forth, in order to regain what we have lost in art's promise. If this is not a perfect example of unlearning, I don't know what is.

GB: Can you expand on this notion of a Mannerist pedagogy, helping readers to understand mannerism, pedagogy, and its connection?

JB: If there is such a thing as *reassurance*, this must be offered as a *manner*. As both *a way of doing* but also a *demeanor*, a manner may well suggest a *modus operandi* that could appear to be moved by an ultimate plan. Yet one could invert this and argue that as a demeanor, the manner is just an excuse to move away from acceptability. Taking a sideways view of the expected, the manner could be a vehicle that rejects those central assumptions over which education is regarded as something equivalent to learning. To put it bluntly, the manner recommends a rejection of anything that we learnt to expect.

Those who believe that learning is premised on progress and growth would rather pejoratively consider Mannerism as a form of unlearning. Here I want to borrow the notion of *maniera* as it was attributed to a phase in Western art found somewhere between the end of the Renaissance and the emergence of Baroque. However, conceptually, Mannerism recurs throughout the history of art, as found in late Hellenism and in the origin of Modernism, as prefigured in Symbolism and Surrealism (Hauser, 1965).

For those who may be rusty on their art history, one could approach Mannerism by putting alongside each other works like Leonardo da Vinci's *Last Supper* (1495–98) and that by Tintoretto (1592–94), or Raphael's *Visitation* (1517) and that by El Greco (1604–14). Far from just a change in "style," in Tintoretto and El Greco we find a radical rejection of the certainty by which art was supposed to reach its ultimate perfection in the Renaissance. If we were to capture the idea of art as unlearning (as a rejection of re-learning), then we should begin to approach the fallacy of progression through Mannerism, where in refusing to accept a linear kind of artistic evolution, artists confirm how art history is far more staggered and paradoxical.

While the Renaissance is wrongly regarded as a resurgence of the scientific precision and skill of the Classical Greeks and Romans which was somewhat "lost" in the Middle Ages, what we find in Mannerism is a rejection of this notion of progressive direction.

What is often seen as a decadence of reason in periods like Mannerism is actually a recognition of the other senses by which we understand our human existence. The social historian and philosopher of art Arnold Hauser captures this when he says that "the artists and writers of the mannerist period were not only aware of the insoluble contradictions of life, they actually emphasized and intensified them; they preferred reiterating and drawing attention to them to screening or concealing them" (Hauser, 1965, p.15). In Mannerism, art appears to decline vis-à-vis what was regarded as canonical in the Renaissance. Yet in this apparent decline one finds a perpetual sense of ascendancy. Far from disparaging, art's *maniera* regales us with a sense of liberation.

This is why Mannerism seems to recur in history. With the onset of Modernism, the Impressionists were rejected from the Academy as they appeared crude. Picasso and others were regarded as close to being decadent. Yet these instances show a willed unlearning that is conscious and that has nothing to do with a lack of skills or a decadence in civilization.

Here an approach to education that has moved away from the instrumentalized assumptions of schooling finds itself rearticulated by what Nietzsche identifies as "something completely incapable of being educated" (Nietzsche, 1997, p.130). Only through art's art of forgetting, understood in the Mannerist way of rejecting the possibility of re-learning, could we begin to understand how an uneducable possibility could ever find its points of departure.

GB: Thank you very much.

References

Atkinson, D. (2011). *Art, Equality and Learning: Pedagogies Against the State.* Rotterdam: Sense.

Baldacchino, J. (2012). *Art's Way Out: Exit Pedagogy and the Cultural Condition.* Rotterdam: Sense Publishers.

Baldacchino, J. (2013). Willed Forgetfulness: The Arts, Education and the Case for Unlearning. *Studies in Philosophy and Education, 32*(4), 415–430.

Baldacchino, J. (2014). *John Dewey: Liberty and the Pedagogy of Disposition.* The Netherlands: Springer.

Baldacchino, J. (2015a). ART ± EDUCATION: The Paradox of the Ventriloquist's Soliloquy. *Sisyphus: Journal of Education, 3*(1), 55–71.

Baldacchino, J. (2015b). Art's Foreignness as an "Exit Pedagogy". In T.E. Lewis and M.J. Laverty (Eds.), *Art's Teachings, Teaching's Art: Philosophical, Critical, and Educational Musings* (pp.19–31). Dordrecht: Springer.

Baldacchino, J. (2017). Art's Ped(ago)gies: Education Is Not Art. Art Is Not Education. In j. jagodzinski (Ed.), *What is Art Education? Essays after Deleuze & Guattari* (pp.163–236). London: Palgrave Macmillan.

Biesta, G.J.J. (2006). *Beyond Learning: Democratic Education for a Human Future.* Boulder, CO: Paradigm.

Biesta, G.J.J. (2014). *The Beautiful Risk of Education.* London: Routledge.

Biesta, G.J.J. (2017). Don't Be Fooled by Ignorant Schoolmasters: On the Role of the Teacher in Emancipatory Education. *Policy Futures in Education. 15*(1), 52–57.

Bingham, C., & Biesta, G.J.J. (2010). *Jacques Rancière: Education, Truth, Emancipation.* London: Bloomsbury.

Dewey, J. (1958). *Experience and Nature.* Mineola, NY: Dover.

Dewey, J. (1997). *Experience and Education.* New York: Touchstone.

Garoian, C.R. (2013). *The Prosthetic Pedagogy of Art. Embodied Research and Practice.* Albany: State University of New York Press.

Greene, M. (1973). *Teacher as Stranger. Educational Philosophy for the Modern Age.* Belmont, CA: Wadsworth Publishing.

Greene, M. (1988). *The Dialectic of Freedom.* New York: Teachers College Press.

Greene, M. (2001). *Variations on a Blue Guitar. The Lincoln Center Institute Lectures on Aesthetic Education.* New York: Teachers College Press.

Hauser, A. (1965). *Mannerism. The Crisis of the Renaissance and the Origin of Modern Art.* New York: Alfred A. Knopf.

Illich, I. (2000). *Deschooling Society.* New York: Marion Boyars.

Illich, I. (2001). *Tools for Conviviality.* New York: Marion Boyars.

jagodzinski, j. (Ed.). (2017). *What Is Art Education? After Deleuze and Guattari.* London: Palgrave Macmillan.

Laclau, E. (2005). *On Populist Reason.* London: Verso.

Nietzsche, F. (1997). Schopenhauer as Educator. In D. Breazeale (Ed.), R.J. Hollingdale (trans.), *Untimely Meditations.* Cambridge: Cambridge University Press.

Plato. (2002). Meno. In *Five Dialogues* (pp. 58–92). Indianapolis, IN: Hackett Classics.

Rancière, J. (1991). *The Ignorant Schoolmaster: Five Lessons in Emancipation.* Palo Alto, CA: Stanford University Press.

15

WALKING THE MUSEUM

Art, artists and pedagogy reconsidered

Gert Biesta

Introduction

How should one conduct oneself in a museum? How, in other words, should one 'walk a museum'? This question came to my mind when I was reading the chapters that make up this book and was pondering a possible response – a critical reflection, as the saying often goes. I'm not a frequent visitor to museums but have become better at it, perhaps having gained a bit more patience over the years, but also having become better at the visual, at looking and seeing (despite the fact that I'm fairly colour-blind and therefore always wonder whether I might be missing something). One of my favourite museums is the National Portrait Gallery in Edinburgh. It is relatively small, so not too intimidating or too difficult to navigate, and although it focuses on only one 'genre', that of the portrait, it does so in ways that are always exciting and engaging. What I particularly like about portraits – although it is a feature of all art that seeks to represent – is their double quality, that is, the fact that portraits both *depict* and *express*. Portraits are clearly about something or, more precisely, about someone, so a portrait always raises the question of the relationship between the portrait and the one being portrayed. This is the question of accuracy and perhaps also the question of truth (see Derrida, 1987). But at the same time a portrait is always more than 'just' a depiction, if the latter is possible in the first place. So there is always also the question of what the portrait is trying to say or trying to show, which may also be understood as a question of what the portrait is trying to say to me, is trying to show me, and is asking of me (see Biesta, 2017 for more on these themes).

'Walk this way'

Walking the museum can be done in the way in which some tourists travel significant distances to see what they already knew they would see there: the Eiffel Tower,

Big Ben, Times Square, the Leaning Tower of Pisa, the Forbidden City, and so on. This is a seeing of what in a sense is already familiar (something that in the age of the abundance of the image has become much more difficult to stay away from). Walking the museum can also be a form of shopping: 'I like this', 'I don't like that', 'this appeals to me', 'that doesn't appeal to me'. Such shopping goes fairly quickly, though is not necessarily insignificant, as one can never be sure of traces that might resurface (much) later. And there is also a way of walking a museum that looks more respectful and more attentive (although it can also just be slow). My walking of the portrait gallery is probably a combination of these approaches. Sometimes there is the simple joy of recognition, of the 'I've-seen-that-before-but-am-now-seeing-it-with-my-own-eyes'. There are also portraits that appeal immediately, that generate pleasure, so to speak, and portraits that do the opposite, that seem to 'have' nothing and 'do' nothing. There are portraits that intrigue, that kind of speak to me. Portraits where I begin to wonder what is going on, technically – 'How did they do that?' – and aesthetically – 'What is happening here?' And there are portraits that, more than just catching my eye, seem to have caught *me*. That I do not just *want* to go back to but feel I *need* to go back to, which sometimes leads to some difficult manoeuvring, particularly on a busy day.

Reading the chapters in this book has felt quite similar to walking the museum, and readers may recognise some of this in their own reading. There are chapters that are familiar, which is helpful because they give a sense of orientation, of knowing where one is. There are chapters that immediately appeal, and chapters that do the opposite, and not always for the same reasons. There are chapters that intrigue, that make me curious about what's going on, about what the authors are trying to do – and sometimes it's just a phrase or a sentence that does this. And there are chapters that seem to have caught me, that keep nagging, so to speak, where I feel I need to go back and have another proper look.

What makes my own reading a little more complicated is the fact that many of the chapters are also portraits. They portray thinkers and thoughts, writers and writing, and I cannot deny that next to Deleuze and Guattari, but also, for example, Whitehead, Green, Lyotard and Merleau-Ponty, I am one of the people being portrayed in several of the chapters. This not only puts me in a privileged position vis-à-vis the chapters, but also in a slightly awkward one, because it delivers the question of accuracy right on my doorstep, so to speak, even if I am not sure whether the one being portrayed is automatically the best judge of the portrait. It would be disingenuous, however, to pretend that the question of accuracy doesn't exist, so let me start with a few observations on this, mainly to get this question 'out of the way' and focus on the far more important issue of what the chapters in this book help us to see about art, artists and pedagogy.

'Every picture tells a story'

As may have been clear from my own chapter in this book, my main concern with contemporary educational discourses and practices, including those that focus on the arts and/in education, is that they counter stifling top-down approaches to education – the ones that turn schools into exam factories and that are currently driving the global league-table industry – with expressivist conceptions and practices that put the 'learner'[1] at the centre of the educational process and that seek to provide opportunities for 'learners' to construct their own knowledge and understanding and to creatively express themselves. I have nothing against expression as such, but I do think that education that just seeks to promote opportunities for expression without asking the more difficult question about the *quality* of what is being expressed, does not take its responsibility seriously enough.

The point, though, is that in the past this responsibility has often been taken up in moralising and authoritarian ways, where it was seen as the task of the educator or teacher to decide for the one being educated what right, good and correct ways of thinking and being were. The response to such authoritarian forms of education, which are not interested in the possibility for students to exist as subjects in their own right, has generally been to do away with the position and identity of the teacher altogether. Thus we have ended up in a universe of learning and learners with teachers as facilitators of such learning, often without asking what the learning is supposed to be for, or about (other than producing measurable test scores that can be used for identifying who is better and who is best; see Biesta, 2010).

Rather than seeing the work of the teacher as telling students what they should think and how they should be, I see the work of the teacher as 'interruptive', that is, bringing the question of the quality of what is being expressed, or, in other words, the desirability of what is being desired, into the lives of students, *not* as a question that can be answered once and for all, but as a question that is worth asking in each new situation, as a question that is worth carrying with oneself throughout one's life. To carry this question with oneself, as a 'living question', is what it means to try to exist in and with the world in a 'grown up' way, always 'measuring' one's own desires (including one's desire for identity) against the desires of others, always asking whether what I desire is desirable for my own life, and my life with others on a planet with limited capacity for fulfilling all our desires.

Such a way of thinking about 'grown-up-ness' has nothing to do with development towards 'grown-up-ness', which also means that 'grown-up-ness' is not a state one can achieve. 'Grown-up-ness' rather denotes a way of trying to be 'at home in the world', to use Hannah Arendt's phrase (see Arendt, 1994, pp.307–308). Being at home in the world denotes the middle ground between world-destruction – where we pursue our desires without any consideration for the world, social or natural, in which our desires can become real – and self-destruction – where, in meeting a world that offers resistance to what we desire, we withdraw from the world, and thus from the possibility to exist in the world, as subject.

What is at stake here educationally is neither about teaching as facilitation, nor about teaching as empowerment – it is more akin to disarmament (see Masschelein, 1997) – and also not about teaching as emancipation in the way in which it is understood in traditions inspired by neo-Marxism and the Frankfurt School. It is teaching as interruption: the interruption of desires, not in order to overcome desires but to figure out which desires are going to help in our attempts at existing in and with the world in a grown-up way, and which desires are going to hinder us in that task. It is, as Spivak puts it, about education as the 'uncoercive rearrangement of desires' (Spivak, 2004, p.526). Such teaching requires suspension – providing time, space and forms to meet our desires and work on them – and sustenance – support for the difficult encounter with the question of the desirability of our desires. Teaching so conceived is always a powerful intervention, and hence an act of power. The only one who is able to transform such *unilateral* power into *relational* authority (Bingham, 2008) is the student. Yet whether such 'authorisation' of the teacher's power will ever happen remains an open question, which, in my view, is the most profound way in which education is a 'risky business' (Biesta, 2014).

It has been rewarding to see how many of the authors have engaged with these ideas in order to get closer to the educational dimensions, or perhaps we can say the educational potential of the arts. As the one being portrayed I just want to introduce a few refinements in the way in which the ideas have been depicted and taken up. In contrast to what jan jagodzinski suggests, I wouldn't characterise what I am trying to do as 'a psychoanalytic model of empowerment', not only because I do not see education as a process in which teachers give power to their students or authorise their students – the opposite is actually the case – but also because the process is not about *becoming* grown-up as a result of this, but of encountering and carrying the question of grown-up-ness as a living question in one's own life. I see similar traces of a developmental reading of grown-up-ness in some of the conclusions Nico de Vos reaches. His explorations of intercorporeity – *in* dance and *as* dance, I would be inclined to say – give further depth and detail to the idea that our subject-ness is not in our own hands, is not an achievement we produce, but is always 'out there', occurring in the 'inter'. But grown-up-ness, as I see it, is not a 'developmental path', not a matter of development, nor part of the child's 'learning and developmental activities'. Rather than a 'result' or 'outcome', it remains something ahead of us, always at stake and always in question.

Jessie Beier and Jason Wallin get much closer to an existential reading of grown-up-ness also because they connect it very helpfully to a question they take from Deleuze, which is the question of (reasons for) believing in the world, which I see as closely connected to the question of wanting to be in and with the world. Where their reflections perhaps remain a bit too much on the expressive side of the educational spectrum is in their emphasis on the value of newness – new ways of acting, new ways of believing and new ways of being. Here I would like to emphasise that newness in itself is not 'enough', so to speak, because there is always the question of the quality – or more precisely: the desirability – of what is new or announces itself as new, and it is the encounter with this question where the educational 'moment' can be found. The educational fascination with the new is not a contemporary phenomenon. Rousseau's famous sentence in *Emile* (1762) – 'Everything is good as it leaves the hands of the author of things, everything degenerates in the hands of man' – continues to provide a powerful articulation of it, one that still holds sway in contemporary thought and practice as can, for example, be clearly seen in the excerpts Julianne Moss and Anne-Marie Morrissey present in their chapter. It shows an articulation of educational practice that, in my view, only goes half way. Yes, it can be good that children become and 'feel more confident expressing themselves', and it can also be good that they gain 'a heightened sense of autonomy and agency in learning, as well as a deeper awareness of the self', but it is not automatically or necessarily good, which means that pedagogical artistry always needs to raise the 'What if?' question, and not only needs to find (artistic) forms and ways of posing that question, but also needs to find (artistic) forms and ways of allowing children to *work through* this question.

There is a very blunt but nonetheless extremely helpful 'test' in order to judge whether statements about education 'connect' with the educational question and that is to think of (historical) examples that would 'fit' the statements but nonetheless are deeply problematic. Or to be even more precise (and more blunt): over time the Nazis also became 'more confident expressing themselves' and also gained 'a heightened sense of autonomy and agency … as well as a deeper awareness of the self'. And that is why it remains important to make the distinction between identity and subject-ness (although the terms matter perhaps a little less than the importance of the distinction in itself), where identity is the question of who I am – something that obviously can be expressed – and subject-ness is the question of how I am, how I exist in the world – which is not a matter of fact but with the 'how' already raises the question of the *quality* of our existing.

'Stuck in the middle with you'

What many of the chapters do very well in my view, and this may well be one of the major contributions this volume is making to the field of art education, is the exploration of the possibilities and complexities of the 'middle ground', the place between self-destruction and world-destruction and, more specifically, an exploration of what the arts have to offer here. Robyn Ewing and John Saunders, for example, do this in a very explicit way by examining what theatre and literature have to offer in 'practising grown-up-ness', that is, in my language, providing forms, space and time in order to figure out what it means to encounter the reality of the world and other human beings and 'come to terms' with this reality. Ewing and Saunders do this partly along more cognitive lines, stressing, for example, the importance of emphatic understanding. Drama, however, also offers possibilities that are much more existential and experiential, such as the example of the 'trust walk', which we may perhaps also read as practical intercorporeity, as de Vos calls it, that is, as a kind of dance.

David Lines does something similar when he looks at free jazz as a middle ground, that is, free jazz as an 'exercise in grown-up-ness' (my phrase). Lines not only points at the responsibility of the players in a free jazz ensemble – a responsibility towards each other but, if I understand Lines correctly, also a responsibility to the music itself. Interestingly, Lines also explores the difference between grown-up and infantile jazz, relating the latter to the problem of overcoding, that is, where the playing sticks perfectly to the particular 'code' of a jazz performer or composer, without, so we might say, taking any responsibility *in relation to* the music. A perfect copy where, in a sense, nothing happens, nothing occurs and no *one* occurs.[2] But the 'solution' for this is not the absence of boundaries – that, so one could say, is also an infantile desire. The 'solution' is precisely to stay and play in the middle ground. As Lines explains: 'From a jazz perspective this would mean a player finding ways to keep forms of creative openness in their musical actions all the while being attentive to the limiting tendencies of powerful blocks of "striations".' The only question I would have here, is whether 'improvisation' is the best word to capture what Lines makes visible about the 'middle-groundly' quality of free jazz. In the domain of music it seems to make sense to use the phrase 'grown-up jazz' to denote the particular potential of free jazz Lines makes visible. In the domain of education I would be tempted to use a phrase like 'jazz pedagogy' rather than the 'pedagogy of improvisation', but that may be more a matter of taste.

I also read the chapter by Jessie Beier and Jason Wallin as an exploration of the middle ground, the place of suspension and, to use their term, endurance. With Deleuze, Beier and Wallin turn to cinema and its potential, as they put it, 'to actualize ways of seeing beyond ordinary or habitual vision by producing new perceptual circuits between humans and the world in turn suggesting that *something else is possible*' which, as they emphasise, is particularly important for 'producing new belief in the world' and hence, in my own words, for arousing the desire for wanting to be in the world in a grown-up way. One important point Beier and Wallin explore with Deleuze, is the extent to which it is possible to 'think' this in non-anthropocentric and non-phenomenological ways (on this see also Biesta, 2006, chapter 2). This also means, and this is another interesting theme they add to the discussion, that the possibility of the end of the existence of human beings – they use the phrase 'teaching *at the end of the world*' – is being considered. This means, and I agree, that we should move beyond the idea of 'education as that holy space of possibility, a space where hope is born and optimism prevails' because, as I am inclined to put it, there is something more important and urgent at stake in our lives than that. There are similar sentiments in jan jagodzinski's contribution, particularly his analysis of the precarious character of (contemporary) human existence. He argues that the task of education in this context – which he specifies as 'an education in design and art' – is to orientate students to a 'post-anthropology' and a 'post-ontology'.

In my view Nico de Vos also does quite a lot of 'groundwork' towards an understanding of the educational possibilities and complexities of the middle ground, particularly through his explorations of the body and (its) intercorporeity. Dance, so the chapter seems to indicate, thus reveals another important quality of the middle ground and what it means to stay in the middle ground, as it is not an encounter of isolated bodies or identities. De Vos rather tries to highlight that the middle ground, or the condition of middle-ground-ness, if this is linguistically possible, comes first. It is there that we not just encounter others and their bodies, but also our self. In my view, and here I perhaps slightly disagree (see also above), this *is* the educational space, the space of suspension, rather than that education is needed to 'lead' the child or student towards it.

'Art for art's sake'

To explore the educative quality of the arts in terms of the middle ground and the middle-ground-ness of art also implies something about how we look at and understand art. David Cole's chapter moves towards these questions with the help of Deleuze's book on Francis Bacon and ideas from Whitehead. It is beyond my competency to try to summarise what Cole is doing, though I do want to highlight one important insight, which is Cole's conclusion that '(t)he truth of applying Deleuze to the arts' has to do with art's 'ability' '*to produce sensation, and to thus extend the levels by and through which art can penetrate subjectivity*'. It is this 'event' (my term) of penetration which, in my view, connects art with the question of grown-up existence – where art is not an 'object' or 'thing' or 'event' outside the subject, to be perceived or appreciated, for example, but rather that which 'pulls' us into the world. I would encourage the reader to consider Chris Naughton's chapter with this in mind, as it provides a further and more detailed exploration of what Cole describes as the arts' production of sensation, and what this means for the relationship between art and the subject, and the role of percepts, affects and concepts in it. What I particularly like about Cole's conclusions for education is his challenge of developmental thinking in the arts curriculum, and his foregrounding of rhythm which, if I read it correctly, adds a further dimension to how we might understand what the middle ground 'is' and how it 'works', bearing in mind that the middle ground neither simply 'is' nor simply 'works'.

Cole's chapter with Margaret Somerville can be seen as a further development of these themes, but also contains a crucial reminder for the discussions in this book, namely that 'art' itself is not a neutral category and that we should therefore be extremely careful to call everything art that, with 'our' eyes, looks like art, because there are other eyes, to formulate it rather clumsily, where art is actually something else. Aboriginal 'art', as they show convincingly, is actually something else. On the one hand we can therefore read their chapter as an expansion of the common conception of art, though I would tend to go in the opposite direction and read their chapter first and foremost as an exposure of a colonial tendency in the use of the category 'art'. We should be mindful that what looks like art in our eyes may not at all be that in the eyes of others – which raises important questions for art education and also for the very conception of 'art'. Through their discussion of Aboriginal 'art' Cole and Somerville begin to show a very different 'reality', which, so I wish to argue, is both important to raise questions about preconceptions we may have about art and hints at very different possibilities for 'art education', which, after this chapter, we should perhaps consistently be putting in quotation marks.

Whereas Cole and Somerville thus make the familiar strange, I am intrigued, but perhaps also puzzled by the way in which they want to 'capture' the idea of 'thinking through Country' with 'Western' philosophical categories. Perhaps rather than trying to 'capture' what Aboriginal art is, rather than trying to *make sense* of Aboriginal art, which, elsewhere (Biesta, 2015), I have characterised as the gesture of learning – How can I make sense? How can I understand? – there is a different set of questions that might be brought into play here. These questions – What is this trying to say? What is this asking of me? – are not questions of learning but questions that have to do with the gesture of teaching and being taught. They are questions, to use Cole's phrase, that have the potential to 'penetrate subjectivity', to 'call' the (grown-up) subject into the world.

Teaching for the possibility of being taught: the question of pedagogy[3]

This brings me to the final topic I wish to highlight in response to the chapters in this book: the question of teaching and the teacher or, in terms of the title of this book, the question of pedagogy and the pedagogue. Mary Ann Hunter's chapter goes, in a sense, straight to the heart of the matter by focusing on the artist as teacher through a discussion of two artists who participated in an artist-in-residence project in Tasmanian schools. She highlights the fact that in both cases the artists did what the artist-in-residence 'label' actually says: they resided in schools as artists. Hunter distinguishes this explicitly from more 'didactical' approaches to artists-in-residence, that is, where they are 'expert visitors charged with instructing and mentoring students'. Yet what she brilliantly shows is that precisely their residing as artists, their acting and being 'unteacherly', was of huge educational significance as it interrupted the 'normal' state and flow of affairs in order, as I would like to put it, to (re)turn students to the world. As she writes: 'Artists' way of being may therefore resonate well with aspirations for "grown-up-ness" in environments of necessary containment. ... Artists may interrupt in subtle and potentially educative ways.' What Hunter alerts us to is what we might call a kind of 'oblique teaching', a teaching that does not instruct, that does not moralise, and that also – and this is important too – does not model what grown-up-ness looks like, but rather is a form of oblique, unteacherly teaching where artists, through their 'material presence and practising of their work [bring] to light what should matter'.

Oblique, unteacherly teaching, echoes with what in the interview with John Baldacchino is discussed as unlearning. Unlearning, if I read it correctly, is an attempt to regain the educative. Baldacchino emphasises that his qualm is not with education as such:

> but with how the educative, that which we engage with as a human way of living and growing, has become embroiled in what Dewey wanted to avert us from: an illiberal world that finds itself stuck in the promise of certainty while we are slowly being deprived from our inability to unlearn what was ingrained in us within and round the schooled society.

Just as such unlearning cannot be taught – so that, in a sense, it remains autonomous vis-à-vis schooling, Baldacchino also emphasises the importance of art's autonomy 'so that it can function in a heteronomous world' rather than being usurped by it (which I also read as an important argument for his claim that art cannot and should not be construed as an 'act of learning'). That unlearning cannot be taught – it's not some kind of method or technique – doesn't mean that there is no role for the teacher but, again, the work of the teacher, so we might say, becomes oblique. And it is not just interesting that Baldacchino 'encountered' unlearning in his own teaching practice, but also that the unteacherly work in relation to unlearning has a pedagogy, namely the pedagogy of mannerism as a form of 'willed forgetting'.

And this, in my view, connects with what John Roder and Sean Sturm explore in their chapter, not just with vivid examples of what the work in the middle ground looks like, but connecting this explicitly to the – can I say it once more: oblique and unteacherly – work of the teacher. They start with something early childhood teachers 'discovered' in their work with artists, that it is 'all about letting go'. Rather than that they dis-covered this, one could perhaps say that this was un-covered for them; epiphany more than construction, being-taught more than having-learned. This is partly a detail and partly not, because what Roder and Sturm carefully and imaginatively do, also brings the main theoretical strands of this book together, to show that what looks like the ultimate learnification of education – refusing to teach, refusing to be a teacher, and handing it all over to what I have sometimes referred to as 'amorphous' learning processes, is actually the complete opposite of learnification. These lines say it all:

> The teacher did not shift pedagogical responsibility onto the children, he opened up a 'literal and metaphorical space' (Biesta, 2017, p.18), for the children to effect an inquiry into their subjectivity. There was thus letting go, not only of teacherly control, and the traditional aligned curriculum, and even the dance canon. However there was no letting go of the responsibility to suspend time and space, and to sustain students (plural) in the middle ground.

They also highlight, and this is indeed an important addition, that what occurs in such situations – or at least may occur – is not just individual subjectification but perhaps first and foremost collective subjectification. And that is perhaps the strongest argument why today we still need places called 'school' and should not hand everything over to personalised on-line learning.

'The end'

Walking through the chapters of this book has indeed been like walking (through) the museum: I have found things that I liked and things I didn't like; I have seen things I think I had seen before, and was pleased to encounter them again; things have caught my eye, and things have caught me. Out of this we can't forge a new theory of art education, if that was ever an ambition in the first place, but the chapters, in their attempts to 'let go' of what we know in order to see again, are shedding new light on the interconnections between art, artists and pedagogy and have sought to find the educational and the educative in these possibilities, rather than just celebrate newness. That, in my view, is what should remain central to everything we endeavour in education, with or without the arts, but ideally with them.

Notes

1 I put 'learner' in quotation marks because in my view the re-labelling of students to learners has contributed to the rise of expressivist conceptions of education, also in relation to the rise of constructivist theories of learning and sense-making and neo-liberal modes of 'managing' education (see particularly Biesta, 2014).
2 A friend of mine once explained that some jazz, such as that of Coltrane, runs a much higher risk of generating such overcoding – because it is itself in a sense already strongly coded – than the jazz of others. I can't judge whether this is true, but it is an interesting observation in relation to Lines' chapter.
3 All other sections in this chapter have the titles of pop songs. Interestingly, I haven't been able to find any pop song with teaching in the title, other than a few instances that are problematic rather than playful. Perhaps this says something about teaching or at least about the representation of teaching in contemporary popular culture.

References

Arendt, H. 1994. Understanding and politics (the difficulties of understanding). In J. Kohn (Ed.), *Essays in Understanding 1930–1954* (pp.307–327). New York: Harcourt, Brace and Company.
Biesta, G.J.J. (2006). *Beyond learning: Democratic education for a human future.* Boulder, CO: Paradigm Publishers.
Biesta, G.J.J. (2010). *Good education in an age of measurement: Ethics, politics, democracy.* Boulder, CO: Paradigm Publishers.
Biesta. G.J.J. (2014). *The beautiful risk of education.* Boulder, CO: Paradigm Publishers.
Biesta, G.J.J. (2015). Freeing teaching from learning: Opening up existential possibilities in educational relationships. *Studies in Philosophy and Education* 34(3), 229–243.
Biesta, G.J.J. (2017). *Letting art teach: Art education 'after' Joseph Beuys.* Arnhem: ArtEZ Press.
Bingham, C. (2008). *Authority is relational. Rethinking educational empowerment.* Albany, NY: SUNY Press.
Derrida, J. (1987). *The truth in painting.* Chicago: University of Chicago Press.
Masschelein, J. (1997). In defence of education as problematisation: Some preliminary notes on a strategy of disarmament. In D. Wildemeersch, M. Finger & T. Jansen (Eds.), *Adult education and social responsibility: Reconciling the irreconcilable?* (pp.133–148). Frankfurt: Peter Lang.
Spivak, G.C. (2004). Righting the wrongs. *South Atlantic Quarterly* 103(2/3), 523–581.

INDEX

Aboriginal: onto-epistemology 72–3, 75–6; onto-epistemology and art 73, 74, 79, 81; flat ontology 77, 81
Adorno, T. 14, 57
aesthetic 8, 14, 21, 47, 59, 66–7, 89, 91–2, 98–9, 118, 121–2, 140, 148
affect 1–6, 43–50, 53, 72, 84–90, 127, 135, 153; affective 54, 61, 66–9, 86, 98, 135
Anthropocene 6, 8, 83–90, 92–5, 120, 121, 125; anthropocentric 7, 87, 116–19, 121–2, 152
Anti-Oedipus 127, 136
Arendt, H. 3, 15, 19, 37, 40, 68–9, 149, 156
assessment 2–4, 10, 27–8, 32, 37, 96, 108–9, 111–14
assemblage 54–5, 89–90, 93, 112, 123, 132, 135

Bacon, F. 4, 21–30
Baldacchino, J. 8, 12, 19, 137–9, 140–6, 154–5
Barad, K. 32–6, 38, 40, 85–9, 94
becoming 5, 23–7, 35, 40–6, 50–8, 77–8, 85–9, 92, 104, 111–12, 122–7, 130, 134–6; becoming-curriculum 131, 136; *becoming-imperceptible* 123–5; *becoming grown-up* 68
being 5, 7–8, 17–18, 22, 32, 34, 36–7, 40, 45, 47, 49–50, 53–4, 60, 63–4, 68, 74, 76, 80–1, 86, 89, 94, 116, 128, 144; being-together 65, 69; *being-subject* 83; human being 18, 61, 62, 63, 64, 65, 67, 68, 87,

128, 137, 144, 151, 152; ways of being 36, 37, 39, 40, 150, 154
being in the world 28, 62, 97, 116
Bergson H. 51, 72
between 4–7, 22, 80, 83, 92, 99, 107, 121, 123, 134, 151; between the body and world 61–6; in-between 22, 29
Biesta, G. *see* creativity; educational task; existence; expression; gift of teaching; good education; grown-up-ness; infantile; interruption; learnification; measurement; middle ground; responsible; quality; suspension
body 6, 17, 21–8, 47, 58, 63–9, 85, 92–3, 98, 119, 132–3, 135, 141, 152; human body 21, 24, 61, 62; as meat 23–5, 28
body without organs 4, 24–8
Bogue, R. 43, 47, 50
Braidotti, R. 32, 34, 36–7, 41, 52, 54, 60, 122–3, 125
Britzman, D. 107, 108, 113n1
Burroughs W. 26
Butler, J. 43, 50, 111

capitalism 2, 6, 9, 11, 24, 57, 72, 75
centre: subject centre 6, 32, 44, 62, 149; human centred 7, 64, 75; centre of the world 15–16, 36, 40; decentred 54, 84
Cézanne, P. 5, 44, 46–7
cinema 7–8, 117–24, 126, 136, 152; cinematic thought 115, 119; visionary cinema 117–18, 120–4

Cole, R, D. 9, 23, 28–30, 46, 48, 51, 58, 60, 72–3, 82, 153, 154
Colebrook, C. 45–7, 121, 125
concept 1–9, 14–17, 23, 29–30, 36, 44–51, 53–9, 62–9, 74, 78, 85–7, 97–9, 101, 112, 116, 122, 129, 130, 137, 139, 141–3, 153
Conrad, J. 23, 30
counter-actualise 47, 130
creativity 3–4, 11–14, 19, 27, 30–3, 41, 52, 93, 98, 138, 139, 143
curriculum 2–15, 26–40, 49, 58, 61, 69, 71–81, 96, 98–100, 105, 107, 108–10, 114–15; arts curriculum 98, 135–6, 153, 155; emergent curriculum 131

dance 2–9, 26, 35, 43, 46–51, 54, 61–70, 74, 79, 80–1, 93, 131–2, 135, 150–5
De Carvalho, S. 4, 31–2, 35–6
DeLanda, M. 72, 82
Deleuze, G. *see* Bacon; Difference and Repetition
Deleuze, G, & Guattari, F. *see* affect; Anthropocene; Anti-Oedipus; assemblage; becoming; body without organs; counter actualise; desire; difference; disjunctive synthesis; expression; fabulation; flat ontology; immanence; immanent materialism; lines of flight; material image of thought; materiality; minoritarian; molecular; movement; nomadic; palpate; percept; plane of immanence; refrain; rhizome; rhythm; sensation; striation; territoriality; *Thousand Plateaus*; *What is Philosophy?*
Derrida, J. 3, 147, 156
Descartes, R. 62, 29, 141
desire 4, 7–8, 15, 17–18, 21, 40, 43–4, 47–8, 50, 58, 66, 83, 97, 109, 111–12, 117, 120–1, 123, 127–9, 132, 135, 149–50, 152
Dewey, J. 3, 7, 8, 137–8, 141, 146, 154
dialogue 4, 7, 15–18, 57, 97, 102, 109, 131–2
difference 3, 10, 23, 52–3, 57, 59, 63–6, 72, 89, 98, 109–10, 116, 118, 124, 128, 134, 151
Difference and Repetition 60, 95, 130, 136
disrupt 6, 8, 32, 36, 86, 108, 118, 127, 131, 135
disjunctive synthesis 3, 72, 90, 91
drama 2, 7, 9, 26, 28, 59, 96–105, 119, 133, 151

early childhood 1, 8, 10, 98–100, 109, 113, 127, 130, 135, 155

Earth 6, 8, 11, 63, 74, 76, 84–90, 93, 120, 121
educational task 8, 19, 32, 35, 37–9, 57, 62, 68–9, 83–7, 90, 93, 97, 107, 111–12, 118, 121–2, 124, 128–9
element(s) 3, 5, 6, 25, 48–9, 54–6, 58–9, 63, 71, 75
entanglements 33, 36, 38, 76, 89–90, 102
existence 7, 16, 29, 53–8, 61, 62, 64, 72, 92, 107, 115–19, 123, 139, 140; grown-up-existence 19, 68, 128, 153; human existence 16, 61, 117, 145, 152; middle ground existence 48; modes of existence 117, 122
existential 14, 16, 83, 116, 119, 150–1, 156
expression 3–4, 13–14, 19, 22–3, 48–9, 53, 56–9, 63, 71, 88, 98, 100, 140, 149

fabulation 46–7, 87, 92, 117, 119, 125
film 7–9, 28, 31–2, 43, 46, 49, 110, 117, 119, 121, 123, 125n1
flat ontology *see* ontology
Foucault, M. 3, 84, 108, 113, 136
Freire, P. 83, 143

gift of teaching 33, 37, 39, 40
good education 32, 37, 39, 40, 156
Greene, M. 7, 97–8, 104–5, 141, 146
grown-up-ness 1, 5, 7–8, 29, 32, 36–7, 40, 68, 97, 99, 107, 149–51, 154
Guattari, F. *see* Deleuze & Guattari

Haraway, D. 85, 94
Heidegger, M. 3, 51, 54, 55, 60, 94
Hindmarsh, L. 4, 35, 36, 37, 38, 41
human: all-too-human 116, 117, 119, 120, 121, 124, 125; human existence *see* existence; inhuman 69, 84–7, 90, 92, 116, 119; non-human 5–6, 22, 28, 32, 35, 44, 46, 48, 50, 72, 84, 116, 118; post-human 28, 119

identity 7, 12–15, 19, 21, 29, 34, 72–3, 90, 107–8, 122–3, 151; identity subjectness 151; musical identity 54; teacher identity 111–13, 149; Aboriginal identity 73, 76–7
immanence 1, 3, 5, 23, 72; plane of immanence 22, 48, 49, 72; art's immanence 138; immanent materialism 6, 57, 73, 82
improvisation 5, 52–8, 60, 152; pedagogy of improvisation 52–4, 56–9
individual 3, 4, 14, 21, 26, 31, 43, 47, 55, 59, 64–9, 72, 77, 86, 97, 102, 104, 108, 118–19, 123, 129, 144, 155

infantile 4, 17, 56, 151, 152
instrumental 3, 12, 13, 111,
    121, 145; instrumentalism 81;
    instrumentalist 139
interconnectedness 62–4, 67, 68
intercorporeity 6, 62–9, 150–2
interruption 4–5, 8, 31–2, 34, 37–40, 48,
    50, 83, 97, 99, 116, 118, 122, 124, 127–8,
    131, 135, 149

jagodzinski, j 6, 44, 51, 86, 141, 146,
    150, 152
jazz *see* jazz pedagogy

Kant, I. 5, 25, 48–9, 85, 87–8

Lather, P. 108, 113, 156
learning 2–3, 30, 36, 38, 40–2, 51, 69,
    104–5, 109, 112–13, 127, 140, 146,
    149, 154, 156; authentic learning 7;
    learning outcomes 11, 13, 32–3, 39, 58,
    98; learning experience 33, 52, 100,
    128, 143; learning journey 101, 110;
    learning pathways 79, 110; learning to
    communicate 99, 102; learning to teach
    112; transformative learning 86, 96,
    98, 105; unlearning 8, 11, 13, 18, 21–2,
    24–8, 137–9, 141–5, 154–5; rhythmic
    learning 27
learnification 39, 127, 155
Levinas, E. 3, 14, 19
Lines, D. 5, 48, 49, 51, 53, 54, 59, 60, 135,
    151, 152, 156n2
lines of flight 57, 93, 134
Lyotard, J. F. 5–6, 55–6, 60, 66–7, 69, 148

Move, Act, Play, Sing, (MAPS) 51, 127,
    130, 135
material 5–7, 15, 23, 27–8, 32, 35, 43–5,
    47–8, 53–4, 61, 69, 86, 89, 91, 94, 124;
    immanent materialism *see* immanent;
    material bodies 48, 65–9, 131; material
    interaction 5; material presence 40, 154;
    materialistic differential 65; materialist
    philosopher 23; material event 48, 66,
    67; materiality 5, 6, 44, 46, 47, 50; new
    materialist 28, 30, 40
measurement 3, 156; measurable outcomes
    11, 13, 96, 109, 149; unmeasurable 56
Meirieu, P. 15, 20
Merleau-Ponty, M. 6, 30, 62–5, 68–9, 148
metaphysics 23, 26, 72, 78, 90, 94
middle ground 1, 2, 4–5, 16, 48, 56–7,
    59, 97, 102, 116, 122, 129, 135, 149,
    151–3, 155

minoritarian 86, 89–90, 92
molecular 6, 89, 90–1
movement 4–6, 10, 22, 24, 52–9, 63, 93–4,
    99, 121, 131, 133, 135
music 2, 5, 9, 26, 43, 48–9, 51–60, 66,
    79, 151–2

Nancy, J.-L. 6, 64–70
nature 2, 7, 14, 29, 42, 46, 47–50, 59,
    65, 67, 78–9, 85, 91–2, 94–5, 117, 120,
    125, 129, 138, 146; Nature 6, 79, 86,
    88–9, 91, 95
Nietzsche, F. 46, 51, 58, 60, 137–8, 145–6
nomadic 5, 57

Olsson, L.M. 10, 20
onto-epistemology 71–3, 75–6, 79, 85
ontology 6, 64–6, 73, 78, 84, 89–90, 93;
    differential ontology 72, 82; flat ontology
    6, 71–3, 75, 76–7, 81; post-ontology 85,
    93, 152
outside 14, 26, 32, 37–9, 53–7, 79, 88–90,
    97, 101, 117, 121, 129, 138, 143, 153

palpate 118
pedagogy 1–3, 5, 12, 32, 58, 107, 121, 129,
    144, 154; arts pedagogy 50, 58; creative
    pedagogy 104; critical pedagogy 143; jazz
    pedagogy 53–4, 152; mannerist pedagogy
    144; pedagogical artistry 39, 52, 91, 107,
    109, 111, 112; pedagogical life 115, 124;
    pedagogy of affect 135; pedagogy of
    improvisation 5, 50, 53–4, 56–9, 152;
    pedagogy of learning 142; pedagogy
    of unlearning 138, 155; pedagogical
    thinking 58; quality pedagogy 52,
    96, 98–9; teacher education
    pedagogy 108
percept 5–6, 43–8, 50, 89, 90, 153;
    perceptual 46, 116–19, 122, 152
Peters, R. 13
phenomenology 62; phenomenological 1,
    56, 115, 117–19, 152
post-truth 83–4, 90
psychoanalysis 22, 111; psychology 122;
    psychological 22, 122

quality: quality arts education 35, 96,
    98–100, 149–50, 153; rhizomatic quality
    52; teacher quality 107, 111–12, 124;
    middle ground quality 152

Rancière J. 38, 83
refrain 5, 15, 52–3, 89
relationality 2, 31, 36, 75

relationship 33, 67, 78, 85, 88, 97, 107, 141;
  Aboriginal and settler relationship 75;
  artist student interrelationships 39, 103,
  123; relationship between art and the
  subject 6, 24, 29, 44, 69, 153; relationship
  between bodies 61–9; relationship to
  land 73, 77–8; relationship with desires
  120, 128–9; relationship with the world
  26, 62, 119; teacher student relationship
  33, 68, 102, 110–11; transformative
  relationships 101
responsible 124; responsibility 5, 14, 36,
  40, 55, 83, 97, 107, 110, 128, 135, 149,
  151–2, 155
resistance 4–5, 9, 15–18, 57, 89, 123, 149
rhizome 57, 58; musical rhizomes 57;
  rhizomatic 5, 52, 58; rhizomatic
  expression 57; rhizomatic
  movement 5, 59
rhythm 4, 22–9, 49, 55, 59, 130, 132, 153;
  rhythmic 53, 77, 89; rhythms of dance 65;
  rhythm in arts-based education 29

St.Pierre, E. 28–9
science 12, 14, 34, 58, 72, 75, 79, 81, 85,
  87, 90–1, 129, 137; science fiction, 92,
  117, 123
self-destruction 16, 57, 116, 149, 151
Semetsky, I. 36, 42–3, 50–1, 129, 130, 136
sensation 4, 22, 24–6, 43–4, 48, 50, 89–90,
  119; bloc of sensation 5–6, 45–6, 48–9,
  50, 89; sensation and art 26, 44–7, 153
Simondon, G. 88, 94, 95
Spinoza, B. 49
Spivak, G. 18, 20, 128, 136, 150, 156
standards 32, 37, 107, 109; teacher
  education standards 112
striations 3, 57, 152
subject(s) 2, 4, 7, 14–16, 23, 43–4, 48, 54,
  56, 61–2, 68, 90, 108, 111, 113, 116,
  120–3, 129, 133, 149; human subject
  6, 25, 44, 56, 61–2, 64, 116, 118–19;
  inter-subjectivity 61–2, 68–9; perceiving
  subject 89, 119; subject in the world
  15–18, 28, 128, 149, 153–4;
  subjectification 57, 129, 155;
  subjectivation 86, 89, 136;

subjectivisation 129; subject-ness 15,
  68, 83, 128–9, 150; virtual subject 118;
  distributive subjectivity 85–6
subjectivity 7–8, 21, 22–6, 29, 35, 61, 68–9,
  107–8, 110–12, 118–19, 121–3, 135, 153,
  154–5; human subjectivity 56, 118
suspension 8, 65, 83, 111, 118, 120, 124,
  128–30, 140, 143–4, 150, 152–3
sustainability 86, 91

teaching 96, 99–100, 102, 104–5, 107–13,
  120–1, 125, 127–9, 135, 142–3,
  149–50, 152, 154, 155–6n3
territoriality 2; deterritorialisation 2, 58;
  reterritorialisation 52, 59
Thousand Plateaus 5, 10, 22, 52–3, 60, 71,
  73, 86, 88, 94, 113, 125, 136
transcendental 23, 84, 89, 118;
  transcendence 140; transcendent identity
  122; transcendentalism 89

Vertov, D. 8, 119, 126

What is Philosophy? 10, 50–1, 60, 94
Whitehead, A. 6, 25–6, 71, 76–9, 81–2,
  148, 153
world: Aboriginal world 6, 71–3, 76, 81;
  arts and the world 2–3, 14, 18, 28, 32, 37,
  59, 66, 107, 115; at home in the world
  15, 149; being in the world; *see above*;
  belief in the world; 7–8, 84, 115–18,
  120–1, 124, 139, 150, 152; capitalism
  and the world 91, 116; encounter with
  the world 4, 15, 29, 65, 96, 104, 122–3,
  139, 150; end of the world 116, 120–1,
  125, 152; existing with the world 16–17,
  36, 62–3, 68, 107, 118, 120–2, 128–9,
  149; Kant and the world 25; making
  sense of the world 49, 62, 72, 78, 96, 98,
  110–11, 117, 141; place in the world 15,
  36–7, 97, 117; reality of the world 16,
  28, 65, 84, 87–8, 116, 119, 140–1, 151;
  withdraw from the world 16, 124, 149;
  world as it is 6, 14, 37, 40, 73, 83, 118,
  120, 124; world destruction 16, 57, 85,
  92, 95, 116, 149, 151; world without us
  28, 44, 85, 119–20